D0019301

Representations of Power

Representations of Power

The Literary Politics of Medieval Japan

Michele Marra

University of Hawaii Press
Honolulu

© 1993 University of Hawaii Press

All rights reserved
Printed in the United States of America
93 94 95 96 97 98   5 4 3 2 1

Library of Congress Cataloging-in-Publication Data
Marra, Michele.
Representations of power: The literary politics of medieval Japan/ Michele Marra.
p.   cm.
Includes bibliographical references and index.
ISBN 0–8248–1535–1. — ISBN 0–8248–1556–4 (pbk.)
1. Japanese literature—1185–1600—History and criticism.
2. Politics and literature—Japan.   I. Title.
PL726.33.P6M39   1993
895.6'09002—dc20   93–10236
CIP

The costs of publishing this book have been defrayed in part by the
1992 Hiromi Arisawa Memorial Award from the Books on Japan
Fund with respect to *Tales of Tears and Laughter,* by Virginia Skord,
and *The Aesthetics of Discontent,* by Michele Marra, published by the
University of Hawaii Press. The award is financed by The Japan
Foundation from generous donations contributed by Japanese
individuals and companies.

University of Hawaii Press books are printed on acid-free paper and
meet the guidelines for permanence and durability of the Council on
Library Resources

Designed by Kenneth Miyamoto

Ai miei genitori Anna e Aldo Marra,
che in silenzio tanto hanno sofferto

CONTENTS

ACKNOWLEDGMENTS

I wish to thank my numerous students at the University of Southern California for engaging in discussions and debates on issues of Japanese literature that were becoming dangerously familiar to me. Their thirst for knowledge has kept alive in their teacher a youthful sense of curiosity from which the present research has greatly benefited.

At the University of Southern California I was blessed with the presence of a distinguished scholar, Peter Nosco, who has been a source of intellectual inspiration as well as a truly marvelous friend. I only wish I were able to integrate all his suggestions here. My colleagues Gordon Berger, Bettine Birge, Dominic C. N. Cheung, George A. Hayden, Mieko S. Han, Nam-Kil Kim, Audrey Li, and John E. Wills have made my job at USC truly pleasurable and intellectually stimulating. Professor Marshall Cohen, a very special dean of humanities, has unflaggingly supported my work, helping me to find a healthy balance between the duty of teaching and the pleasure of research.

Parts of the present work were presented to members of two study groups to which I had the privilege to belong. I wish to acknowledge my special debt to a few of them: Bruce Coats of Scripps College; Janet Goodwin of the University of Southern California for sharing with me her impressive knowledge of medieval Japan; Akiko Hirota of California State University, Northridge; Stanleigh H. Jones, Lynne Miyake, and Samuel Yamashita of Pomona College; Herbert E. Plutschow of the University of California, Los Angeles; Eri Yasuhara of California State University, Los Angeles.

My wife Toshie Marra of the East Asian Library at UCLA has helped me to gather an extensive amount of material from collections all over the United States and Japan. She is undoubtedly my best teacher of things Japanese, as well as a patient, loyal, and enduring companion.

This book would not have been published without the constant support and devoted care of three special people to whom I am especially indebted: Professor J. Thomas Rimer of the University of Pittsburgh; Professor Peter H. Lee of the University of California, Los Angeles; and my editor Patricia Crosby of the University of Hawaii Press.

An earlier version of a section of chapter two appeared in *The Journal of Asian Studies* as "The Buddhist Mythmaking of Defilement: Sacred Courtesans in Medieval Japan." I thank the editor David D. Buck for allowing me the use of copyrighted material.

Los Angeles, California
20 January 1993

Representations of Power

Introduction

This book continues a project that I started some years ago on the political implications of Japanese medieval literary texts. I published the preliminary results in a study of cultural displacement —that is, a process of marginalization of authors whose loss of political power forced them to embrace the life and values of reclusion.[1] Because that book addressed the expression of political discontent from the margins of power, the trajectory of my inquiry arose from the place of displacement—the hut of the recluse and the remote mountain villa of politically silent aristocrats—and ended at the center of political power. While representing centers of authority—mainly the Fujiwara regents—as repositories of economic capital deprived of genuine cultural values, my analysis stressed the role played by the counterideological moves of marginal voices as producers and providers of cultural discourses upon which they based their legitimation, and thanks to which they survived their political displacement.

Rather than concentrating on counterideological responses to dominant ideologies, the present study examines the cultural politics of dominant ideologies by reversing this trajectory—that is, by starting from the centers of political production and analyzing the role played by literary texts in the creation and maintenance of political power. The centers of authority in question are the court, the Buddhist temples, the shogunate, and the capital's political unit made up of prominent "Citizens" *(machi-shū).* Focusing on diverse political voices and cultural patterns allows me to avoid the danger of reducing this study to a monolithic view of Muromachi Japan based on a single product, a single author, or a single "genre" that would neglect larger ideological implications. Moreover, the cross-fertilization of different political fields by the same texts and symbols highlights the unbound and constantly open nature of literary works whose "literariness" consists in their perpetual resistance to closure.[2] The political appropriation of any text thus aims at opposing this resistance, locating the work in the closed framework of ideological production.

Although this program fails the deconstructive lesson of decentering the need for classification, it may help to envision an alternative classifying model that is based on the awareness of the need for the "unbound work" *(opus infinitum)* to be ideologically bound by an act of pragmatic reading—reading with a purpose—in order to define itself.[3] Several scholars have recently applied this multiple program of literary investigation to the writing of a monumental history of Italian literature that convincingly proves how far the discipline of literary history is from extinction and how misleading are the predictions of the field's demise. This nine-volume enterprise rethinks the contextualization of literary works in terms of literature and power/institutions, the act of production and consumption, the forms of the text, the problem of interpretation, the relationship between literary and nonliterary texts (music, theatre, and the figurative arts), the geography of literature, and many more questions.[4] The application of the historical approach to literary texts contextualizes the particular inside a larger and more global field by emphasizing a network of relationships that explains the role played by literary artifacts in the very moment of their appropriation—the moment of ideological closure.

The present study touches only the first of the issues listed here, mainly the problem of literature and political power, as well as the literary power of representation. The functional/pragmatic role of representation puts in motion an empowering chain that includes both the producer—for giving imperishable fame to his patron—and the object of representation for being immortalized in the text of tradition. This process of mutual legitimation requires the mastery of a cultural competence that both parties must share and from which patrons and artists derive a cultural justification and legitimation that is central to the exercise of political power. The possession of this code provides the beneficiaries with forms of cultural capital that, being acquired and in a state of constant transformation, integrate and expand the inherited educational capital, reinforcing other forms of capital—economic and social—in the definition of social distinction.

The empowerment of the beholder of cultural capital warrants his mark of distinction in a social structure whose major condition of existence is its ability to create and maintain a sustained degree of "difference" distinguishing itself from other segments of that same structure. This is accomplished because of the fact that "art and cultural consumption are predisposed, consciously and deliberately or not, to fulfil a social function of legitimating social differences."[5]

For a translation of this act of cultural legitimation in the court language of medieval Japan I have chosen to discuss the political and literary disputes between the Northern and Southern courts in the second half of the fourteenth century. The political rivalries between members of the imperial family engendered a need for images of legitimation that the competing Nijō and Kyōgoku schools provided with the announcement of conflicting poetic codes and aesthetic programs. Through an act of mutual legitimation, poets secured the survival of their schools by entrusting themselves to the mercy of political powers and sharing with them the sweetness of victory and the bitterness of defeat. The poetic disputes over the appropriation of "mythical" language and topics—the religious implications of the emperor's sacred regalia—emphasize the importance that the concept of "cultural appropriation" holds in the definition of the relationship between literature and power, as well as in the analysis of cultural politics in the formation of ideological constructs. Poets struggled to legitimize themselves through an exclusive appropriation of the motif of the "Sacred Mirror"—the embodiment of the metaphysical and earthly holy: god and emperor—upon which they wrote a large number of poetic variations in the attempt to legitimize their patron as the only heir to the sun goddess Amaterasu.

The French sociologist Pierre Bourdieu has highlighted the centrality of efforts over "the appropriation of economic or cultural goods" in the formation of political power as "symbolic struggles to appropriate distinctive signs in the form of classified, classifying goods or practices, or to conserve or subvert the principles of classification of these distinctive properties." The maintenance of distinctions can "only exist through the struggles for the exclusive appropriation of the distinctive signs" that empower and legitimate the actors of the political/cultural game.[6] A similar process of appropriation took place with the Buddhist interpretation of the Sacred Mirror that aimed at empowering the political structure of Buddhist institutions by creating a new mythology with the symbols of Shintoism in order to legitimate the Buddhist creed as the source of imperial power. Besides securing Buddhist authorities with leverage over the symbols of imperial legitimacy, the process of appropriation and assimilation guaranteed the Buddhist supremacy in the religious field, as well as silencing potentially rival faiths such as popular beliefs, Shinto, and shamanic practices that were entrenched among the common people.

Textual traces of this process recur in the monumental production of anecdotal literature *(setsuwa)* of the thirteenth and fourteenth centuries as well as in several narratives *(otogizōshi)* of the following two centuries, the late Muromachi. Far from conceiving the process of assimilation as a simple end in itself and as a theory justifying religious distinction, temples gave practical representations of their textuality in the staging of symbolically charged rituals, in which the Buddhist epistemological codes—delivery and staging of sermons, proselytizing practices of evangelism, performances of memorial services for the dead, and the parading of nonhumans *(hinin)*—came together to satisfy a political need: to prove the temples' ability to overcome and domesticate those metaphysical forces that Buddhist mythographers had constructed as dangerous and threatening, and thereby both to shelter the community from supernatural intervention and to provide the social structure with stability and order.

The rich symbolism of rituals exploited the people's fear of the elements of marginalization—death, pollution, outcasts, slaves, prostitutes —that became central to the cultural politics of Buddhist institutions. This need for the peripheral and the excluded to secure the success of the Buddhist enterprise empowered the forces of marginalization—the outcasts populating a geography of defilement—that, realizing the centrality of their role to the stability of the social structure, began to appropriate the ruling means of production by developing their skills as actors, playwrights, and entertainers, thereby strengthening their place of social and economic distinction.

The appropriation of this Buddhist cognitive framework by the Ashikaga shoguns ennobled the producers of theatrical performances, transforming the community's scapegoats of defilement into mythographers of shogunal authority. Writers and performers of *nō* provided the shogunate with cultural capital that gave legitimacy to the shogun's usurpation of imperial prerogatives. A series of cultural appropriations—the Buddhist assimilation of imperial symbolism and the shogunal patronage of an aesthetic outgrowth of Buddhist rituals—secured military rulers with a mythology of power that constructed pastoral representations of a harmonious political order. The shogun's successful presiding over the cosmological process of production and reproduction legitimized his position at the top of secular hierarchies. The ideation of the shogun's cultural ideology provided a "natural" justification of his source of authority—a convincing ground for the shogunal displacement of the emperor from the arena of "real politik" that was based on the belief in "feeling justified in being (what one is), being what it is right to be."[7]

Far from promoting revolutionary changes and catering to subversive trends, the pattern of appropriation and assimilation tended to recenter the discourse on power without ever challenging the notion of authority. Despite a change in rules and players, the game remained essentially the same. The temples' transfer of the social periphery into the center of religious production remarginalized the victims of exploitation by accepting, protecting, and legitimating the hierarchical mode of social classification. By defining human suffering as a precondition for holiness and a step taking commoners up the hierarchical ladder of status—terrestrially from outcast to a member of the imperial family and cosmologically from demon to god along the six modes of rebirth or *rokudō*—the Buddhist concept of assimilation resisted and silenced subversion as an expression of a threatening supernatural force, or "other," to be exorcised and domesticated.

Likewise, the development of the capital's newest unit of power, the "Citizens" *(machishū),* originated as a reaction to the ideological closure of the court, the shogunate, and Buddhist institutions. This new force defined its own ideological program by looking for social and cultural legitimation in the appropriation of "traditional" cultural paradigms that eventually erased the original voice of subversion. The Citizens invested in the culture of an economically decayed aristocracy, inheriting the means of cultural production that allowed them to distance themselves from—and, therefore, to rule over—a traditional literary canon that they transformed with acts of parody and satire. This attack on the unquestioned validity of cultural patterns ceased, however, as soon as the Citizens realized their political potential and achieved a measure of economic, social, and political distinction that provided them with a specific social identity: participation in the urban power of the bourgeoisie. Then a reversal took place in which *"obsequium,* the deep-rooted respect for the established order which sets limits to petit-bourgeois revolt, is also the basis of the social virtues of the new petite bourgeoisie."[8]

The act of appropriation of "higher" values contributed to the Citizens' official identity, while the seeds of subversion and change were displaced and silenced in the aesthetic realm where they survived as a harmless product of the imagination. The confinement of the "other" to artistic representations guaranteed the survival of the hegemonic discourse of political power. Terry Eagleton has recently reminded us of the ambiguous role played by the aesthetic in the field of power, tracing the double-edged process of artistic representation. While it may offer the beholder a model of "political aspirations, exemplifying new forms of autonomy and self-determination," the noncognitive category of the aesthetic hides a secret mechanism of " 'internalised repression,' inserting social power more deeply into the very bodies of those it subjugates, and so operating as a supremely effective mode of political hegemony."[9] The Citizens learned this lesson from their source of legitimation, the aristocracy, whose mastering of the aesthetic code secured them for centuries with monopolistic rights over the process of cultural production. The transfer of cultural capital to members of the new bourgeoisie empowered them with participation in the process of political decision making, as well as legitimizing them as the new guardians of political stability.

CHAPTER ONE

Poetic and Political Disputes: Patronage at the Two Courts

his chapter analyzes the role that the poetic act played in the fourteenth century in providing competing emperors with a political program of cultural legitimation. Our examination focuses on how poets from rival schools appropriated the means of cultural production—courtly language, aesthetic rules, mythological thought—to justify the claims of their imperial patrons to the legitimacy of their position at the center of the political body. A few examples of individual voices belonging to opposite camps illustrate the centrality of poetic discourse in the creation of the ruler's cultural capital that constantly assists him along the path of legitimation.

The Disputes

Since the institutionalization of court poetry under the strict patronage of the imperial house and the aristocracy in the tenth century, the destiny of Japanese poets was rigorously tied to the political circumstances of their patrons. The proliferation of centers of power in the twelfth and thirteenth centuries led to an increased potential for income and personal gain for poets associating themselves with the sources of authority, such as emperors, retired emperors, shoguns, their leading vassals—stewards (jitō) and constables (shugo)—and temples. Ironically, the expansion of opportunities confronted the objects of patronage with new challenges, forcing the poet to promote authorities that might easily have fallen into political disgrace and thus caused the ruin of both the poet and his family. This pattern became widespread particularly during the period of the Northern and Southern courts (Nanbokuchō) from 1336 to 1392.

During these seven decades the country witnessed rule by two different political centers. The Northern court reigned in the capital of Kyoto under the tight control of the Ashikaga shogun; the rival Southern court established its imperial palace in the mountainous region of Yoshino, south of the ancient capital of Nara. The division of the Japanese imperial line was not the result of usurpation on the part of a different dynasty. Although the emperors of the two courts shared the same blood, they represented rival branches of a family that was divided by disputes over the choice of a legitimate heir to the throne. The disputes had begun in the middle of the thirteenth century, when Emperor Go-Saga (r. 1242–1246) was succeeded first by his older son Go-Fukakusa (r. 1246–1259) and then by his younger son Kameyama (r. 1259–1274), neither of whom was ready to relinquish power to the son of his brother. These events led to the formation of two factions: the Jimyōin or senior branch, headed by Go-Fukakusa, and the Daikakuji or junior line of Emperor Kameyama.

Although Kameyama was expected to let the son of Go-Fukakusa ascend the throne after his abdication, owing to the support of members of his line he was able to have his own son proclaimed emperor with the name of Go-Uda (r. 1274–1287). The reaction of the Jimyōin branch was immediate and strong. A temporary diplomatic victory allowed Go-Fukakusa's son and grandson to follow on the throne as Emperors Fushimi (r. 1288–1298) and Go-Fushimi (r. 1298–1301). The succession disputes between the two branches of the imperial family continued even after the retirement of Go-Fushimi. First a member of the Daikakuji line and a son of Go-Uda became Emperor Go-Nijō (r. 1301–1308), followed by a representative of the Jimyōin line, Emperor Hanazono (r. 1308–1318), who was the son of Fushimi and a brother of Go-Fushimi. Matters were further complicated by a split within the Daikakuji line at the time of the premature death of Emperor Go-Nijō whose son, Prince Kuninaga, was too young to take over leadership of the Daikakuji faction. Therefore a brother of Go-Nijō, Go-Daigo (r. 1318–1332; then 1333–1336 in the Northern court and 1336–1339 in the Southern court), was made emperor with the understanding that he would relinquish power to Kuninaga as soon as the boy was ready for office. The Jimyōin line accepted the Daikakuji proposal by establishing a son of Go-Fushimi, the future Emperor Kōgon (r. 1332–1333), in the seat of crown prince.

Events took a totally unexpected turn when Emperor Go-Daigo launched his attack against the Hōjō shogunate; he wished to promote a program of political restoration in the hands of a powerful monarch, namely himself. Go-Daigo's decision resulted in a rout for the Daikakuji faction, eventually forcing it out of the capital. Although successful from 1333 to 1336 in his attempt at imperial renewal—an event known as the "Kenmu Restoration"—Go-Daigo, defeated by Ashikaga Takauji, was forced to retreat to the Yoshino area where he became the first sovereign of the Southern court, leaving Emperor Kōgon of the Jimyōin to legitimize, from the throne in the Northern capital, the power of the real ruler, Takauji. Fights between Northern and Southern troops continued all over Japan until 1392, when the two courts were finally reunited under the rule of a Southern monarch, Go-Komatsu (r. 1392–1412), who was allowed to return to the capital.

In the genealogical table of Figure 1.1, names in capital letters indicate members of the Jimyōin line, while numbers refer to the order of the emperor's reign. The letter "N" stands for Northern court; "S" indicates the Southern court.

This split between the two branches of the imperial family and the resulting creation of rival courts had a great impact on the Japanese literary scene of the time. Since the appearance of the first poetic anthology in the tenth century, the compilation of imperial collections *(chokusenshū)* had become for rulers a means to proclaim their cultural capital. The glory of the emperor's reign was sung in thousands of poems celebrating the seasons, love, grief, and the glorious deeds of the sovereign. At the same time, imperial patronage decided the fate of literary history by assuring lasting fame to the compilers of these collections. The authors became authorities once they were summoned to carry out the imperial command to gather the encomiastic voices of grateful subjects. The politics of selection was, therefore, fundamental to the social, economical,

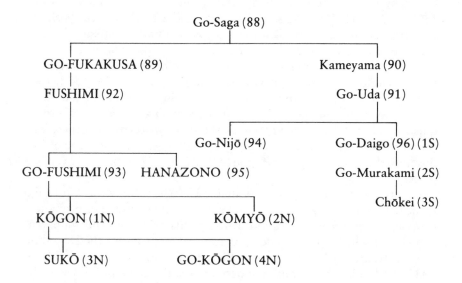

Figure 1.1

and political well-being of the poet, whose status and income depended on the kind of acknowledgment he received from the center of power, the court. To be chosen as selector empowered the poet to perform an authorial act that transferred to him the imperial prerogative in the field of literary production. The selector was the producer of the emperor's cultural domain, just as the emperor's ministers and administrators were in charge of his economic capital. Imperial authority could not do without the producers of poetic myths that were central to the ruler's maintenance of power.

The mechanism of selection put in motion by a compiler in charge of choosing "suitable" poems reproduced on a minor scale the process of empowerment to which he was subjected by a sovereign whose choice was essential to the completion of an act of cultural legitimation. To be included in a body of imperial recognition meant to be acknowledged as part of that body—as a member of an imperial machine that could not function without the presence of all its parts. Inclusion guaranteed the eternal recognition of the selected poet as a functional part of the emperor's body. Exclusion was tantamount to dismemberment. This explains the inevitable feuds among members of the same poetic family fighting for recognition and inclusion. In these struggles for power, components of the same family disjoined themselves in order to be rejoined to the sources of political legitimation, a process that led to the creation of different schools and poetic styles, each proclaiming its legitimacy in handing down the secret tradition of poetry. The political climate of the *Nanbokuchō* period provided an ideal ground for poets fighting for patronage who became the partisans of either the Jimyōin or Daikakuji line.

The relationship between ruler/patron and poet fed on a process of mutual legitimation. While poets lent their rhetorical skills to the creation of images of authority for the immediate benefit of sovereigns, the ruler stamped the official seal of approval on his mythographers and their poetic schools. The poetic act was mobilized to justify the legitimacy of imperial credentials to subjects in need of convincing arguments on the genuineness of the ruler's claims. In order to assert his power, the sovereign was in fact required to display a combined knowledge of economic, symbolic, and cultural notions, the lack of which could endanger the stability of his reign. On the economic side, rights to income *(shiki)* deriving from the supervision of estates *(shōen)* provided the cash for maintenance of the imperial machine. The delicacy of the balance of power between himself, the aristocratic families that were providing him with well-funded consorts, and the shogunate in whose hands were legal and fiscal matters put the emperor in a vulnerable position. Possession of the Three Regalia—Sacred Mirror, Sword, and Jewels—was the condition for the ruler's symbolic appropriation of a divine power that was directly derived from his imperial ancestor, the sun goddess Amaterasu. In the process of imperial legitimation the sponsorship of rituals and public cultural events was a further means to enhance the central position occupied by the emperor in the sphere of political/religious power.

Within this framework of double legitimation emperors in the thirteenth and fourteenth centuries took to patronizing the descendants of the Mikohidari family, which had produced two of the best-known Japanese poets: Fujiwara Shunzei (1114–1204) and his son Teika (1162–1241). The history of the Mikohidari family was quite similar to that of its imperial sponsors, inasmuch as rivalries developed among the sons of Tameie (1198–1275)—the son of Teika who succeeded his father as head of the family. Tameie had two sons—Tameuji (1222–1286) and Tamenori (1227–1279)—from the daughter of Utsunomiya Yoritsuna, who were born in the second decade of the thirteenth century. Four decades later Tameie had two other sons—Tamesuke (1263–1328) and Tamemori (1265–1328)—from a different wife, who is best known by her religious name, Abutsu.

Problems arose at the time of Tameie's demise when his will was made public, leaving the proprietary rights of the Hosokawa estate—the family's major source of income—to the younger Tamesuke who was then taking precedence over his two older brothers. Apart from its economic impact, Tamesuke's inheritance put him at the head of the family, making him the legitimate heir to Teika's poetic tradition. The reaction of his brothers was so fierce that the matter was brought to the attention of the Kamakura shogunate, where the interested parties went to appeal their case.[1] The situation became so tense that the family split in three branches that developed rival poetic traditions. Nijō Tameuji became head of the Nijō school; Kyōgoku Tamenori founded the Kyōgoku school; Reizei Tamesuke took charge of the Reizei school. Whereas poets of the Kyōgoku branch enjoyed the patronage of members of the Jimyōin line, the Nijō school found a convenient ally at court in the Daikakuji faction. The names of the poets involved in this family feud can be seen in Figure 1.2.

On a quantitative scale, poets of the Nijō school were the most successful in securing the patronage of the court. Nijō Tameyo was the compiler of the thirteenth and fifteenth imperial collections—the *Shingosenshū* (New Later Collection; 1303) and the *Shokusenzaishū* (Collection of a Thousand Years Continued; 1320)—both ordered by Emperor Go-Uda in 1301 and 1318, respectively. Tameyo's grandson, Tamesada, was responsible for the compilation of the sixteenth and eighteenth col-

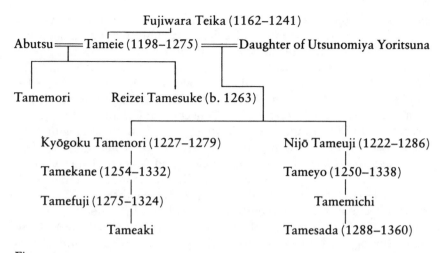

Figure 1.2

lections: the *Shokugoshūishū* (Later Collection of Gleaning Continued; 1325 or 1326) and the *Shinsenzaishū* (New Collection of a Thousand Years; 1359). While the first was sponsored by Go-Daigo, a member of the Daikakuji line, the second had its patron in Emperor Go-Kōgon, a member of the rival Jimyōin. This apparent contradiction may be explained by the fact that by the second half of the fourteenth century the Kyōgoku school was so weak that it could not secure the favors of the Jimyōin line any longer. Moreover, although the *Shinsenzaishū* was officially sponsored by Emperor Go-Kōgon, the request for a new imperial collection had come from the shogun Ashikaga Takauji, who fought for the exclusive right of the Northern court to be considered the only legitimate source of imperial authority.

The Nijō school was also generously represented in a collection of the Southern court that, although never considered a "genuine" imperial collection, was accepted as an "adjunct imperial collection" *(junchokusen)* by the Southern Emperor Chōkei, Go-Daigo's grandson. This was the *Shin'yō Wakashū* (Collection of New Leaves), compiled by a son of Go-Daigo, Prince Muneyoshi (1311–ca. 1385), who completed it in 1381. Against this poetic output of the Nijō line, the efforts of Kyōgoku poets produced only two imperial collections: the fourteenth, the *Gyokuyō Wakashū* (Collection of Jeweled Leaves; 1313 or 1314), and the seventeenth, the *Fūga Wakashū* (Collection of Elegance; 1346). Emperor Fushimi entrusted the first to Kyōgoku Tamekane in 1311; Emperor Kōgon was both the sponsor and the major compiler of the other collection.

With the split of the two courts and the rise of Ashikaga power, the purpose of imperial collections shifted from an act of legitimation of the imperial house to the creation of cultural capital by the Ashikaga shogunate. As in the case of the *Shinsenzaishū* mentioned above, although Go-Kōgon was the official sponsor of the nineteenth collection—the *Shinshūishū* (New Collection of Gleanings; 1364)—the real figure behind the curtains was the new shogun Yoshiakira. The twentieth collection, the *Shingoshūishū* (New Later Collection of Gleanings; 1383), was ordered in 1375 by Emperor Go-En'yū at the request of the shogun Ashikaga Yoshimitsu. The twenty-first and last imperial collection, the *Shinzokukokinshū* (New Collection of Ancient and Modern Times Continued; 1439), was ordered by Emperor Go-Hanazono, who had been requested to put it together by the shogun Ashikaga Yoshinori. These last three collections were all compiled by poets of the Nijō school.[2]

This complicated history of imperial and shogunal patronage highlights the political repercussions of the poetic act whose survival was secured by inclusion into a body of legitimation. In an attempt to gain access to the forbidden city of cultural discourse, poets struggled to appropriate in their representations of imperial power the symbolism that defined the "sacredness" of the imperial family. By reproducing in their poems the mythical images that in the eighth century had won the Yamato clan a position of supremacy in the establishment of imperial rule, court poets fashioned themselves as a new breed of imperial mythographers. Their political/poetic destiny was closely tied to their ability to create convincing images of political/religious power.

The Sacred Regalia

A major goal of courtly structures in times of peace is the creation and preservation of an "unadulterated" tradition in order to establish a system of stability upon which to fall back when a crisis arises. If the crisis leads to the formation of rival centers of power, success befalls those who can prove the legitimacy of their actions and present themselves as the unsoiled representatives of tradition. Credentials are fundamental in the process of claiming legitimacy to sovereignty. In the Japanese case an emperor-to-be could not ascend the throne unless he could prove he possessed the regalia that a tradition going back to the eighth century argued to be the legacy of a deity to her human manifestation: the emperor. The fact that two people claimed legitimacy to the throne at the same time implied doubling of the regalia in the moment of their transmission—a blasphemous idea in the Japanese history of imperial rule. Regalia were kept in the imperial palace, a holy presence close to the human form—the emperor—of the divine. No matter how fragile the wooden structure of the palace might have been, the Sacred Mirror was said to have survived "not the least bit damaged" by the flames that had reduced to ashes the hall where it was kept.[3] The mirror could melt but, because of its peculiarly divine matter, would never disappear.[4]

Besides being threatened by natural disasters, the regalia were also endangered whenever the emperor, in whose sight they were constantly kept, was driven out of the palace. This emergency had occurred during the Genpei war, when the defeated Taira took with them Emperor Antoku in their westward escape from the Minamoto. The records mention that the Sacred Sword was lost in 1185 to the waters of Dan no Ura together with the life of the young emperor,[5] a statement that created a serious problem for the idea of imperial legitimation. A melted mirror and a lost sword could hardly justify the alleged eternity of a legitimate imperial line. This led to the fierce criticism of Kitabatake Chikafusa (1293–1354), the historian of the Southern court, who explained the legitimacy of imperial succession in *The Chronicle of Direct Descent of Gods and Sovereigns* (*Jinnō Shōtōki*, 1339). In order to rescue from pending death the symbolism of the sacred regalia, Chikafusa argued that both the damaged mirror and the lost sword were copies of originals kept respectively in the Ise and Atsuta shrines. Thus they had never perished and continued to guarantee the legitimacy of Amaterasu's mandate to the emperors.[6]

By being driven out of the imperial capital, and thus deprived of the geography of power, the Southern court, whose new palace was a humble cottage in the impervious mountains of Yoshino, needed to demonstrate that they had never relinquished the regalia to the Northern usurper but had brought them to Yoshino in their escape from the capital. Chikafusa's argument on the alleged authenticity of the regalia that were in the hands of the Southern sovereigns aimed at rejecting the right to rule of the Northern emperors by denying their direct descent from the sun goddess.

The topic of the regalia became a major issue for poets concerned with the problem of legitimation. In the preface to the *Shin'yō Wakashū*, Prince Muneyoshi referred to the myth of "the transmission to our country of the Three Treasures from the ancient deities."[7] The same theme reappears at the end of the collection, whose last two poems by Emperor Go-Murakami (r. 1339–1368), the brother of the compiler, argued the presence of the regalia in Southern hands:

Yotsu no umi	The Three Treasures
Nami no osamaru	Have been transmitted to me
Shirushi to te	As a sign

| Mitsu no takara o | Of the pacification |
| Mi ni zo tsutauru | Of the four seas' waves. |

Kokonoe ni	Thanks to the mirror
Ima mo masumi no	Now more than ever shiny
Kagami koso	In the imperial palace,
Nao yo o terasu	Such a bright light
Hikari narikere	Still illumines the world.[8]

Emperor Go-Daigo—the father of both Go-Murakami and Muneyoshi
—was well aware of the potency of the image of the Sacred Mirror that
he considered to be the shiny source of ethical behavior for subjects and
rulers alike. Go-Daigo followed the Confucian interpretation of Shintoism advanced by Chikafusa, who argued that, besides being concrete
proof of Amaterasu's mandate, the transmission of the mirror was for the
emperor a way to absorb from the deity the virtue of honesty *(shōjiki)*
that he would then pass down to his people.[9] By proclaiming the possession of the authentic regalia, Go-Daigo assured his vassals that, thanks to
the power inherited from the sacred object of which he claimed to be the
only legitimate guardian, their hearts, as a reflection of the deity's body,
were kept in a state of constant purity. The emperor voiced this idea in
the following poem:

Mina hito no	Polish the heart
Kokoro mo migake	Of all my people!
Chihayaburu	The Sacred Mirror
Kami no kagami no	Of the everlasting deities
Kumoru toki naku	Is never clouded.[10]

The third Southern ruler, Chōkei (r. 1368–1383), a son of Go-Murakami, continued the attack on the Northern court, accusing his enemies
of legitimating their power by forging the imperial symbols. In a poem
presented in 1375 to the "Five Hundred Rounds Poetry Match of the
Southern Court" *(Nanchō Gohyakuban Utaawase)*, the emperor argued
that, should there be two Sacred Mirrors in the world, then two suns and
two moons should be seen in the sky:

Hoshi utau	As attested even by the voices
Koe ni mo shirushi	Of these singing stars,
Chihayaburu	The Sacred Mirror
Kami no kagami wa	Of the everlasting deities
Tada koko ni masu	Is shining only here.[11]

Judging the contest was his uncle Muneyoshi, who included fifty poems
from this match in the *Shin'yōshū*.

The same symbolism was used by the Northern court in arguing their case for legitimation. They too claimed the authenticity of their mirror that they maintained it could be worshiped only in the Northern palace. The Northern singers were the aristocrats Tōin Kinkata and Kinkage, as we can see from the two following poems collected in the *Fūgashū:*

Kokonoe ni	In the palace
Ama teru kami no	Not even today is
Kage ukete	The Sacred Mirror clouded:
Utsutsu kami wa	It receives the light of the god
Ima mo kumoraji	Shining in the sky.
Amaterasu	How can it be clouded—
Mikage o utsutsu	The bright mirror
Masukagami	Handed down to this world?
Tsutawareru yo no	It reflects the features of the god
Kumori arame ya	Shining in the sky.[12]

An eyewitness to the 1331 enthronement ceremonies of the first Northern ruler, Emperor Kōgon, recorded that the event was marred by the absence of two of the regalia, the Sacred Sword and the Jewels, which had been taken by the former Emperor Go-Daigo in his first escape from the capital to the Kasagi Temple. Kōgon had to use a replica of the Sacred Sword that was kept in the Day Chamber (Hiru no Goza) as a symbolic protection of the ruler.[13] This information comes from the *Takemukigaki* (Record of the Dwelling Facing the Bamboo Grove), a diary compiled by Hino Meishi, who worked as an attendant *(suke)* in the bedchamber of Emperor Kōgon. Meishi certainly expressed the general sentiment of the Northern court when she recorded her joy and a paralyzing sense of awe upon viewing the restitution of the regalia to the Tominokoji imperial palace in the Tenth Month of 1331. She devotes several pages to the ritual accompanying the wrapping of the container where the symbols of imperial power were kept; according to well-established court precedent, the container was carefully tied six times with a rope.

In her representation of the imperial symbols, the poet Meishi highlights the mutual nature of the act of legitimation. Besides providing a justification for the sovereign's legitimacy, a private relationship with the regalia empowers the subject with participation in the legitimate center of cosmic production. In her autobiographical account the regalia become a metaphorical reading of the emperor's physical body. Meishi's pride in having been chosen as a guard to the sword and jewels translates into a scene of self-congratulation in which the woman spends the night lying down in the same room with the emperor's symbolic body, the sacred treasures. There is a connection between Meishi's duty as an attendant to the emperor and her role of guardian of the sacred symbols.

By sleeping with the regalia, the imperial chambermaids *(suke* and *naishi)* continued to perform their nightly duties of attendance upon the sovereign. The sword was certainly the most graphic among the sexual symbols described in Kōgon's enthronement ceremony: Meishi was allowed to carry the Sacred Sword with her own hands—a reference to the woman's handling of the emperor's private parts in the nights of duty. Her joy at being included among the retinue of a dashing eighteen-year-old boy who was "surrounded by thirty consorts" is hardly contained.[14] Since precedent required forty consorts for the occasion, Kōgon was apparently short ten wives at the time of his coronation, a fact that may suggest the difficulties involved in duplicating the same high standards in each of the two courts.

Meishi wrote of the event's holiness in the following poem, which highlights the analogy between the regalia and the ruler's physical body in the woman's representation of the symbols of imperial power:

Te ni naruru	How awe-inspiring
Chigiri sae koso	The destiny that allows me to touch them
Kashikokere	With my own hands,
Kamiyo furinuru	These regalia handed down since the divine age
Kimi ga mabori wa	To protect my Lord.[15]

Meishi mentions the third regalia—the Sacred Mirror—at the time of the Kagura dances held in the Inner Room (Naishidokoro) in the presence of the emperor. She attempts to lend legitimacy to her ruler by acknowledging the divine origin of a ritual that was taking place on the occasion of Kōgon's enthronement. The Sacred Mirror legitimized the central position occupied by the palace and its custodian, the emperor. Meishi interprets the dances as a reenactment of the famous eighth-century myth in which the wild dances of deities restored the sun to the world, putting an end to Amaterasu's disappearance from the sky.[16] The light emanating from the mirror was said to brighten the entire palace and make luminous even the sound of music. Most appropriately the tune for the occasion was "Splendent Star" *(Akaboshi).* The palace appears as a point of light late at night, shining upon and brightening all the surroundings, and making of the night a radiant dawn. The source of the mirror's brightness could only be the divine cave of the sun goddess, as Meishi states in this poem:

Itodo nao	Now more than ever
Kumoi no hoshi no	How bright is the sound
Koe zo sumu	Of the stars on this palace,
Ama no iwato no	Its light coming
Akuru hikari ni	From the cave of heaven.[17]

On this scale of metaphors in which the representations of the deity, the mirror, and the imperial body overlap, the Northern emperor appears released of his material components as a ray of light penetrates all corners and purifyies them on contact. Like the Sacred Sword, this ray of light penetrates, possesses, rules, and owns its object of penetration in an intricate texture of sexual symbolism played on both the microcosmic —the palace—and the macrocosmic or mythical levels. Meishi was treading a path well known to the rulers of the Southern court. She was struggling to demonstrate the authenticity of her sovereign at a time when imperial prerogatives were questioned and credentials closely checked.

Both the Northern and Southern courts launched a program of cultural restoration based on the myths of ancient times. In the case of Emperor Go-Daigo restoration meant the reestablishment of political control in exclusive imperial hands, bypassing the by then unshakable structure of the military government. Go-Daigo's successful attempt to put an end to the rule of the Hōjō clan led to a change of guard at the top of the shogunate with the Ashikaga family taking the lead, but it fell short of fulfilling the emperor's desire to wipe out "the Eastern Barbarians." With Go-Daigo's retreat to the Yoshino area, the resistance against Ashikaga troops lingered for almost three-quarters of a century owing to the Southerners' ability to muster support in the provinces, forcing the shogun in and out of the capital.

In order to disclaim the Northern court's "illegitimate" pretense to power, Emperor Go-Murakami portrayed himself as a descendant in a straight line from the first human emperor, Jinmu (r. 660–585 B.C.), who, according to Chikafusa, "decided to establish his capital at Kashiwara in Yamato province and built a palace there on the model of the palace in heaven above."[18] In the poem that follows, the emperor resurrects the past in order to claim legitimacy for his line:

Takamikura	The curtains
Tobari kakagete	Hanging down
Kashiwara no	From the ceremonial throne:
Miya no mukashi mo	A bright spring like that of the past
Shiruki haru kana	Of Kashiwara palace.[19]

The Southern court never relinquished its imperial prerogatives, jealously guarding the ancient customs and rites of the court which were minutely reproduced in Anō and the other Southern capitals albeit on an inevitably minor scale. Go-Daigo's obsession with form and precedent led the emperor to record in two manuals—the *Kenmu Nenjū Gyōji* (Annual Festivals of the Kenmu Period) and the *Nitchū Gyōji* (Daily Festivals)—the minutest details of annual and daily ceremonies. The reenactment of the annual rites was the link that kept a displaced Southern court tied to its glorious past. The *Shin'yōshū* records a few poems composed by Go-Murakami during traditional rituals, of which the following is an eloquent example:

Toyo no akari	Let me try to return
Amatsu otome no	Along the path of innumerable
	generations
Sode made mo	As turn the sleeves
Yoyo no ato oba	Of the Heavenly Maiden
Kaeshite zo min	During these harvest dances.[20]

Go-Daigo's *Kenmu Nenjū Gyōji* is integral to an understanding of the meaning of the Toyo no Akari festival to which Go-Murakami refers in his poem. The ceremony was usually held in the Eleventh Month, a day after the emperor's offering of the new crops to the deities *(niinae-sai)*. The emperor established his legitimacy by presiding over the reproduction of a mythical dance in a ceremony that witnessed the emperor's symbolic distribution of food and drink to the court aristocracy. Go-Murakami's poem stresses the importance of correct precedent in the execution of a major courtly rite that female dancers brought to a conclusion by rolling up their sleeves five times in imitation of the Heavenly Maiden.[21]

The geographical displacement of the court was the main source of chagrin for an emperor struggling with the problem of self-legitimation. Go-Murakami again gave voice to the distress of the Southerners:

Aoigusa	Accompany,
Kami mo aware wa	Hollyhock,
Kakesoe yo	This sad deity:
Yoso ni miare no	He was born in a different land
Kamo no mizugaki	Along the fence of the Kamo Shrine.[22]

The emperor regrets that he could not celebrate the Kamo Festival in its rightful place, the capital's Kamo Shrine, as precedent required. The festival was an annual invocation to the Kamo deity, Wakeikazuchi, to be reborn in his place of worship. The hollyhock *(aoi)*, which on the fifteenth day of the Fourth Month decorated the entire capital, was a symbolic representation of the deity. Go-Murakami argues that his exile forced upon him by the shogun was equivalent to the exile of the god, who was now sharing the sadness of the Southern court. The emperor aimed at mastering social solidarity and cohesion by having the ritual act performed regardless of whether the festival could take place in its proper location or not. The repetition of the act legitimized the source of authority, creating agreement among the theorists of the Southern court about both the appropriateness of having the festival performed—a fact that we may call social consensus—as well as the meaning that the performance of such action contained—a form of cultural consensus.

As for the common people who may or may not have accepted the Southern court's claims to legitimacy, social solidarity was all that was required from the emperor. The ritual provided it by appealing to the emotional response of the subjects, no matter what their thoughts on the legitimacy disputes might have been.[23] While the nonverbal aspect of ritual was monopolized "to produce harmony of wills and actions without provoking recalcitrance" among the Southern subjects,[24] the poetic act on the part of the emperor appealed to the mythmakers who were committed to legitimize the ruler's source of authority.

On their part, the Northern rulers did not diverge from their concerns with the problem of legitimation. Internal rivalries within the same court increased the competition among intellectuals whose destiny was determined by the side they chose to join. Although they retained the geographical symbol of cultural capital—Kyoto—as the site of their physical being, poets of the Northern court were not immune from displacement and exile. The dismemberment of the imperial body required an even stronger policy of legitimation. Emperor Fushimi (r. 1288–1298) turned his cultural efforts to that end.

A Poetic Voice of the Senior Line: Emperor Fushimi

The ascension to the throne of Emperor Fushimi was the result of internal disputes of the powerful Saionji family whose members exploited the divided court for personal gain. A conflict between the head of the family, Saionji Saneuji, and his brother Saneo had led the latter to leave the main branch and to found a new family line that came to be known as the Tōin clan. Court aristocrats continued the policy that was perfected in the Heian period by the Fujiwaras of marrying their daughters to the emperor, thus assuring themselves the title of regent at the time of their grandsons' ascension to the throne. The Saionjis were no exception. While Saneuji gave his daughter Higashi Nijō-in in marriage to Emperor Go-Fukakusa, Saneo made his daughter Kyōgoku-in the consort of Emperor Kameyama. The Saionji main branch, then headed by Saneuji's grandson Sanekane, risked being pushed to the margins of power by the Tōin when Higashi Nijō-in ended up without children and Kyōgoku-in gave an heir to the emperor, the future Go-Uda.

Go-Fukakusa was already on his way to becoming a monk when an order came from Kamakura proclaiming Fushimi—his son by another consort—as the new crown prince. This unexpected turn of events was brought about by Sanekane, who, as court ambassador to the shogun in

Kamakura *(Kantō moshitsugi),* was able to persuade the *bakufu* to make Fushimi the next emperor. Sanekane then tried to retain power within the main branch by marrying his daughter Eifukumon-in to Fushimi. Although the increasing weakness of the Jimyōin line eventually forced Sanekane to change allegiance and back up the rival Daikakuji, he successfully prevented the collapse of his branch and its replacement by the competing cousins. Figure 1.3 traces the intricate relationship between the Saionji and the imperial family.

After securing Fushimi the throne, the Saionji family started working toward the emperor's accumulation of cultural capital by introducing him to the poet Kyōgoku Tamekane, who became Fushimi's tutor. In 1293 Fushimi ordered the compilation of a new imperial anthology and then summoned the four poets Nijō Tameyo, Kyōgoku Tamekane, Asukai Masaari, and Kujō Takahiro. Although a supporter of Daikakuji policies, Tameyo could count on extensive ties with the court for being included in a group that was patronized by an emperor of the Jimyōin line. Fushimi's accession to the throne had, in fact, brightened the hopes of Kyōgoku poets in finally seeing their names recorded in an imperial anthology. Fushimi aimed at having the two senior poets Asukai and Kujō allied with Tamekane in an attempt to erode the decisional power of Nijō Tameyo. With three compilers on the side of the Kyōgoku school, the selection was expected to favor Fushimi's protégés.

A turn of political events thwarted the emperor's plan, however, forcing Tamekane to resign from his post of Adjunct Middle Counselor *(Gon-chūnagon)* in 1296 and making him an exile the following year on

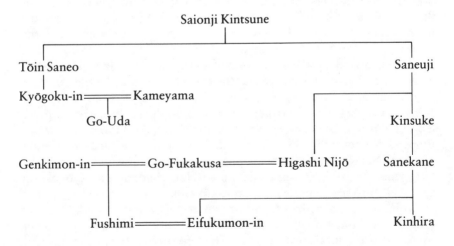

Figure 1.3

suspicion of treason. A victim of a slander fabricated by Tamekane's political enemies in order to discredit him in the eyes of the shogunate, Fushimi was forced in 1297 to abdicate in favor of his son Go-Fushimi (r. 1298–1301), while the new crown prince, the future Emperor Go-Nijō (r. 1301–1308), was chosen from the rival Daikakuji family.

Meanwhile, the death of the poets Masaari and Takahiro put an end to Fushimi's dream of compiling an imperial collection. The transfer of imperial power into the hands of Go-Nijō's father, Retired Emperor Go-Uda, who acted as the actual ruler behind the scenes *(jisei no kimi),* led to Tameyo alone being commissioned with the anthology. The result was the compilation of the *Shingosenshū* in 1303. Fushimi recorded his disappointment in a poem from his private collection, the *Fushimi In Goshū:*

Netamashiki	This chagrined heart
Kokoro no uchi zo	Of mine does not know
Toki mo wakanu	Time anymore:
Sora mo kusaki mo	Even sky, herbs, and plants
Haru wa ukuru o	Are unreliable signs of spring.[25]

Finally pardoned in 1303, Tamekane returned to power in court circles in 1308, at the time of the ascension to the throne of Emperor Hanazono, the second son of Fushimi and a favorite student of Tamekane. Willing to accomplish what he was prevented from doing a few years earlier, Fushimi again entrusted Tamekane with the compilation of an imperial anthology. Claiming that a poet who was exiled by the government had no right to associate himself with court business, Nijō Tameyo immediately appealed to the Kamakura authorities. Tamekane pleaded his case in a memorial, the *Enkyō Ryōkyō Sochinjō,*[26] eventually winning the debate with Tameyo. Commissioned to compile the *Gyokuyō Wakashū* in 1311, he completed it two years later, in 1313, the year when both Fushimi and Tamekane retired from the world and took the tonsure.

The senior line was finally given an official voice in the field of poetry. Far from being an innocent pursuit, the composition of poems in the traditional *waka* meter of thirty-one syllables continued to play a central role in the process of political legitimation. As the example of Tamekane clearly indicates, poets were definitely asked to play political roles. After taking the tonsure Tamekane was exiled again in 1316 by Saionji Sanekane, the same man who several years earlier had introduced him to Emperor Fushimi. Apparently Tamekane's protection of Hanazono was not to the liking of Sanekane, who supported, instead, Hanazono's brother Go-Fushimi (r. 1298–1301). Go-Fushimi's consort Kōgimon-in was, in fact, the granddaughter of Sanekane. Arrested in 1315, Tamekane was exiled to Tosa the following year, unable ever to return to his house in the capital. The fate of the Japanese poet in the late Kamakura period was eloquently sung by Tamekane's rival Nijō Tameaki in a poem on the poet's public role in medieval Japan:

Omoiki ya	To think about it,
Ware shikishima no	Rather than the way of poetry
Michi narade	They end up
Ukiyo no koto o	Asking you
Towarubeshi to wa	The things of this floating world.[27]

Since the poetic voice was central to the creation and maintenance of imperial authority, the poet's destiny was closely tied to the fortune of his patron. Fushimi guaranteed the development of Kyōgoku poetry as long as he could count on strong backing from the aristocracy and the shogunate. With the withdrawal of political support, the poet must acknowledge his loss in the battle for legitimation. What remains as the poet's legacy to his school is his aesthetic program, whose defense was essential to the recovery of power.

Conflicting Codes and Rival Programs

Whether he supported the Jimyōin or the Daikakuji branch, a need for patronage confronted the medieval Japanese poet with a fundamental choice in the political role to be played. A poet was aware of the coexistence of different "traditions"—poetic as well as political—that he was required to embrace and defend, a task made certainly difficult by the fact that the sources of these allegedly different "traditions"—Fujiwara Teika for poets and the sun goddess for emperors—were shared by all parties. While emperors struggled to prove the physical ownership of the "authentic" regalia in order to claim their legitimacy, poets publicized their credentials by compiling poetic treatises that might prove their programmatic filiation from Teika, the source of legitimation. When Teika was felt to belong to a "modern" tradition, legitimation would be sought in more ancient poetic practices.

No work could play the legitimating role better than the *Man'yōshū*—the first anthology of Japanese poetry and poetic counterpart of the book on ancient Japanese myths, the *Kojiki*. It is from this monumental collection that the Kyōgoku school claimed its aesthetic descent. The reason for this choice can be found in the Kyōgoku poets' desire to achieve a degree of distinction that would legitimize their "difference" from rival schools of poetry. Scholars have identified this differential quality as the "revolutionary" style of the Kyōgoku school that sets it apart from the more "traditional" Nijō poetic practices.[28] This alleged novelty is customarily explained on the ground that Kyōgoku poets drew their inspiration and techniques from poems of the *Man'yōshū,* which a line of "mythical" exegesis presents as the "pure" and "uncontaminated" source of Japanese poetic expression. However, the argument can easily be reversed to mean that, far from desiring to ground their distinction in a "revolutionary" approach to poetry, Kyōgoku poets aimed at being more "traditional" by predicating their art on "more traditional" practices.[29]

In his *Notes on Poetry* (*Tamekanekyō Wakashō,* ca. 1285–1287), an essay written for the instruction of his pupil Fushimi, Tamekane confesses the difficulties involved in attempting to differentiate between legitimate and illegitimate (*jashō*) poetic traditions. However, Tamekane argues that a solution may be found in the examination of the levels of sincerity contained in a poem, an achievement that was mastered particularly by the ancient poets of the *Man'yōshū.* While at the same time quoting Teika's advice to the shogun Sanetomo to imitate the poetry of the Six Poetic Geniuses (Rokkasen), Tamekane reminds his student that the *Man'yōshū*—the wellspring of the Japanese poetic voice—may serve even better the purpose of inspiring genuine poetry. For Nijō poets who used to polish their compositions until all signs of "vulgarity" had finally disappeared, keeping literary and ordinary language clearly distinct, nothing could be more removed from the rules of poetic practice than Tamekane's program:

> At the time of *Man'yōshū,* poets wrote exactly as they felt in their hearts and did not hesitate to say the same thing twice. They made no distinction between informal and formal, and did not differentiate between poetic and ordinary speech. They followed what they felt in their own hearts and expressed themselves just as they wished. Relying on their own innate qualities, they skillfully expressed the feelings that moved their hearts. In sentiment and wording, form and character, their poems are superior. And because the strength of their poetry is extraordinary, it is elevated, profound, and impressive. . . .
>
> There is obviously a difference between using words to describe an emotion and imbuing your words with the flavor of your true emotions. Whatever the subject of your poem may be, when you address your subject you should become one with it. It is not just a matter of entering into its outward appearance, but of harmonizing completely with its internal and external aspects. There is a vast difference between doing this in principle and actually entering into the emotional experience.[30]

This passage should not be taken as a defense of an allegedly romantic theory of poetic inspiration. Far from being a precursor of modern poetic practices, Tamekane's theory derived from the philosophy of one of the earliest Buddhist schools to enter Japan in the seventh century, the Hossō school. The sect's basic philosophical assumption was that outward appearances are nothing but the product of human imagination. Thus one must attribute "the existence of all the outer world to inner ideation —in short, holding that nothing but ideation exists,"[31] a program that explains the academic name of the school, "Mere Ideation" (Yuishiki).

When Tamekane argued that the poet should become one with the subject of his poem, his use of the word "yoking" *(sōō = yoga)*[32] referred to a basic Hossō principle according to which subject and object must be "yoked" together in order for the subject to realize that the object of the mind's ideation cannot be taken as an "objective" reality. Since reality was held to be the mere ideation of the mind, the language expressing this reality must be one with it, the result of a free process springing from the mind, and not the artificial product of techniques as the Nijō poets claimed in their treatises.

The impact of the tenets of the Hossō school on the theoretical principles of Kyōgoku poets has been analyzed by the Japanese scholar Iwasa Miyoko, who has focused her attention on a relevant passage from Tamekane's *Notes on Poetry* that we need to discuss.[33] She interprets the text as Tamekane's translation in poetic language of the "Five General Mental Functions" that were classified by philosophers of the Hossō school in their analysis of the elements of existence ("One Hundred Dharmas" or *Hyaku Hō)*. Tamekane's passage reads as follows:

> Be it blossoms or moonlight, daybreak or the same as dusk, (1) whatever your subject may be *(koto ni mukite wa)*, (2) try to make yourself one with it *(sono koto ni narikaeri)* and (3) express its true essence *(sono makoto o arawasu)*. (4) If you absorb its appearance *(sono arisama o omoitome)* and (5) let the reactions that it evokes penetrate your heart deeply *(sore ni mukite waga kokoro no hataraku yō o mo)*, only then entrusting these feelings to words, then your words will be captivating and attractive. As you are only bringing out the scene, merely letting out what is within you, there is no reason to be bothered by what others say.[34]

Iwasa sees a symmetric correspondence between the five sentences that I have marked above with numbers and the role played by the five mental functions during the activation of consciousness. The following are the five resulting equations: (1) = touch *(sparśa)*; (2) = volition *(manaskara)*; (3) = sensation *(vedanā)*; (4) = idea *(saṃjñā)*; (5) = thought *(cetanā)*.[35]

Seen from the perspective of Hossō philosophy, the expression "heart" *(kokoro)* should then be taken to mean "consciousness" *(vijñāna)*, so that "to penetrate your heart deeply" underscores the idea that the object must be "yoked" *(sōō)* to the consciousness producing it, since subject and object are the products of the same mental process. Belief to the contrary leads to a split between object and representation that in reality does not exist. Words "unyoked" from the object deny the process of ideation and erroneously take objects as a separate entity from its originating mental process.

Moreover, Tamekane argued that "words must be perfumed with consciousness" *(kokoro no mama ni kotoba no nioi yuku to wa),*[36] an expression well known to Hossō scholars who conceived the base consciousness *(ālayavijñāna),* in which diverse mental processes are stored, as a changing substance "perfumed" with cognition and action that provide it with a transient form.[37] Far from attempting to overthrow the poetic tradition, the freedom of expression advocated by Tamekane was a struggle to bring that tradition back to its original, mythical past when words—no matter how "vulgar" and crude—always matched perfectly the poet's intention/ideation. This point recurs in the *Bunkyō Hifuron,* a ninth-century poetic treatise by the monk and philosopher Kūkai (774–835), to which Tamekane often resorted for quotations.[38]

Addressing the topic of the *Man'yōshū,* Tamekane stated that "consciousness uses its specific characters *(kokoro jisei o tsukai)* to skillfully express the feelings that moved the poet's heart."[39] The expression "specific characters" (Skt. *svabhāva;* Jpns. *jisei*) is a Buddhist word referring to the nature of all the elements of existence *(dhārma)* that are produced by the mind. Tamekane argued that the creative process of *Man'yōshū* poets was a mental movement that led to the formulation of an ideal reality as these poets envisioned it in their mind and then entrusted it to paper. According to Tamekane, it is the mental process of these poets that should be imitated, not necessarily their ancient style. This accounts for the small number of poems from the *Man'yōshū* that were included in the imperial anthologies compiled by members of the Kyōgoku school, despite the master's reverence for this ancient collection. The *Man'yōshū* stood in the mind of Kyōgoku poets as the enlightened source of the poetic act. The theories of a Buddhist school provided them with a poetic strategy with which to challenge their professional and political rivals.

An attack on Tamekane's poetic principles came in the Ninth Month of 1295 with the compilation of the *Nomori no Kagami* (Reflections in a Field Guard's Mirror), which was written from the partisan view of the Nijō school. Originally attributed to the poet Rokujō Arifusa, this treatise, according to Fukuda Hideichi, seems to be the product of a Tendai monk who was challenging the legitimacy of Tamekane as the heir to Teika's line.[40] In fact the text makes the point that, should Tamekane really be the guardian of Shunzei, Teika, and Tameie's poetic practice, he would not be encouraging poets to take the *Man'yōshū* as their model.

The philosophy of a more recent Buddhist school, the Tendai, replaces the Hossō doctrine of mere ideation in the *Nomori no Kagami*'s explanation of the nature of poetry and its legitimation of Nijō supremacy in the poetic field. Tamekane was accused of mistakenly privileging a statement from the preface of the first imperial anthology, the *Kokinshū* (905), according to which "words take the mind as their seed *(sore waka wa sono ne o kokochi ni tsuke)*."[41] The *Nomori no Kagami* argues that Tamekane neglected one of the basic principles of the Tendai dialectical explanation of reality, in which the acknowledgment of contingency must be followed by its denial before reality can eventually be perceived in its final and correct form. The text blames the poet Ki no Tsurayuki for the omission in his preface of the fact that, while "words take the mind as their seed," they also "should not take the mind as their seed," since the mind is both good and bad and, therefore, poets should respect the Buddhist command "while taking the mind as your master, do not take the mind as your master."[42]

Since, according to the author of the *Nomori no Kagami,* an explanation of reality in its base, vulgar form is nothing but the product of a bad mind, Tamekane's belief in the need to match every single word with the reality of the external world is perceived as a device to present with "vulgar" language the product of a deficient mind. Tamekane, therefore, was urged to learn the practice of Nijō poets who instead "dress up their poems with words"[43] that describe a reality in its final, enlightened form. The treatise attacked Tamekane's act of turning his back on an entire tradition of proper, restrained, and polished poetic language as a vulgar desire to "show publicly one's private parts," a betrayal of the alleged purpose of poetry—"to see what cannot be seen, to hear what cannot be heard, to think what cannot be thought, and to sing what is not."[44]

The attack on Tamekane was based on the Tendai teaching of the Three Truths that Fujiwara Shunzei originally applied to his own poetic practice.[45] This doctrine interpreted reality according to the three stages of void *(kū)*, provisional *(ke)*, and mean *(chū)*. Although reality was held to be basically void, it still had a provisional existence, which is the one usually experienced by people. The true state of reality beyond both void and the momentary (or transitory) was the third truth—the mean or middle—a state of Thusness leading those endowed with the correct state of mind to the realization of reality in its true being of nonduality.

According to the *Nomori no Kagami,* poetry is required to explain this triple process and provide the same representation of reality that appears to the mind of the enlightened. Members of the Nijō school accused

Tamekane and their Kyōgoku rivals of stopping in their poetic practice at the stage of the provisional, where things were taken to be what the eye sees and not as an enlightened mind would perceive them. The treatise provided Tamekane's enemies with potent arguments against the poetic/political system in which Tamekane was grounding his program of legitimation.

Unsatisfied with the relative "modernity" of the Tendai tradition which went back no further than the early Heian period and upon which the patriarch Shunzei had built his philosophy of art, Tamekane aimed at recapturing the original authenticity of the poetic act by referring to the anthology of "mythical" times—the *Man'yōshū*—and by using the philosophy of a Buddhist sect of the Nara period—the Hossō school—as a framework for his theoretical speculations. By implying that the legitimating source of his poetry was even more ancient than Shunzei's, Tamekane put himself and the Kyōgoku school in the center of the process of Mikohidari production, claiming legitimacy over his rivals as the heir to the tradition of his ancestors Shunzei and Teika. He appropriated for himself and his school the "consciousness" *(vijñāna)* of the imperial body, of which Tamekane became the major spokesman in the discussions over the heart and mind *(kokoro)* of the poetic enterprise.

This theoretical apparatus continued to play a central role among the imperial defenders of the Kyōgoku tradition in their rivalry with the Nijō school. The marginalization of the Jimyōin line from the center of power forced the descendants of Emperor Fushimi increasingly to displace their political frustrations into the realm of cultural production.

A Guardian of the Kyōgoku Tradition: Eifukumon-in

With the exile of Kyōgoku Tamekane and the death in 1317 of Emperor Fushimi, it was Eifukumon-in (1271–1342)—Fushimi's first consort—who became the guardian of the Kyōgoku poetic tradition and the center of a group of poets whose most representative members were Eifukumon-in's adopted son Go-Fushimi; Tamekane's sister Tameko; the daughter of the Kujō Minister of the Left, Enseimon-in Shindainagon; Kazan-in Iechika and Iemasa; Hino Toshimitsu; Taira Tsunechika; Fushimi's consort, Shinshi; and the daughter of Nijō Noriyoshi.

The geographical center of Eifukumon-in's activities was the residence of the Saionji family, known at the time as the Kitayama villa, which was located in the area where today we admire the Golden Pavilion (Kinkakuji). After the death of her father Sanekane (1322) and her brother Kinhira (1325), Eifukumon-in became, in fact, the senior member of the Saionji clan and a spokesperson for the Jimyōin branch of the imperial family. When in 1326 the designated successor of Emperor Go-Daigo, Prince Kuninaga, suddenly died, her grandson—the future Emperor Kōgon (r. 1332–1333)—was made crown prince and put in charge of the Jimyōin mansion that Eifukumon-in had jealously guarded for many years before moving to the Kitayama residence. After Fushimi's death, Eifukumon-in exercised a close watch over the emperor's descendants by managing the finances of the residents of the Jimyōin mansion, starting from Emperor Go-Fushimi and his consort Kōgimon-in—the daughter of Saionji Kinhira and, therefore, a niece of Eifukumon-in—as well as their son Kōgon and the abdicated sovereign Hanazono, Go-Fushimi's brother.[46]

Beside directly managing her powerful household in the matters of daily life, Eifukumon-in also exploited the authorial power of the poetic act in order to politically legitimize the might of her family members through the game of rhetorical skills. The empress entrusted the poetic act with the creation of cultural and symbolic power that were required to justify the central position she was taking as a major figure in the politics of the Jimyōin family.

From the very moment of her marriage to Emperor Fushimi and her "official" acceptance into the Jimyōin line, Eifukumon-in confided in the power of the written word, producing a poetic exchange with her husband in which she legitimizes herself as both an object worth recording and the subject empowered to produce the act of recording. The trope is a variation on the symbolic act of transferring a precious instrument—a *koto* that was originally possessed by Emperor Go-Fukakusa—to the hands of the family's newest member. The encoded message was that, by passing the instrument over to his wife, Fushimi was honoring his father's command to entrust it to deserving hands. Since the Saionji family was well known for its musical skills, this symbolic "enthronement" ceremony was addressed to the empress as well as to her clan. The *koto* was to Eifukumon-in what the regalia were to her husband in the process of legitimation. The exchange occurred in 1305, one year after Go-Fukakusa's death, and was recorded in the *Gyokuyō Wakashū,* one of the two imperial collections compiled by Kyōgoku poets. Fushimi wrote:

Tamazusa no	Since the string of this life
Sono tama no o no	Is now broken,
Taeshi yori	This jewelled instrument
Ima wa katami no	Is now his memento:
Ne ni zo nakaruru	Its sound brings tears to my eyes.

Eifukumon-in answered:

Inishie o	Viewing this jewelled instrument
Kakuru namida no	That moves you to tears

Tamazusa no	Hiding the past
Katami no koe ni	I add my tears
Ne o zo soenuru	To the sound of this memento.[47]

The political reality of the fourteenth century produced a change in the tone of Eifukumon-in's poetry that from encomiastic soon became more silent and private. The representation of the empress's ascension into the mythical dimension of eternity is replaced by a more distressed description of reality that becomes for Eifukumon-in a source of deep grief, a "bondage" turning her life in an unexpected direction. Far from being welcomed, the role that she must play as the jealous guardian of the traditions of her adoptive family becomes a cause of personal strain and at times an unbearable responsibility. This private representation of the negative side of power became the topic of a poem that she wrote "at the time of Go-Fukakusa's death":

Omowazarishi	Autumn's dew
Fuji no tamoto no	Falls on the mourner's dark sleeves
Aki no tsuyu	As I never expected it to happen:
Kakaru chigiri no	Now I understand
Aware o zo shiru	The sadness of this bondage.[48]

The empress had become a witness to a situation of political fragmentation that extended to all levels of authority: between the two rival branches of the imperial family, within the branches themselves, between members of the most aristocratic as well as military families. She compared the political uncertainty of the time to a mountain stream that at the beginning flows in a single course, only to split eventually into countless minor currents pouring into an equal number of falls. The power of a potentially mighty river was weakened by the excessive number of feeble streams that, should they ever reunite in a single, powerful course, would then produce an impressive cascade—a role that the poet associated with the emperors of the Jimyōin line. The metaphor of the mountain stream appears in *Eifukumon-in's One Hundred Round Poetry Contest with Herself (Eifukumon-in Hyakuban Onjika-awase)*:

Yamagawa no	The mountain stream
Tada hitosuji no	Flowing
Nagare koso	In a single route
Amata no taki ni	Parts its waters
Ochiwakarekere	In a myriad falls.[49]

Two occurrences made clear to the empress that her family was far from becoming the mighty cascade: The first was Go-Fushimi's loss of power in 1333, when Emperor Go-Daigo in an unprecedented turn of events returned to the capital from his place of exile, thus resuming the functions of the ruling sovereign; the second was the execution in 1335 of Kinmune, head of the Saionji family, by the soldiers of Go-Daigo. The death of Go-Fushimi the following year left the Jimyōin in a situation of particular vulnerability. The emperor's abdication followed by the tonsure had already weakened the hopes of Eifukumon-in, whose exchange with her adoptive son was included in the *Fūga Wakashū,* the second collection by Kyōgoku poets. Go-Fushimi's poem is followed here by Eifukumon-in's reply:

Aki o matade	I finally decided
Omoitachinishi	Without even waiting for autumn:
Kokegoromo	How can I hereafter dry
Ima yori tsuyu o	This mossy robe
Ikade hosamashi	The dew drenched more than ever?
Omoiyaru	Thinking of you,
Koke no koromo no	My tears add to the dew
Tsuyu kakete	On your mossy robe
Moto no namida no	Reducing the sleeves
Sode ya kuchinamu	To rags.[50]

There is no reason to believe that the acceptance of Eifukumon-in into the imperial family did not result in "a sad bondage." Not only did she have to worry about the loss of power on the part of the Jimyōin branch; the situation of the Saionji clan was no more promising. Kinmune—the son of Sanehira and Kinhira's grandson—became, in fact, the victim of his own brother Kinshige, who, wishing to replace Kinmune in the leadership of the clan, exposed a plot in which Kinmune was involved: a conspiracy to overthrow Go-Daigo and reinstate Emperor Kōgon to the throne. Kinmune's political fate was decided. This event, known as the Chūsendai Rebellion, led to Kinmune's exile to Izumo province as well as to Kinshige's promotion to the headship of the Saionji family. The *Taiheiki* narrates the dramatic end of Kinmune, who was strangled in front of his own wife Meishi.[51] There is no record of this episode in Meishi's diary, the *Takemukigaki.* The relationships and intrigues among the descendants of Saionji Sanekane may be clarified by referring to Figure 1.4.

After Kinmune's death, Eifukumon-in invited Meishi and her little son Sanetoshi, who was born after the death of his father, to live with her in the Kitayama villa. Eifukumon-in was planning to have the leadership of the family returned to Kinmune's line. She evidently hoped that Sanetoshi would restore prosperity to the family, returning it to the glorious age of Sanekane.

The metaphorical representation of authority was provided by the

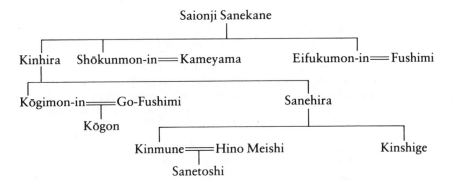

Figure 1.4

evergreen pine—the young Sanetoshi—whose resistance to the rigors of winter makes it the only survivor in a field of withered plants. The strong rain falling on the tree hints at the uncertain future awaiting Sanetoshi, who cannot avoid fights and intrigues if he wishes to succeed to the leadership of the Saionji clan. This representation of Sanetoshi's political initiation highlights Eifukumon-in's dream of restoration in which opponents are definitively silenced. The poem appears in the *Fūga Wakashū:*

Muramura ni	A young pine tree
Komatsu majireru	Grows amid
Fuyugare no	Myriad winter plants:
Nobe susamajiki	Furiously the evening rain
Yūgure no ame	Falls on the withered field.[52]

Meishi's diary records that Sanetoshi's arrival at the Kitayama villa was especially welcomed by Kōgimon-in—daughter of Saionji Kinhira, wife of Emperor Go-Fushimi, and mother of Emperor Kōgon—who became one of Sanetoshi's first partners in the courtly practice of poetic exchange. To the boy's complaint that the new environment was forcing him to spend all his energy studying, Kōgimon-in answered that efforts must be made in order to ensure the Saionji clan a strong leader and the rulers of the Northern court a reliable guardian. Kōgimon-in argues that Sanetoshi was bound to reestablish a deep tie between his family and the new rulers. In her two poems in response to Sanetoshi, Kōgimon-in used the metaphor of the footprints of a bird, which in the tradition of Japanese poetry is reminiscent of the shape of the Chinese characters written with a brush. In this exchange Sanetoshi's poem comes first:

Yuki furite	How terribly sad
Samuki ashita ni	To be scolded and forced

Fumi yome to	To do my homework
Semeraruru koso	On a cold morning
Kanashiu wa are	With the snow falling.
Fumisomuru	Now I see
Waka no koshiji no	That those bird's prints
Tori no ato ni	Will never cease to appear
Nao o taesenu	In the North, treading for the first time
Ima zo miekeru	The path of poetry.
Sakōbeki	For as long as
Yado no aruji no	The lord of this flowering house
Ikutose ka	Lives,
Taenu miyuki no	I shall see the unceasing footprints
Ato o mirubeki	Of imperial visits.[53]

Meishi's uncle, Hino Sukeaki, shared with Eifukumon-in and Kōgi-mon-in the same hope when, on the occasion of Sanetoshi's coming of age in 1341—the boy was only eight at the time—he addressed him with a congratulatory poem:

Sakōbeki	The white snow
Yukisue kakete	Piles up on a house
Shirayuki no	Whose ancient glory
Furinuru uchi ni	Continues
Ato zo kasanaru	In a flowering future.[54]

Eifukumon-in was unable to witness the political restoration of the Saionji family. The fact that her later poems remain essentially private acts removed from officialdom illustrates the political displacement of which she had become a victim. She spent her last lonely years grieving the death of close relatives and friends such as her adoptive son Go-Fushimi, her sister Shōkunmon-in (a consort of Emperor Kameyama), her adoptive daughter Shōgimon-in, and Hanazono's natural mother, Kenshinmon-in—the last daughter of Tōin Saneo. Three years before dying, in the spring of 1339, she mentioned her reclusive life to Retired Emperor Hanazono, who at the time was living the life of a monk at the Hagiwara residence, the site of today's Myōshinji, not far removed from Eifukumon-in's mansion. In two poetic exchanges with Hanazono, Eifu-kumon-in invited him to bring solace to her loneliness and to admire the cherry blossoms together, now that she felt entirely forgotten. Hanazono argued that he was so estranged from public life that he could not find the strength to shake off the reclusive mood to which he had sadly become accustomed. The first and third poems, both by Eifukumon-in, were sent "together with a twig of cherry blossoms":

Toki shiranu	Please, come and visit
Yado no nokiba o	The full bloom of the cherries
Hanazakari	On the eaves of a dwelling
Kimi dani toe na	That has forgotten time:
Mata tare o ka wa	Otherwise, who else should come?

Haru utoki	Estranged from spring,
Miyamagakure no	Absorbed in my thoughts,
Nagame yue	Hidden in a mountain,
Toubeki hana no	I forgot the time
Koro mo wasurete	When the cherry blossom should be
	contemplated.[55]

Sakichiru mo	Until which spring
Shiru hito mo naki	Should these flowers wait
Yado no hana	For you to come see them,
Itsu no haru made	These garden cherries that no one notices
Miyuki machiken	Having blossomed and already scattered?

Yoyo o hete	It has been such a long time
Miyuki furinishi	Since my last visit through the years
Yado no hana	To the garden flowers:
Kawaranu iro mo	This unchanged color
Mukashi kourashi	Seems to like the past.[56]

Hanazono's unwillingness to please the woman and pay his respects may have been motivated by reasons different from those adduced by the emperor—his decision to forget the pleasures of the world and embrace the path of reclusion. More personal considerations may have affected his determination, particularly his bitterness against Eifukumon-in and the Saionji family who strongly supported his half-brother Go-Fushimi. As the daughter of Tōin Saneo and of one of Saneo's minor consorts—the daughter of a priest of the Kamo Shrine—Hanazono's mother, Kenshin-mon-in, was descended from a collateral branch of the Saionji. She was no match for Eifukumon-in, who was in charge of the destiny of Fushimi's successors.

If we must judge from Kyōgoku Tamekane's fondness for his ability as a poet, Hanazono was intellectually more gifted than his brother Go-Fushimi. The fact that Tamekane rallied support for Hanazono raised the suspicions of Saionji Sanekane, who by protecting the interests of Go-Fushimi eventually caused Tamekane's exile. Therefore, one should not be surprised by Hanazono's eagerness to protect Tamekane's legacy and ensure that the Kyōgoku poets did not stray from the "legitimate" path. In the obituary that he wrote for Tamekane, Hanazono recalls the time when the poet "certified me [as a poetry master]."⁵⁷ Hanazono must have felt that he, not Eifukumon-in, was the true heir to Tamekane and the real guardian of the Jimyōin cultural capital.

Eifukumon-in's reluctance to accept Hanazono's claim was grounded in her understanding of the political implications of the poetic act. Her willingness to defend her public role as a patron of the arts was only strengthened by her displacement from the public arena of politics. This unwavering determination on the part of the empress followed the public humiliation she suffered on account of Tameyo, the head of the rival Nijō school. The incident occurred at the time of Tameyo's compilation of the *Shokusenzaishū* (1320), when Eifukumon-in entrusted the poet with one of her compositions to be included in the anthology. Tameyo did so, but only after making unauthorized revisions of the empress's poem. His violation of Eifukumon-in's authority went well beyond the alteration of two among the five lines of the poem; Tameyo refused to return it to the author even though the empress had requested its withdrawal in order to avoid public humiliation. Given the political undertones associated with the people involved in this incident, the episode was less trivial than it may appear to us today. As the head of an influential poetic school, Tameyo was forcing his poetic/political ideas on a major representative of a rival faction. Eifukumon-in's silent acceptance of this abuse was tantamount to a bestowal of legitimacy upon her political enemy. She could only bow to the supremacy of the double Nijō/Daikakuji line.⁵⁸

Hanazono leveled a severe criticism against Eifukumon-in's poetic practice, which he claimed betrayed the rules set by Kyōgoku Tamekane. The retired emperor believed his stepmother to be unfit to represent the Kyōgoku tradition. In the entry for the twenty-fourth day of the Third Month 1332 from his diary, the *Hanazono Tennō Shinki,* he records that he sent for Tamekane's sincere opinion about a few rolls composed on the occasion of poetry contests that were judged by Eifukumon-in.⁵⁹ Basing his remarks on the Chinese *(mana)* preface to the *Kokinshū,* according to which "empty language billowed up like clouds as the times grew frivolous and as extravagance and license became the rule; flowery expressions gushed forth like a spring,"⁶⁰ Hanazono argues that Eifukumon-in's poetry is made of "frivolous, flowery expressions *(fuen)* packed with too much content *(yojō).*"⁶¹

Seen in the light of the *Kokinshū* tradition, Eifukumon-in's use of flowery expressions was compared to a tree that, although it may be at the peak of blossoming, refuses to produce any fruit. This mistake violated Tamekane's firm belief in the need to avoid artificial expressions that did not match the objective situation. Poets of the Kyōgoku school considered "flowery beauty" *(en)* a characteristic of female production that was best represented by the poetry of Ono no Komachi, "beautiful but weak," according to the *mana* preface.[62] The fact that Eifukumon-in was packing her poems "with too much content" was again in open contradiction to Tamekane's prescription of a perfect balance in the composition of poetry between the word and the external reality. An exaggerated outburst of passion deflected the poet from a truthful representation of his/her object, leading to a mere emotional explosion with no objectively perceivable image.

Hanazono's attack on Eifukumon-in's poetic production must have been prompted by the retired emperor's fear that the person at the very center of the Jimyōin political and cultural process was leaning toward an artificial and emotional kind of poetry that conformed to the canon of the rival Nijō school—the "weak" tradition according to Kyōgoku standards. It is no wonder that the poems by Eifukumon-in which were selected in the two Kyōgoku anthologies—the *Gyokuyō Wakashū* and the *Fūga Wakashū*—all adhered to the Kyōgoku style, with images defined in a precise language and balance found between subject and object.

The controversy between Hanazono and Eifukumon-in is a further example of the political implications of the poetic act and, as well, of the central role played by poetic matters in the battle over political legitimation. The inheritor of the Kyōgoku poetic tradition was Emperor Kōgon (r. 1332–1333), a son of Go-Fushimi and a grandson of Fushimi. With him the legacy of Kyōgoku Tamekane seemed to prosper again, only to be eventually silenced by the insuperable power of the Nijō school.

The Closure of the Kyōgoku Tradition: Emperor Kōgon

Kōgon's reign lasted for about three years—from the time of Go-Daigo's exile to Oki in 1331, following the failed Genkō revolt against the shogunate, to the emperor's return to the capital in 1333 and his reinstatement to the throne. When the creator of the Kenmu Restoration was again ousted by the Ashikaga in 1336 and forced to escape to the Southern region of Yoshino, Kōgon's younger brother ascended the throne as Emperor Kōmyō (r. 1337–1348). In 1348 Kōmyō abdicated in favor of Kōgon's son, who became Emperor Sukō (r. 1349–1351). Kōgon, Kōmyō, and Sukō learned the bitter taste of exile in 1351, when Go-Murakami's troops led by Kusunoki Masashige occupied the capital and took the three emperors as prisoners to the Southern capital of Anō.

As soon as Takauji was able to reconquer Kyoto, another son by Kōgon, Prince Iyahito, was enthroned as Emperor Go-Kōgon (r. 1353–1371). In 1354 the hostages were transferred to Kongōji Temple in

Kawachi province and then finally were released, Kōmyō in 1355 and the other two in 1357. Kōgon spent his last years in religious practices that he performed in the seclusion of three temples: the Kōgon'in—a small temple north of his Fushimi residence, the Jōshōji in Tanba province, and the Daikōmyōji—a temple built in the capital by Kōgon's mother Kōgimon-in and entrusted to the Zen monk Shun'oku Myōha, where Kōgon finally died in 1364.[63]

Kōgon and his uncle Hanazono fulfilled the dream of Fushimi and that of his consort Eifukumon-in by compiling an imperial collection, the *Fūga Wakashū*, that was based upon poets of the Kyōgoku school. The work was completed in 1349, one year after the death of Hanazono, to whom scholars attribute both the Chinese *(manajo)* and the Japanese *(kanajo)* prefaces. From its very beginning the anthology reveals Kōgon's poetic program. In an effort to establish the Kyōgoku school as the legitimate descendant of Shunzei and Teika, the collection starts with a poem by Kyōgoku Tamekane—the master of the Kyōgoku school—followed by verses of Fujiwara Shunzei. Then comes a verse by Tadamichi, a major political patron of the Mikohidari house and the grandfather of Kujō Yoshitsune, author of the *kana* preface to the *Shinkokinshū*. The fourth poem is by Emperor Go-Toba—the sponsor of the *Shinkokinshū* and a victim of exile after the Jōkyū disturbance of 1221—followed by supporters of the Kyōgoku school such as Saionji Sanekane, Emperor Fushimi, and one of his daughters. Completing Kōgon's short but eloquent version of the history of Japanese poetry is the ninth poem, a privileged space reserved to Fujiwara Teika.[64]

The transparency of this arrangement is apparent in its political implications. The direct descendants of Emperor Fushimi appropriated and displayed the cultural capital of the Northern court by stressing their direct relationship with a poetic line—the Kyōgoku school—that claimed to be the legitimate heir to the tradition of Shunzei and Teika. Furthermore, they searched for political legitimation by associating the Northerners with the names of the most prominent politicians of all time, names such as Tadamichi and Sanekane.

Moreover, as Hanazono states in the *mana* preface to the *Fūgashū*, poetic language is essentially political inasmuch as it contributes to the creation of a "legitimate" and moral world. Since the imperial institution was called upon to ensure the country's order and stability, the problem of legitimation was central to the ruler's performance of his duty. Double courts and double standards could not result in what was expected of a Confucian sage who, in Hanazono's opinion, was the true model for flawless leadership. The preface to the *Kokinshū* provided Hanazono with a pragmatic theory of literature as well as a Confucian interpretative framework that was applied to a poem, the *Naniwazu,* quoted by the retired emperor in his own preface.[65] This congratulatory expression of "natural" regeneration was credited with being first recited by a Korean scholar of the Kudara state, Ōnin, at the time of the enthronement of Emperor Nintoku (r. 313–399), a ruler whose government was traditionally associated with the ideas of benevolence, justice, and social and political order.

Naniwazu ni	Flowers on the trees
Saku ya ko no hana	In bloom at Naniwazu
Fuyugomori	Say, "Now winter
Ima wa harube to	Yields its place to springtime!"
Saku ya ko no hana	Flowers blooming on the trees.[66]

Hanazono protested against the contemporary neglect of the political implications of poetry, which he claimed was originally intended to guide rulers in the peaceful running of the country. He criticized the aesthetic approach to poetry, which was mainly concerned with matters of love, as an artificial reading by modern poets who were lost in questions of poetic technique and misunderstood the pragmatic role of poetic production. Openly turning his attack against members of the Nijō school,[67] Hanazono argued in the Japanese preface that the poetic act was the beginning of a didactic process in which poetry was expected to "teach people and admonish rulers."[68] His source of legitimation was the ancient Chinese *Book of Songs (Shih Ching),* which the retired emperor claimed to be the product of a mythical age in which poets were known for their loyalty to truth *(makoto)* as well as for their resistance to the use of either fabrication or embellishment. Hanazono perceived the act of collecting the *Fūga Wakashū* as a way of maintaining peace in the country now that "the wild horse was no longer tethered and the waves of the four oceans had finally calmed down."[69] He was referring to the relatively peaceful period from 1344 to 1346, one of the very few truces in the conflicts between the two courts.

Kōgon shared with Hanazono a similar view of poetry. He believed that he was deterred by political circumstances from embodying the true virtues of the benevolent ruler and that his performance as a sovereign would be judged according to the prosperity enjoyed by his subjects. In the harsh assessment of his own government that the emperor voiced in several poems, Kōgon traced the cause of his failure to an inscrutable Buddhist destiny that put him at the top of secular hierarchies without giving him direct control of the political situation. In this reversed and negative representation of imperial authority, Kōgon acknowledges his failure in living up to the standards of the Confucian sage, while his sub-

jects are portrayed in the act of starvation, the victims of ravaging wars
that the guilty emperor was unable to stop:

Samukarashi	When I think
Tami no waraya o	Of people's straw-thatched houses
Omou ni wa	In this bitter cold,
Fusuma no naka no	How shameful I feel
Ware mo hazukashi	Inside my sliding doors![70]
Totose amari	For more than ten years
Yo o tasukubeki	I longed to help the world,
Na wa furite	But now it belongs to the past:
Tami o shi sukuu	I did nothing
Hitokoto mo nashi	To assist my people.[71]

The goal set by Confucians in matters of government could not be
reached unless power was restored to one ruler and an end was put to the
fragmentation of power—a point upon which the emperors of both the
Northern and the Southern courts consistently agreed. Go-Daigo had
implemented an entire policy of restoration in order to put his bookish
knowledge of Confucianism into practice. The Northern sovereigns were
heading in the same direction: toward the reunification of the imperial
family in a single line that would stop internal disputes as well as external
conflicts with military leaders. Political restoration also meant poetic rec-
tification, the reestablishment of the "correct way of poetry" (*shikishima
no tadashiki michi*), as Hanazono stated in the preface to the *Fūga
Wakashū*.[72] Divisions hindered the path of benevolence, peace, and prosperity. The restoration of order implied a resurrection of the "original"
truth and the reinstatement of a mythical past in the practices of the
present.

As a poet, Kōgon captured his nostalgia for the lost paradise of the
past (*furuki*) in an image that secretly unveils the emperor's bitterness at
the thought of a divided dynasty. His rhetorical camouflage hides his
anger (*urami*) beneath the image of the tides' ebb and flow leaping over
the bay (*uranami*):

Yotsu no umi	When I think
Sumigataki yo no	Of this world in the four oceans
Omoide ni	That is so hard to live in,
Furuki ni kaere	I wish the wave of poetry
Waka no uranami	Would return to the bay of old.[73]

The political/poetic reunification did not take place during the emper-
or's lifetime. Contrary to an ancient belief in the actualization of verbal
expression (*kotodama*), the spoken word (*koto*) did not have the power

to imprint its message onto the page of reality *(koto)*. The ruler's inability to fulfill the restorationist duty of harmonious reconciliation displaced Kōgon's political dream into the textual space of poetry, in the unrealizable attempt to resurrect the idea that "to utter the word was to give rise to reality itself."[74] The two following poems are examples of the imperial rite of "verbal actualization." The first is a prayer addressed by Emperor Kōgon to the Iwashimizu deity, while the second is Hanazono's representation of the legitimacy of the Northern court:

Tanomu makoto	I trust in your truth,
Futatsu nakereba	God of Iwashimizu, and think:
Iwashimizu	If only I could live
Hitotsu nagare ni	In one single stream,
Sumu ka to zo omou	And there were not two.[75]

Minakami no	The gods decided
Sadameshi sue wa	That the current
Tae mo sezu	Of the Mimosuso River
Mimosusogawa no	Would ceaselessly flow
Hitotsu nagare ni	In one single stream.[76]

The poet and the emperor filled two different spaces as separated as words are from reality. The priest of the sacred governed over a cultural capital that was dispossessed of its fundamental counterpart: political power. Kōgon's poetic act continued to produce images of authority. Far from working for the sake of imperial authority, however, his poetic representations channeled the results of authorial participation into the power structure of a wise shogun who knew the benefits deriving from the poetic game. While from a political point of view Kōgon and his successors were puppets in the hands of the Ashikaga family, from a cultural perspective they were producers of images of power legitimizing shogunal authority. Kōgon's awareness of this political/cultural fracture, which eventually forced him to retire from the world and take the tonsure, was voiced in two poems:

Osamaranu	How wretched for me
Yo no tame no mi zo	To be in charge
Urewashiki	Of an ungovernable world:
Mi no tame no yo wa	As for my personal destiny,
Samo araba are	Be what it may![77]

Natsukusa no	Leaving aside
Shigemi o sutete	The thicket of summer plants
Nogareiru	How fresh the dew moss
Yamaji no koke mo	Of the mountain path
Tsuyukekarikeri	Where I find my escape.[78]

In 1342, the year of Eifukumon-in's death, Emperor Kōgon took the
tonsure at the Saihōji Temple and made himself a disciple of Musō
Kokushi (1276–1351), then abbot of the Tenryūji which was to become
a major center of Zen Buddhism. This was the result of pressure exerted
by Ashikaga Takauji, who in 1340 demanded that the emperor offer part
of his land in Tanba province—the so-called Chōkōdō property—in
order to defray expenses for the construction of the Tenryūji. By building
this majestic temple the Ashikaga shogunate intended to pacify the spirit
of their imperial enemy, Go-Daigo, who had died the previous year
(1339). Jealously guarded by the Northern court, the Chōkōdō property
was passed over from Go-Shirakawa to Go-Fukakusa, eventually becoming the symbol of Kōgon's economic legitimation. The shogun's decision
to pacify his enemy at the expense of the Northern court's economic capital must have created resentment, though it has gone unrecorded. The
situation was exploited instead by the shogun's mythographers who
silenced the emperor's private reaction and organized a public display of
grace and harmony on the occasion of Kōgon's dismissal. This theatrical
ruse was devised by a prominent shogunal ideologue, monk Musō
Kokushi, who voided the reality of Kōgon's political fall by planning the
emperor's acceptance into the Buddhist world and describing it as a
serene and felicitous event.

The highlight of the ceremony was the exchange of congratulatory
poems between Kōgon, Ashikaga Takauji, his brother Tadayoshi, Abbot
Musō, and Saionji Kinshige, the one responsible for the incrimination
and execution of his brother Kinmune. The celebration of the emperor's
political funeral afforded Takauji an occasion to announce publicly that
he had succeeded where both courts had failed in incorporating the virtues of a sage Confucian ruler. He presented himself as the restorer of
peace and prosperity to the people. The impact of the announcement was
largely produced by the might of the poetic act.

Amekaze mo	Following the attitude
Kimi ga kokoro no	Of their lord,
Mama ni shite	Rain and wind
Nodoka ni hana no	Stare at the flowers in blossom
Sakari o zo miru	With a pacified heart.
	—The Retired Emperor [Kōgon]

Hana no iro	The color of these flowers
Kotoba no tama mo	Is now brightened
Kimi ni ima	By the jewelled words
Migakarete koso	Of the lord's
Hikari sōrame	Refined brush.
	—Musō Kokushi

Yamakage ni
Saku hana made mo
Kono haru wa
Yo no nodoka naru
Iro zo miekeru

The calm colors
Of this world
Appear in this year's spring
Even in the flowers
Blossoming in the mountain's shadow.
—Shogun Takauji

Nagaraete
Yo ni sumu kai mo
Arikeri to
Hana miru haru zo
Omoishiraruru

Looking at the blossoming flowers
In spring
I have come to understand
How precious it is
To live a long life in this world.
—Tadayoshi

Mezurashiki
Kimi ga miyuki no
Matsu kaze ni
Chiranu sakura no
Iro o miru kana

Here I see
The beauty of a cherry blossom
That was spared
By the wind awaiting
A rare imperial visit.
—Chikurin Minister of the Center Kinshige[79]

The history of Kōgon's patronage of Kyōgoku poets had finally ended. Takauji struck the last blow to the school when he ordered Crown Prince Naohito—Kōgon's first or possibly second son—to be replaced by Kōgon's third son, the future Emperor Go-Kōgon. Go-Kōgon was already preparing himself to become a monk at the Myōhōin Monastery when he was confronted with Takauji's command. Utterly untrained in the arts of poetry and government, Go-Kōgon was the perfect choice for an autocratic military leader who was stepping over imperial authority on the ground that he was more "benevolent" and "virtuous" than any legitimate ruler.

After the Kyōgoku school had lost the support of the Northern sovereign, Regent Nijō Yoshimoto (1320–1388) had no obstacles in making the Nijō school the official voice at court, thus putting an end to the fortunes of Kyōgoku poetry.[80] Participation in the Nijō school, however, did not always secure the poet with private and public stability, particularly when that poet was a member of the Southern court.

A Voice from Exile: Prince Muneyoshi

Formal affiliation with the powerful Nijō school was not a guarantee of political success if the poets were forced to perform their poetic activity from the margins of exile. The physical separation from the center of legitimation cut poets off from a cohesive structure that justified their performance and provided them with the solidarity of fellow poets and the safety—sometimes dangerous—of the institution. The banishment of the poet was essentially political displacement, a fall "from grace and from the craft or occupation that has made it possible for the writer to devise works" and legitimize or delegitimize authority.[81] The exiled poets must create their own institution, searching for solidarity among those voices inspired by similar feelings of dissatisfaction.

Solidarity was easily found in medieval Japan, where the two courts channeled their respective discontent in the sponsorship of legitimizing political/poetic bodies. The Southern court could count on the major voice of Prince Muneyoshi (1311–ca. 1385)—also known as Munenaga—the son of Emperor Go-Daigo and Nijō Tameko and, therefore, a grandson of the influential Nijō poet Tameyo.[82] Muneyoshi himself displayed his credentials as a poet in a letter that he addressed to the Southern loyalist Kazan-in Nagachika, a letter in which he mentions the time spent as a teenager in poetic gatherings at the old house of Fujiwara Teika, together with the major Nijō poets Tameyo, Tamefuji, and the lay priest *(hōin)* Sadatame.[83] Not only did he qualify as a leading voice of the school; as one of Go-Daigo's numerous sons, he played a key role in his father's political career. Muneyoshi was first appointed chief abbot *(Tendai zasu)* of the Tendai sect in the capital's foremost temple, the Enryaku-ji, and then was sent as an ambassador to the eastern provinces with the task of mustering alliances for the Southern cause.

Referring to the beginning of Muneyoshi's religious career, the *Taiheiki* describes the prince's entrance into the Myōhōin cloister, where he was known as monk Sonchō. The chronicler acknowledges his poetic talent, claiming the superiority of Muneyoshi's poetry to that of Jien—a very distinguished poet and an earlier Tendai abbot descended from the main branch of the powerful Fujiwara family—and its comparability to the poetry of Saichō, founder of the Japanese Tendai sect.[84]

In 1330, catering to the nepotistic policies of his father, Muneyoshi replaced his brother Son'un (Prince Moriyoshi) as leader of the Tendai sect. By placing his sons at the head of major temples, Go-Daigo was preparing his attack against the Hōjō shogunate, forcing the belligerent monk-soldiers of Mt. Hiei to defend the imperial cause. Alerted by Yoshida Sadafusa of the imminent insurgence, the shogunate exiled Go-Daigo and two of his sons, Princes Takayoshi and Muneyoshi.

The event was recorded by Takayoshi in a poetic exchange with his sister, Princess Keishi, who by then had already become a nun. The woman encourages the defeated brother not to join the margins of power by taking religious vows, but instead to keep fighting from the center of the political body. Keishi argues that, far from being a move to relinquish authority to the enemy, the religious path must be considered a means to maintain power only in times of social stability. She implies that, seen from the perspective of the governing body, religious epistemes must contribute to the formation of ideological structures legitimizing and maintaining political authority. They were not aimed at the creation of decentered and alternative models for religious/cultural power dissociated from the practice of government.

> When, at the beginning of the Genkō era (1331), he heard that she had become a nun because she was so distressed at the state of the world, [Prince Takayoshi] sent a poem to Princess Keishi:

Ikade nao	How can I avoid
Ware mo ukiyo o	Now more than ever
Somukinan	Turning my back on this sad world?
Urayamashiki wa	How envious I am
Sumisome no sode	Of the nun's black sleeves.

> The princess answered:

Kimi wa nao	Don't turn
Somuki na hate zo	Your back on this world now
Tonikaku ni	Not, at least, as long as
Sadamenaki yo no	This unsettled world
Sadamenakereba	Does not settle down.[85]

Muneyoshi's poetic representation of the same event was an unreligious outburst of the "religious" man. He blames the protective deity of Mt. Hiei for not fulfilling his promise and turning his back on the chief priest of the mountain. The prince highlights the political implications of an office that was at the head of the major religious institution of the time —the Enryakuji: a contract between the emperor, the abbot, and the sacred that the deity refuses to honor. The explanation for the god's betrayal was drawn from the poetic tradition, a reference to the fact that the event occurred in the Tenth Month, known in Japanese as "Godless Month" *(kaminazuki):*

Ika ni semu	What can I trust in
Tanomu hiyoshi no	During this Godless Month
Kaminazuki	Here at Hiyoshi?
Terasanu kage no	Only in the winter showers falling
Sode no shigure o	On my dark sleeves that never dry.[86]

Go-Daigo was exiled to Oki Island, Takayoshi to Tosa, and Muneyoshi to Sanuki. During the journey toward the margins of power the prince struggled to retain poetic authority by appropriating the *loci classici* of poetic production that would legitimize his performance of the poetic act. The geography of exile provided him with topics of legitimation. For example, it was to Sanuki that Emperor Sutoku (r. 1123–1141) was exiled two centuries earlier; and Muneyoshi's grandfather Tameyo put a stamp of approval on the prince's poetic authority by sending him a poem that most propitiously reached Muneyoshi at Matsuyama, the "Waiting Mountain." The exchange is translated here—first the poem by Tameyo, followed by Muneyoshi's answer:

Matsuyama wa	How many thoughts
Kokorozukushi ni	Come across my mind
Ari totemo	Thinking of Waiting Mountain:
Na o nomi kikite	How sad to just listen to its name
Minu zo kanashiki	Without seeing it!
Omoiyaru	It is to no avail
Kokorozukushi mo	To keep on thinking
Kainaki ni	From afar:
Hito Matsuyama to	Waiting Mountain
Yoshi ya kikareji	Cannot hear you.[87]

Following his father's return to the capital in 1333, Muneyoshi was reinstated to the abbacy of the Enryakuji, receiving in 1336 the First Rank, the highest honor a monk had ever received until that date. Muneyoshi's prosperity was as brief as his father's rule in the capital. By 1336 Go-Daigo was driven out of Kyoto by the troops of the Ashikaga shogunate, forcing Muneyoshi to experience a second painful exile that would last almost fifty years. While Go-Daigo and the regalia found temporary refuge at the foot of the sacred mountain in Eastern Sakamoto, Muneyoshi left for Ise province with the general—and historian—Kitabatake Chikafusa. Meanwhile, Muneyoshi's brothers, Tsuneyoshi and Kaneyoshi, worked on the institutional and military establishment of what would be known later as the Southern court, together with Shijō Takasuke, Chūin Sadahira, and Nitta Yoshisada. At the end of the year Go-Daigo had already settled in the Yoshino area and begun his endless quarrel against Ashikaga Takauji and Emperor Kōmyō.

Muneyoshi voiced his displacement from the center of political power in several poems that develop the image of a lonely cuckoo-bird (*hototogisu*) singing in the mountains. He sent one of them to his half-sister Kanshi, daughter of Go-Daigo and Saionji Yoshiko. The disclosure of the addressee's name is crucial to an understanding of the poem's political overtones. As a consort of the Northern ruler Kōgon, Kanshi was held hostage in the enemy's camp. The poem appears in Muneyoshi's private collection, the *Rikashū*:

Hototogisu	Cuckoo-bird,
Itsu no satsuki no	On which day

Itsu no hi ka	Of that Fifth Month
Miyako ni kikishi	Was it that I last heard you
Kagiri narikemu	Singing in the capital?[88]

Muneyoshi was entrusted by his father Go-Daigo with the recruitment of troops in the eastern provinces, a new role for the poet-prince that accounts for his travels between the Southern capital and the castle of his host, Ii Michimasa of Tōtōmi province—present-day Shizuoka prefecture. In 1340 Muneyoshi and the Ii clan were forced to leave the castle because of repeated attacks from the shogunate. While his wife—either the daughter or sister of Michimasa—and his son Tadayoshi retreated into the mountains, the prince continued wandering in the eastern provinces, around the time when Kitabatake Chikafusa was taking Ota Castle (1341) at the foot of Mt. Tsukuba in today's Ibaragi prefecture.

By allowing him to play the double role of ambassador and poet, exile afforded Muneyoshi with an opportunity to create with his second activity an image of authority that would prove beneficial to his more strictly political function. The prince's position as an ideologue of the Southern court was no less formidable than the one held by the more famous Chikafusa. By traveling and surveying the eastern provinces, Muneyoshi organized the resistance against the Northern court, which found in his poetic activity a convincing cultural legitimation.

When the eastern allies of the Southern court lost their castles to the supporters of the Ashikaga cause, the ambassador Muneyoshi was left with poetry alone to remind his friends of the Yoshino court and Emperor Go-Daigo. The poetic act never ceased to function as the producer of representations of authority, no matter how negative the poetic image, no matter how weak Muneyoshi's position in eastern Japan had become. The portrayal of an absent power was a constant reminder of the causes for war to both the marginalized Southern court and the scattered allies in the east. The prince's poetic output functioned as a means of propaganda to encourage the Southern loyalists to keep the conflict alive, and his rhetoric continued to reinforce the poems' political message that came to be incorporated in his geography of exile.

After reaching the village of Shirasu in Kai province, for example, Muneyoshi employs the double meaning of local names—*kai* signifying both the homonymous province and "to be worthy of," *shirasu* denoting the village as well as the act of "governing"—to lament the lack of political supporters in the region:

Karisome no	Although I hear
Yuku kai to wa	That it is quite worthy
Kikishikado	To temporarily reach Kai province,

Iza ya shirasu no	No person waits at Shirasu,
Matsu hito mo nashi	No ruler.[89]

The poet fled Kai after the province was attacked by the constable *(shugo)* of Shinano, Ogasawara Sadamune. Forces loyal to Go-Daigo were led by Yoshimune—a son of Nitta Yoshisada—in an attack against Shinano in 1340, but they were forced to retreat to Echigo by Uesugi Noriaki, whose offensive pushed Muneyoshi further north to the port of Teradomari on the Sea of Japan. By comparing himself to a goose instinctively heading north, Muneyoshi claimed that his northern retreat was a natural repossession of the native land. He refused to play the role of exile, taking exception with those who perceived him as a man alienated "from his native ground" *(ex solo)*—which, by the way, is the etymology of the Latin expression *exsilium*.[90] He argued that his escape from the enemy's armies was a return—an "insile"—to the native ground.

This concealment of reality derived from the prince's argument that the entire land belonged to the emperor and, therefore, every village, no matter how small or how far from the capital, was the native place of the imperial house. Naturally Muneyoshi was thinking of Go-Daigo's house. He made this point in a poem collected in the *Rikashū* and dated 1341, although, like most poems in this collection, the event took place one year before the recorded date:[91]

Furusato to	The cry of the returning goose—
Kikishi koshiji no	The bay gets farther and farther.
Sora o dani	Flying in the sky of Echigo
Nao ura tōku	That she heard
Kaeru karigane	To be her native land.[92]

In the spring of 1342 Muneyoshi moved to Nago Bay in Etchū province, present-day Toyama prefecture, where he stayed until 1344 at the Kibune Castle of Ishiguro Shigeyuki. By that time the prince seems to have accepted the idea of the exceptionality of his absence from the center of power, an experience that he increasingly tends to identify with the pain of exile. The images of remoteness and loneliness traditionally associated with the theme of exile surface in the following exchange between Muneyoshi and his cousin Nijō Tamesada, whose reply wishes the prince a safe return to the capital:

Ima wa mata	No one again
Toi kuru hito mo	Comes and visits
Nago no ura ni	Nago Bay.
Shiotarete sumu	Would they recognize this fisherman
Ama to shiranamu	Living covered by salt?

Ayu no kaze	Blow fast, eastern wind,
Haya fukikaese	And return to us the fisherman
Nago no ama no	Of Nago Bay,
Shiotare koromo	Without leaving a trace of resentment
Urami nokosade	On his robe crusted by salt.[93]

The more Muneyoshi was kept from exercising his official role because of victories by the shogun's troops in the east, the more his poetry became a private act lamenting the hardships of exile. Three years, from 1341 to 1343, he spent in the cold region of Etchū:

Naniyue ni	Why would I spend
Yuki mirubeku mo	Three years in the winter
Aranu mi no	Of the Etchū region,
Koshiji no fuyu o	Whose snow there was no reason
Mitose henuramu	To come and see?[94]

By 1343 the troops of the Southern court were forced to withdraw from the entire Kantō area under the pressure of Kō no Morofuyu. After losing Ota Castle in 1341, Kitabatake Chikafusa was now on his way back to Yoshino. The other loyalist general who still remained in the area, Kasuga Akikuni, was killed in 1344, the year Morofuyu triumphantly entered Kamakura. In northern Japan Muneyoshi found an ally in the Suwa family, which was in charge of the Upper and Lower Suwa Shrines. There the bitterness of political defeat was further compounded by Muneyoshi's failure as a poet: News reached him that none of his poems was included in the new imperial collection, the *Fūga Wakashū*. No doubt was left in the prince's mind that his eastern adventure was unsuccessful. The initial purpose of inspecting the land in order to muster support for the Southern court had foundered, leaving behind an unarmed politician and a forgotten poet. Tamesada conveyed the news to the prince, who sent to the Nijō poet the following expression of disappointment:

Ika nareba	How can I be heard
Mi wa shimo naranu	If even the words
Koto no ha no	Of this unsettled self
Uzumorete nomi	Are eventually
Kikoezaruramu	Buried?[95]

With Kō no Morofuyu's arrival in Kamakura the Kantō area enjoyed seven years of relative peace in the hands of the troops of the Northern court. Muneyoshi spent this time in the mountains of Ōigawahara. The situation remained more tense in western Japan, where Kusunoki Masayuki, the son of Masashige, was trying to increase his influence by fighting in Kii, Kawachi, and Settsu provinces. Prince Kaneyoshi was acting as the western shogun, raising armies in the Bungo province of Kyūshū.

In 1347 Yoshino fell, forcing the new Southern emperor, Go-Mura-kami, to escape to Anō. The disintegration of the Southern court was destroying a historical reality that the poet's authorial intervention wished to revive by appealing to the memory of the founding Emperor Go-Daigo. The two imperial brothers presided over the celebration of the past in a poetic/political act that was recorded in the *Rikashū*. A bitter Muneyoshi accuses his brother of responsibility for the fall of the Southern court and is reassured by Go-Murakami that the court still enjoys the protection of their father:

Tarachine no	Where shall we go,
Mamori o sōru	Now that we leave
Miyoshino no	The precious mountain of Yoshino,
Yama oba izuchi	Where paternal protection
Tachihanaruramu	Was granted us?
Furusato to	Although we have left
Narinishi yama wa	The mountain
Idenuredo	Which once was our capital,
Oya no mamori wa	The protection of our father
Nao mo aruramu	Is still here with us.[96]

An internal struggle within the Ashikaga family gave Go-Murakami the opportunity to attack Eastern Kawachi and advance as far as Sumi-yoshi in Settsu province. Nitta Yoshimune rushed to Kamakura, while Kitabatake Akiyoshi and Kusunoki Masayoshi defeated Takauji's son, Yoshiakira, and marched on the capital. Needing time to settle the dispute with his brother Tadayoshi, Takauji made a temporary peace with the Southern court that led to the reunification of the Shōhei era in 1352, a pact in which Go-Murakami was recognized as the ruling emperor. The rulers of the Northern dynasty—Kōgon, Kōmyō, and Sukō—became hostages of the Southern court. Muneyoshi was appointed eastern shogun, an office that had not been renewed since the fall of the Kenmu empire in 1336.

With the prince's reinstatement in the center of power, his poetry assumes once again the public tone of officialdom. He felt that the time had finally come to carry out his father's command: the reunification of eastern and western Japan under the sway of a single ruler. In the two examples that follow, the private voice becomes once more the proud voice of the state. The recluse Muneyoshi who for years had withstood the harshness of the Eastern climate represents himself again as the ruler in charge of the natural order in a celebration of natural/political power:

After living for such a long time in a faraway province, not only had I forgotten the manners of the capital, but I dedicated all my efforts to the way of the bow and horse. Surprised by my appointment to the office of shogun, I composed the following poems:

Omoiki ya   How could I have thought of it,
Te mo furezarishi   Birchwood bow, untouched by my hand
  Azusayumi   For so long a time?
Okifushi wagami   And yet I always expected it
Naremu mono to wa   To happen some day.[97]

  Yomo no umi no   However ebullient you are inside,
Naka ni mo wakite   Calm down,
  Shizuka nare   Sea of the four directions:
Waga osamubeki   Now I shall rule on the winds
Ura no namikaze   And waves of the bay.[98]

The truce was very short. In the Third Month of 1352, while Takauji was defeating Yoshimune and reconquering Kamakura, Yoshiakira returned to Kyoto to put an end to the brief Shōhei reunification. Meanwhile Muneyoshi was waging war against the Ashikaga troops at Kotesashihara. Now that the Southerners were once again part of the central body of government, the prince exhorted his men to the final sacrifice, should that be required by the well-being of the "legitimate" court. Five hundred years later, Muneyoshi's call for loyalty and unselfishness became the slogan of Sakamoto Ryōma (1835–1867) during the Meiji Restoration:

Kimi no tame   If this life
Yo no tame nani ka   Has value when we shed it
  Oshikaramu   For sovereign and country,
Sutete kai aru   Why should we regret
Inochi nariseba   Losing it?[99]

In 1359 the Northern Emperor Go-Kōgon ordered Nijō Tamesada to compile the eighteenth imperial anthology, the *Shinsenzai Wakashū*. Tamesada was an experienced poet and the compiler in 1323 of the *Shoku Goshūi Wakashū* at the request of Emperor Go-Daigo. Since he had trained Muneyoshi in the art of poetry, Tamesada led the prince to believe that a few of his poems might be included in the new collection. Times, however, had changed profoundly. The Nijō school was enjoying the patronage of the Ashikaga shogunate, and no poet of the Southern court could gain access to the anthology, not even a disciple of the compiler.

Muneyoshi voiced his disillusion and anger—which eventually led him to compile an anthology of Southern poets, the *Shin'yō Wakashū*—in the following poem:

Ika ni semu	How can I stand it
Iwaneba mune ni	Without saying anything—
Mitsu shio no	A rising tide—
Kokoro no uchi ni	Bitter hatred
Karaki urami o	Welling up in my heart.[100]

No record shows that Muneyoshi ever bore any grudge against Tamesada, whose choices were dictated by mere political necessity. Although Tamesada failed to include poems by members of the Southern court in the *Shinsenzai Wakashū,* he remained Muneyoshi's only link to the center of cultural power. When Tamesada died in 1360, Muneyoshi composed fifty elegies in his memory, including them in the *Rikashū*. He sent them to Tamesada's eldest son, Tametō, from Shinano province where he was living the life of a recluse. The use of the same imagery employed in the ninth century by Ariwara no Narihira during his exile in the eastern provinces—the "capital bird" *(miyakodori)* to which the poet entrusts a message to be delivered in the capital—underscores the role played by the late Tamesada as messenger of the exiled poet.[101] He provided the prince with a rare channel of communication with the capital. With his death Muneyoshi mourns the unfulfilled hope that his poetry might finally be recognized in the center of power and accepted in the capital's hall of fame:

Omou hito	What shall I ask you,
Nashi to wa kikitsu	Capital bird,
Miyakodori	Now that I have heard
Ima wa nanichō	That the one for whom I cared
Koto ka toubeki	Is no more with us?[102]
Tamahirou	If only I could pick up the beads
Koto mo araba to	And take you back to life!
Waka no ura ni	How desolate now
Tanomu kokoro no	This heart that trusted
Ima wa hakanaki	The haven of poetry.[103]

Once his weak ties with the Northern capital were destroyed, Muneyoshi turned again to the Southern court of Go-Murakami around whom the Southerners were organizing their resistance in the eastern and western provinces. Several poems were exchanged between the two brothers that testify to the common target of their political struggle. In 1360 the *bakufu* forced Go-Murakami to retreat further to the Kongōji and establish a new capital at the Sumiyoshi Shrine in present-day Sakai. The poetic correspondence between the emperor and his brother indicates Go-Murakami's desire to be joined in Settsu province by Muneyoshi in order to rebuild a shattered political body. The lament is the basic mode of these poetic exchanges in which circular arguments take the place of the concrete images of power that were usually employed in similar circumstances, as if the Southern court had totally lost control of the political situation.

In the two exchanges translated here, the first and third poems, by Go-Murakami, are followed by the answers of his brother:

Itsu made ka	Until when
Ware nomi hitori	Shall you leave me
Sumiyoshi no	Alone in Sumiyoshi
Towanu urami o	Together with my bitterness
Kimi ni nokosamu	Which I never sought?

Waga isogu	If you only knew
Kokoro o shiraba	How my heart looks forward
Sumiyoshi no	You would not feel bitter
Matsu hisashisa o	Waiting such a long time
Uramizaramashi	In Sumiyoshi.[104]

Meguriawamu	For a life
Tanomi zo shiranu	With no promise
Inochi dani	Of ever meeting again
Araba to omou	Nothing is more vain than the hope
Hodo no hakanasa	Of our meeting.

Meguriawamu	What about the man
Tanomi arubeki	Who grows old alone
Kimigayo ni	In the reign of our lord,
Hitori oinuru	The lord who should instead be confident
Mi o ika ni sen	Of our meeting?[105]

Since Go-Murakami died in 1368, the meeting never took place. The prince found a new confidant in a different brother, Kaneyoshi, who was vigorously fighting in Kyūshū against the Northern troops of Imagawa Ryōshun. In 1371 Muneyoshi sent him a poem exhorting Kaneyoshi to continue his fight in those distant regions. The poem is a perfect balance of private reminiscence and public celebration, lament and eulogy—a rare instance in Muneyoshi's later production and a meaningful closure to his private collection:

Kusa mo ki mo	I do not wish to listen
Nabiku to zo kiku	To the autumn wind's lament
Konogoro no	Of the present time,

Yo o akikaze to	During which I hear herbs and trees
Nagekazaranamu	Bow to your power.[106]

In 1374 Muneyoshi finally returned to Yoshino after an absence of thirty-seven years. The celebration of mourning became a central issue in Muneyoshi's poetic production. Most of the major loyalists were dead, including Shijō Takasuke, Kitabatake Chikafusa, Tōin Saneyo, and Emperor Go-Murakami. Only memory was left to the prince to sing a world of ashes:

Onajiku wa	Oh, if only I could meet
Tomo ni mishi yo no	Those same people
Hito mogana	I once met in the past,
Koishisa o dani	And make them talk at least
Katariawasen	Of the dear old days![107]

In 1376 Muneyoshi visited Nyoirin Temple in Yoshino in order to celebrate the ninth anniversary of Go-Murakami's death. Now that their position in the political arena was almost totally compromised, the Southerners could only cling to the power of representation, the memory of the past. The prince, Abbot Raii, and Emperor Chōkei were responsible for this process of poetic resurrection. The abbot, who officiated at the memorial, was so close to Muneyoshi that he had fourteen poems included in the *Shin'yō Wakashū*. The first of the three poems translated here is by Muneyoshi, followed by the abbot's and the emperor's:

Iku haru ka	For how many springs
Chirite misuramu	Will you keep showing off
Tsurakarishi	Your falling flowers,
Hana mo mukashi no	The falling of which today
Wakare nagara ni	Is like that cruel parting of old?

—Muneyoshi

Shitaedomo	The spring that showed the falling
Mishi yo no haru wa	In spite of people's yearning
Utsurikite	Has changed:
Adanaru hana ni	His face remains
Nokoru omokage	In this transient world.

—Raii

Yotsu no toki	He came back
Koko no kaeri ni	At the Fourth Hour
Narinikeri	In yesterday's dream,
Kinō no yume mo	When I was not yet
Odorokanu mani	Awake.[108]

—Emperor Chōkei

By 1373 all the major strategic points of Kii province that were once held by Kitabatake Chikafusa had fallen under the powerful attacks of the shogun's armies. Anō Palace had burned down, and a very modest dwelling was housing Emperor Chōkei and his guests. Both political and cultural power were seriously threatened. Excluded from the poetic/political activities of the capital, the Southerners ritualized the poetic act by gathering around the poet-prince Muneyoshi.

In 1375 the prince served as the judge of the "Five Hundred Round Poetry Contest of the Southern Court" *(Nanchō Gohyakuban Utaawase)* that was sponsored by the emperor. Fifty poems from this contest were included in the *Shin'yō Wakashū,* which became with the thousand poems selected by Chōkei in 1377 the basis of the Southern anthology. In 1376 Muneyoshi was again the judge of the "Hundred Round Palace Poetry Contest" *(Dairi Hyakuban Utaawase).* The mood was essentially private, a lament of the Southerners' decay, as the judge himself underscored in his own composition:

Yama takami	On the high mountain
Ware nomi furite	Snow falls and my head whitens:
Sabishiki wa	The sad thing is to see
Hito mo susamenu	Dawn in the snow
Yuki no asaake	Where no one prospers anymore.[109]

The final blow to the Southern court came with the death of Kaneyoshi in 1383 and the abdication of Chōkei in favor of his son Go-Kameyama —a meaningless ritual act. Although the date of Muneyoshi's death is unknown due to a lack of records on his activities after 1381, he failed to witness the reunification of the two courts in 1392. As his last years went unrecorded, he most probably spent them in exile.[110] The best poetic representation of what might have been his last moments was provided by Muneyoshi himself several years earlier in a reply to a poem by Kazan-in Nagachika—a disciple of Muneyoshi and the author of a poetic treatise, the *Kōun Kuden.* The prince employs the image of the old woman who, having become an economic burden to her family, is abandoned on Mt. Obasute—the Mountain of the Discarded Woman—and left alone to die. In the exchange Muneyoshi's reply follows Nagachika's poem:

Omokage mo	To look
Mishi ni wa ika ni	At your face,
Kawaruramu	How vast must be the change!
Obasute naranu	The moon on the edge of the mountain
Yama no ha no tsuki	Where no woman is discarded.

Mi no yukue	To this heart
Nagusamekaneshi	That cannot find consolation
Kokoro ni wa	For the way life turned out,
Obasute yama no	Even the moon on the Mountain
Tsuki mo ukariki	Of the Discarded Woman was sad.[111]

Muneyoshi's exile played a major role in the formation of the Southern court's ideological discourse. His poetry turned images traditionally related to marginalization and decentralization into the myths of power and authority legitimating the rule of Emperors Go-Daigo and Go-Murakami. Whenever the political circumstances silenced the Southern rulers, Muneyoshi leaned toward a more private use of the poetic act. The lament then replaced the encomium, but only to remind Southerners of their "mythical" past and sustain the legitimacy of their claims to power. Whether performed in a private or public capacity, the poetic act could hardly be dissociated from the political role that Muneyoshi, as well as the other poetic voices of the fourteenth century, consistently asked poetry to play.

CHAPTER TWO

The Aesthetics of Impurity:
A Theatre of Defilement

The sense of refinement and grace engendered by the presentation on stage of a *nō* play is well known to a spectator whose exegetic power is put to the task of penetrating layers of complicated symbols. The arrival on the scene of the main actor draws the viewer into the realm of mythological quest. Reality is displaced in the aesthetic sphere of representation wherein historical events undergo a process of aestheticization—a "purification" of the subject matter that speaks the language of a "high," noble, aristocratic arena of culture. This representational choice bespeaks the nature of production and consumption of an art form that was appropriated by patrons either belonging to the top of the social hierarchy or advancing claims to that end.

A study of the historical development of *nō* clarifies this relationship, placing two major moments of the history of *nō* in the house of the de facto highest power in the country: the shogun. Both aimed at obfuscating the popular origins of *nō*, transforming it into the symbolic representation of the patrons' "high" values. The fact that Zeami Motokiyo (1364–1443) is considered today the genre's major producer and adapter indicates the favor that he encountered both in his time, when he enjoyed the patronage of the Ashikaga shogun Yoshimitsu (1358–1408), and in the seventeenth century, when the formal structure and subject matter of *nō* were finally codified during the Tokugawa period. Zeami's treatment of language and topics pleased the Ashikaga and Tokugawa shoguns for bringing into their cultural capital aristocratic elements that were associated with the center of mythical/symbolic power—the court—from which the military leaders were largely excluded even though they were centers of economic/political power. Zeami's incorporation into *nō* of courtly language and tropes provided the military class with access to the secrets of the aristocracy's forbidden literary tradition.

Zeami was confronted with a formidable task: the transformation of a popular/religious/magic/pragmatic/temple-oriented art form known as *sarugaku* into an elitist/entertaining/representational/military-oriented artistic practice that had to please the new patrons of *nō*. The Japanese counterpart of the European sacred representation of the Middle Ages lent its religious symbolism to representations of secular power that benefited the Ashikaga shoguns. The staging of *nō* plays on their behalf provided them with a doubly enriched cultural capital: a mastery over refined aristocratic expression as developed within court circles as well as the power of the marginalized other—the so-called "low culture"—that aristocrats feared and upon which temples built their symbolic authority.

In the previous chapter we dealt with the court's conflicts of legitimation that were based on battles over the appropriation of refined expressions. This chapter focuses on the power of language to represent the margins of refinement—the feared and the rejected—and on the appropriation of this world of exclusion by Buddhist institutions (temples) that capitalized both economically and politically from their sponsorship of *sarugaku*. The conclusion analyzes how the excluded world was eventually aestheticized in new versions of *nō* that provided military leaders with representations of authority and power.

Beginnings: Backstage Sarugaku

Confronted with the issue of origins, Zeami fabricated a mythical account of the beginning of his art that concealed the popular roots of *sarugaku*, emphasizing instead its religious connotations through linkage with the Indian history of the Buddha's life. What better legitimation could be provided to an art form that was struggling to gain shogunal favor? Zeami's obfuscation of historical reality attempted to provide his art with an aura of authority and legitimation. He argued that an act of *sarugaku* by pious disciples of the Buddha took place during a sermon delivered by Śākyamuni. Their purpose was to put an end to an uproar by religious dissidents who were disrupting the master's speech. The staging was so successful that silence was restored to the temple and the historical Buddha could safely finish his lecture.

This legend—of which no source has so far been found in any Buddhist scripture—is recorded in one of Zeami's theoretical works, the *Fūshikaden* (Style and Flower). Zeami states that the first mythical *sarugaku* performance took place at the rear entrance of a hall of the Indian Jetavana Monastery *(ushirodo)*, a reference that indicates his knowledge of an earlier religious practice known as "backstage *sarugaku*" *(ushirodo no sarugaku)*. The legend has recently been translated as follows:

In the country of the Buddha, a wealthy man named Sudatta had built a Buddhist place of retreat, the Jetavana Monastery. At the dedication ceremonies, the Buddha preached a sermon. Devadatta and a throng of unbelievers cried out and danced wildly, holding branches and bamboo grass in which they had placed *shide,* making it more difficult for the Buddha to carry out the ceremony. The Buddha then signaled his disciple Śāriputra with his eye, and Śāriputra, through the power of the master, had the idea of arranging for flute and drum music to be played at the rear entrance to the hall *(ushirodo).* Then three of the disciples—the learned Ānanda, the wise Śāriputra, and the eloquent Pūrna—performed sixty-six entertainments. The heretics, listening to the sound of flute and drum, assembled at the rear entrance and fell silent observing the spectacle. During this time, the Buddha was able to continue on with the dedication service. Such were the beginnings of our art in India.[1]

Despite this attempt at erasure and obfuscation, scholars have successfully recovered the historical truth beneath this mythological account. Today they accept backstage *sarugaku* as the prototype of *nō,* although no definitive conclusion has been reached on the subject. We know that a performance of backstage *sarugaku* took place at the Hōshōji Temple on the twelfth day of the First Month 1251 in the presence of a retired emperor. The occasion was a political as well as a religious event: the celebration of the New Year festivals *(shūshōe)* that took place every year from the eighth to the fourteenth day of the First Month in order to beseech the deities for protection of the country. Our source is a passage from a diary, the *Ben no Naishi Nikki,* that states:

> When the emperor arrived at the Hōshōji on the occasion of the New Year's celebrations *(shūshōe),* the moon was beautifully bright. The performance of backstage *sarugaku (ushirodo no sarugō)* was particularly appealing and I was enchanted by the magicians *(zushi)* and the sound of the jingling bells.[2]

This is the only surviving statement from a witness of backstage *sarugaku* belonging to the aristocracy. All other documents are records kept by temples, a fact that may indicate the secretive nature of this kind of performance. The presence of magicians is a basic link between the public event—a Buddhist ritual of national relevance in which emperors, retired emperors, and all the major aristocrats participated—and the unfathomable power of inscrutable deities. Their role was fundamental in addressing the wrath of gods who were thought to resist the performance of the ritual and jeopardize its outcome unless their fury was placated and mistakes were avoided in the handling of sacred matters. The attention that Buddhist monks paid during the festival to buddhas and bodhisattvas was, in fact, a liability inviting the retaliation of envious Shinto gods *(kami)*, whose disapproval could easily compromise the successful result of the religious performance. This accounts for the secrecy in which subrituals related to Buddhist / Shinto syncretic issues were conducted at the time of the main *shūshōe* ceremony. The evil influence of a *kami* had to be kept under strict control at least until the end of the festival.

Several scholars have recently argued that backstage *sarugaku* was addressed to one of these Shinto deities, Madarajin, whose spirit was believed to dwell in a sacred and secret area behind the Jōgyō Hall of Tendai temples. Already in the eleventh century Shinto shrines reserved sacred spaces—hidden behind the hall or beneath its floor—to deities. Niunoya Tetsuichi reports that the Jūzenshi complex of Hiyoshi Shrine had a room beneath the floor where a deity was enshrined and its statue surrounded by several people—most of whom were beggars—whose confinement required them to regularly perform purification ceremonies.[3] It is not surprising to see this practice transferred to Buddhist temples in an age of burgeoning syncretic movements.

Niunoya argues that the performers of backstage *sarugaku* lived in the rear of the hall where Madarajin was worshiped, acting as temple employees and servants to the deity.[4] A reference to the role played by Madarajin in Buddhist temples appears in the *Jōgyōdō Raiyuki,* a document of Kōryūji Temple in Kyoto, in which we read that "a statue of the deity was enshrined in the rear of the [Jōgyō] Hall as a guardian of the Buddha."[5] The statue faced the dangerous northeastern direction *(ushitora)* that since early times was believed to be the demons' entrance into the capital. The magicians *(zushi sarugaku)* to whom Ben no Naishi refers in her diary were assigned the dangerous task of confronting the mysterious power of the unknown.

Hattori Yukio argues that *sarugaku* actors performed a series of dances in front of the divine statue.[6] Yamaji Kōzō reaches the same conclusion, acknowledging the fact that the dances performed for Madarajin belonged to the "old man" *(okina)* type—a congratulatory dance and an invocation to the deity to come and guard the sacred performance— which is still staged today. The rites conducted in front of the statue were so central to the well-being of both temple and government that members of the local police *(kebiishi)* supervised the activities of magicians and actors, living together with them in a state of total isolation at the rear of the hall for a period of seven days, in order to ensure the successful completion of the main *shūshōe* ritual.[7]

Further evidence for the derivation of *nō* from backstage *sarugaku* comes from the presence of an "old man mask" *(okina)* in the Jōgyō Hall, the same mask that actors use today to impersonate an elderly character. Amano Fumio contends that a mask symbolizing an old man was kept in the Jōgyō Hall of a Tendai temple at Tōnomine, where it was worshiped as Madarajin. Basing his hypothesis on a passage from a theoretical treatise on *nō* by Zenchiku (1405–?1471), the *Meishukushū,* he argues that an entire array of performances known as "the sixty-six *sarugaku* pieces" *(rokujūrokuban sarugaku)*—which included *imayō, rōei* songs, and dances by female dancers *(shirabyōshi)*—were performed in front of the mask/deity. All performances were followed by rounds of *sake,* so that even the mask hanging in the hall was said to eventually become red with the excitement.[8]

The presence of the *okina* mask among the performers of backstage *sarugaku* helps us to identify their social status. We know, in fact, that since the mid-Kamakura period the same mask was worshiped as the guardian of outcasts *(hinin)* and the protector of their shelters. Beside symbolizing Madarajin, the mask also stood as a representation of Monju (Skt. Mañjuśrī), a deity worshiped by lepers and other victims of exclusion who, either for their sickness, deformity, poverty, or their involvement in unconventional activities, were rejected as "different" by a social structure that perceived itself to be healthy. Monju and the *okina* mask were objects of worship at the Hannyaji, a temple at the center of the religious activities of monk Eizon of the Ritsu sect, who spent his life among outcasts. The temple was located in the area called the Slope of Nara (Narazaka), which was famous in medieval Japan for sheltering the largest number of outcasts in the Yamato area.[9]

Besides dancing in front of Madarajin and attending to his needs, magicians and actors staged an important act on the last night of the *shūshōe* festival. Known as the "Exorcising Ritual" *(tsuina),* it involved the chasing and beating of the demon Vināyaka—the disrupter of cosmic order—by two guardian deities, Ryūten and Bishamonten, whose victory over the demon restored order and purity to the temple's main ritual. Sometimes the deities would appear with masks representing the guard dogs of shrines and temples—Aun and Komainu—one with an open mouth, the other with its mouth closed.[10] The performance took place inside the hall, while outside a group of temple employees threw stones at the demon. The symbolic act required that the doors of the hall remain closed in order to avoid contamination of the sacred area should the stones enter the hall. Medieval documents such as the *Chūyūki* (fourteenth day of the First Month 1130), the *Hyōhanki* (fourteenth day of the First Month 1152), and the *Kanchūki* (eighteenth day of the First

Month 1289) record that while magicians *(zushi)* played the role of Ryūten and Bishamonten, the serfs of liminal areas owned by the temple *(sanjo)* acted as the chased demon and the stone-throwing mob.[11]

It is very difficult to reconstruct the events of this ritual—particularly because of the limited data delineating the exact social status of the performers. Modern scholars tend to agree that most of the participants in the *shūshōe* festival were owned by local proprietors who sheltered them from the heavy burden of taxation. They inhabited special lands—we can call them "liminal areas"—that were annexed as special belts to the estates *(shōen)* of temples and the imperial court. These people were recruited whenever a temple needed their services. In the case of festivals, the "priests of the liminal area" *(sanjo hōshi)* performed according to their skills. The performers of the devil-chasing scene were undoubtedly more endowed with theatrical ability than those entrusted with the throwing of stones. Historical records testify to the presence of "priests of the liminal area" who lived around the western gate of Daigoji Temple and performed the *shūshōe* festivals in the twelfth century.[12]

Liminal areas provided temples with a large pool of manpower. Among the performers at religious festivals were several categories of artists from the less skillful stone-throwers to the more sophisticated magicians *(zushi)*, whose act comprised fast footsteps, jumping, and running *(hashiri)*. In between there were the actors of *sarugaku* whose main role consisted of acts of mimicry and the inducement of laughter from the audience. Magicians were distinguished from *sarugaku* actors by the sophistication of their colorful costumes, as well as the larger rewards that they received from the temple. A record of the Jōshōji dating to the end of the Heian period, the *Jōshōji Nenjū Sōsetsuchō,* states that on the occasion of a *shūshōe* festival each of the seventeen magicians was given seven rolls *(hiki)* of silk, while the twenty-five performers of *sarugaku* were each rewarded with one simple roll.[13]

This situation continued until early Kamakura times, when the magicians' act was still followed by the actors' imitations. A deep transformation occurred during the middle years of the Kamakura period, when the actors began increasingly to marginalize and replace the magicians—a change that explains the choice of the name "backstage *sarugaku*" *(ushirodo no sarugaku)* to define the temples' secret and most important ceremony at the beginning of each year. Because of lack of evidence on the participation of magicians and actors in the *shūshōe* of the fourteenth century, it is difficult to establish whether or not they still took part in the Buddhist ritual at that time.[14] *Sarugaku* came to be sponsored by shrines both in the capital and in the provinces. The Kamo (Kyoto), Sumiyoshi (Osaka), Matsuo (Yamashiro), and Kasuga (Nara) shrines became the major patrons of an art form that came to be increasingly appreciated on its own terms, apart from its original ritual function, although the pragmatic role of *sarugaku* was never erased.

The Geography of Exclusion

Besides providing us with a link to the development of *nō*, the presence of the old-man mask in both *nō* and "backstage *sarugaku*" establishes a further relationship between the performers and special-status groups that were known in medieval Japan as "base people" *(senmin)*, "professionals" *(shokunin)*, "people of the riverbanks" *(kawaramono)*, and "nonhumans" *(hinin)*—people who "were owned by other individuals and did not have 'the right to be taxed.' "[15] This broad classification of the excluded and marginalized encompasses members of diverse occupations —from artisans to artists to beggars—whose only common bond was their nonresident status, their lack of a permanent address. They lived between the spaces reserved for the settled people (peasants)—also known as "common people" *(heimin)*—in the cracks and interstices of the ordered social structure: at the settlement's "boundaries, such as along riverbanks, under bridges, or near slopes."[16]

The discrimination to which outcasts—as I will be calling the special-status groups—were subjected by those recognized with status was prompted by their continuous exposure to defilement, for the job of outcasts was mainly related to the disposal of the dead. The fear engendered among all social classes by the concept of death and impurity led the common people to a contradictory perception of the low/other/marginalized. On the one hand, they confined the "polluting" elements of society to areas of liminality—spaces between being and not-being, life and death—divesting them socially of their status and cosmologically of their participation in the most privileged of the six Buddhist realms *(rokudō)*: the world of humans *(ningen)*. On the other, the outcasts' connection with the secret and inscrutable power of the unknown—death—surrounded them with a divine aura that commoners could never claim. Unable to trace their ancestors, the outcasts were known as "the children of god."[17] This contradiction which marginalized the outcasts as human beings while centralizing them as symbols of exorcised chaos and reestablished order explains the temples' use of nonhuman carriers of impurity in their efforts against defilement. The outcasts became the subcontractors of temples that were acutely unwilling to make defilement their central business.

Our major source for the study of *sarugaku* in the Heian period, the *Shin Sarugaku Ki* (ca. 1052) by Fujiwara no Akihira, records the areas where actors were residing at the time. All these zones—Sakanoue, Modoribashi, Sesonji, Ōhara, and Ono—were parts of a liminal map marking places reserved either to the destitute people of riverbanks, bridges, and slopes or to the serfs inhabiting annexed areas *(sanjo)*. The toponymic designations of the most famous actors of the time confirm this linkage: Kikumasa of Sakanoue (slope), Tokutaka of Modoribashi (bridge), Kikutake of Ōhara *(sanjo),* and Fukumaru of Ono *(sanjo).*[18] A closer analysis of this map of defilement is necessary if we are to understand the central role that actors and other "defiled" employees of temples played within the structure of religious institutions.

BOUNDARIES: SLOPES AND RIVERBANKS

Outcasts ensured their means of survival through their ability to function as an "intermediate and taboo-loaded category"—an attempt to exploit marginalization for their own benefit, making symbolically central their social peripherality and exempting the central segments of society from the performance of similar duties.[19] They made death their way of life, capitalizing on the social rejection that their occupation brought them. In medieval Japan death was thought to be the major cause of defilement, a taboo *(imi)* that ought to be avoided at all costs. When facing the impurity of death, a purification ceremony *(misogihare)* was required to cleanse the object of defilement as well as everything that might have come into contact with it.

The obsession of the medieval Japanese with death and defilement is documented in the *Goryōsha Bukkiryō* (An Ordinance to Subjugate the Spirits of the Dead; 1403), a detailed list of impurities that specifies the amount of time required for cleansing several kinds of exposure to contamination. It was, in fact, believed that the victims of defilement who came into contact with an impure object would produce "secondary" defilements that attached to those who had inadvertently approached them.

The record mentions different types of defilements, including the impurity derived by a woman from blood both during her monthly periods—at which time she was sheltered from public view for eleven days—and at times of birth, which required a confinement of only ten days. Abortion was considered a most defiling act because of the presence of blood and death: Seven days was the penalty for the woman acting in the first three months of her pregnancy, thirty days for those procrastinating further. Persons who ate the meat of deer and wild boars defiled themselves for five days, while the consumption of the animal's legs—which, being closer to the ground, were more defiled—demanded two more days. To encounter the corpse of an animal inadvertently required five days of total reclusion. Seeing a human corpse could mean economic disaster for a man who had to wait fifty days before resuming his daily activities. The penalty was reduced to a short week, however, if the corpse belonged to a deformed man.[20] The death of an emperor or shogun was considered "a national defilement," causing cohorts of diviners *(onmyōji)* to be summoned to cleanse the nation.

The Japanese attitude toward the polluting nature of death remained unchallenged during the entire Middle Ages. Nobody was sheltered from the threat of the afterlife, not even temples that earned a good part of their income from the business of tombs. A humorous story of the twelfth century from the *Konjaku Monogatari* relates how an old man and his two companions exploited the monks' resistance to confronting a corpse in order to steal the temple's bell. While the old man pretends to be dead under the bell, no one among the villagers accepts responsibility for removing the corpse on the grounds that "since the shrine's festival is approaching, we cannot defile ourselves." Purporting to dispose of the body, the old man's two companions steal the bell, knowing that thirty days must pass before the monks will finally dare to enter the hall for fear of defilement.[21]

On a more tragic note, the Muromachi scholar Sanjōnishi Sanetaka (1455–1537) confesses in his diary, the *Sanetakakō Ki,* that on the sixth day of the Eleventh Month 1505 he dismissed a female servant who was dying of pneumonia. The woman was abandoned in the Imadegawa area, on the bank of the Kamo River, for fear that Sanetaka's residence might be exposed to the defilement derived from viewing a corpse.[22] The woman spent her last days among the outcasts living along the river *(kawaramono),* whose permanent state of defilement shielded them from Sanetaka's concerns.

The government established the banks of the Kamo and Katsura rivers as the capital's burial sites. In an attempt to protect the court from exposure to death, an edict which is recorded in the *Nihon Kōki*—twenty-fifth day of the First Month of 797—was promulgated just three years after the transfer of the capital to Heian, according to which farmers of Otagi and Kadono villages in Yamashiro province were forbidden to bury members of their family near their homes as they had customarily done for generations. The penalty for transgressors was painfully severe— exile from Kyoto and the Kinai region.[23]

Earlier we noted the area of Sakanoue in connection with the actor Kikumasa. Japanese scholars identify this region with the slope of Kiyomizu Temple in the capital, which by the end of the Kamakura period was populated by more than a thousand outcasts, most of whom were in charge of burials. In 1445 Tōji Temple stipulated a contract with the outcasts of Kiyomizu slope (Kiyomizuzaka), giving them a complete monopoly on funerals. The temple circumvented the problem of defilement by providing the means of production, requiring their "nonhuman" employees to supply the labor.[24]

Besides providing temples and shrines with manpower, outcasts played a fundamental role in the economic life of the country as artisans and food gatherers. The *Tengu Zōshi,* a picture scroll *(emaki)* of the late Kamakura period, contains the picture of a boy hunting with a falcon in front of a garden where the skin of either a horse or a cow is hung out to dry. On the right side of the picture a man plucks the wings of captured birds, preparing them for sale in the capital.[25] A contemporary anthropologist describes the daily activities of medieval outcasts as follows:

> The "defiling occupations" included butchers, falconers, tanners, makers of leather goods, cormorant fishermen, undertakers, caretakers of tombs, executioners, *tatami* floor mat makers, and sweepers. All of these occupations involved dealings with culturally defined impurity which derived from death and "dirt." Butchers and falconers handled the bodies of dead animals. Tanners and makers of leather goods handled the hides of dead animals. Undertakers, caretakers of tombs, and executioners were associated with human corpses. . . . The special status people who engaged in these occupations were "the specialists in impurity." . . . They specialized in removing impurity and thereby spared others the inevitable problems of dealing with culturally defined dirt and impurity. Nevertheless, they were seen to be defiled themselves.[26]

The *Tengu Zōshi* is an invaluable source for the study of medieval outcasts. The explanations *(kotobagaki)* accompanying the pictures of the fifth chapter of the "Miidera roll" mention the words "outcast" *(eta)* and "boy outcast" *(eta warawa)* in relation to the inhabitants of the banks of the Kamo River. They are credited with an even higher degree of defilement than the *tengu,* mythical figures that the superstitious illustrator portrays as long-nosed mountain goblins. The scroll narrates the story of a *tengu* who, having lost his way, finds himself wandering in the Shijō Kawara area—the bank *(kawara)* of the Kamo River along Kyoto's fourth ward (Shijō). Far from engendering terror among the local population, the *tengu* himself becomes the victim of a starving outcast who kills the goblin in order to satisfy his hunger.[27]

The consumption of the *tengu*'s meat by the outcast underlines the contempt with which commoners regarded the people of the riverbanks, a mixture of fear and disbelief toward an "inferior" species. However, a literal reading of the episode fails to convey the deeper implications of the fact that the *tengu* in question was a metaphorical representation of the minister of the Buddhist Law: the monk. Indeed, the *Tengu Zōshi* defines the seven types of *tengu* as follows: "the monks of Kōfukuji, Tōdaiji, Enryakuji, Miidera, Tōji, the mountain priests *(yamabushi),* and the recluses *(tonsei).*"[28]

The author emphasizes the overdefiled nature of the nonhumans by having an outcast butchering a disciple of the Buddha. No crime, in fact, could surpass the harming of a holy man. To kill him and feed on his body definitely excluded the outcasts from participation in an ordered social structure. The fear and contempt in which they were held by commoners provided the nonhumans with a safety valve protecting them from acts of retaliation. Moreover, their marketability in the line of pollution made them a potent presence that was contained in marginalized areas of displacement. The Shijō Kawara circuit was under the direct control and protection of Gion Shrine, which employed the outcasts to bury the dead and cleanse the sacred area.[29]

BOUNDARIES: BRIDGES AND GATES

Another actor mentioned in the *Shin Sarugaku Ki* is Tokutada of Modoribashi, or "Tokutada from the Returning Bridge," a reference to an area in the capital around the bridge of First Avenue (Ichijō Modoribashi). The rich symbolism associated with this area nurtured the vital contradiction that made outcasts objects of both respect and contempt on the part of the hierarchical society. Even when emptied of its particular contextualizing meaning, the bridge is a potent carrier of symbolism in its functional purpose of letting someone pass from one space to another by an act of crossing over a third, less defined, and more fluid zone. Bridges convey the ambiguity of symbols—the inability to grasp their "definite" meaning that made outcasts fundamental players in the game of the absolute and the unknown.

By taking the leap across the bridge, outcasts empowered themselves with answers to the absolute question of meaning. Because of this "privileged" position, *hinin* became a badly needed workforce that was sought after by religious men who made the unknown their profession, as well as by secular members of society who wanted to be sheltered from the risks of knowing it. It also created the positive side of the outcast's existential contradiction—an acceptance, sometimes even respect, triggered by fear. In order to get closer to the problem of meaning, however, they had to die as human beings, exposing themselves to all sorts of defilements, and constantly enduring public rejection.

The trajectory of the history of *sarugaku* performers follows the ambiguity of the symbolic bridge. First rejected by society as an image of defilement—at once both a scapegoat and a votive offering—the actor eventually came to be regarded as the deity's means to manifest himself onstage: a sacred image empowering the ideological discourses of religious and political institutions. This is the potent trajectory of ambiguity, which anthropologists have defined as "a kind of bridge that allows us to run back and forth from one kind of meaning to another, until we take firm resolve to cross the bridge into new, and fixed, meanings."[30]

The two meanings addressed by the actors and by all the specialists of defilement are the two sides of one coin: the riverbanks of life and death spanned by the bridge of First Avenue. The association of this bridge with the realm of the unknown comes from a legend of the Kamakura period which was anthologized in the *Senjūshō*, a collection of Buddhist anecdotes. According to the story, monk Jōzō was undergoing ascetic training in the Kumano area when he was informed of the death of his father, Miyoshi Kiyoyuki. Upon returning to the capital, the monk witnesses a most astounding occurrence: While the corpse is being carried over the bridge during the funeral procession, Kiyoyuki comes back to life and lives an additional week, thanks to Jōzō's prayers to *kami* and buddhas. The bridge was then named "the Returning Bridge of First Avenue" (Ichijō Modoribashi) for this miraculous event.[31]

No one profited more than temples from the contradictory and ambiguous symbolism embodied by the outcasts that temples exploited to their advantage. The stigma attached to the nonhumans was a product of the Buddhist epistemology that defined outcasts *(eta)* as those carrying many *(ta)* impurities *(e, kegare)*. Whether these originated from illnesses *(yamai no kegare)* or crimes *(tsumi no kegare)*, the prime cause stayed with the destiny (karma) that individuals brought upon themselves in a past existence. Buddhist monks fostered and justified the contempt in which outcasts were held by preaching that, should one fall in the net of wrongdoing and disparage the Buddhist teachings, he will become a vehicle of defilement. Therefore, since they had stained themselves with the "dirt" of sin, outcasts deserved the severe punishment of their status.

The areas to which the nonhumans were confined provided preachers with concrete examples of the effects of karma, a visual experience that monks could offer as a tangible visualization of their sermons to believers approaching the off-limit area of the sacred. The scriptural legitimation of the presence of the "other" and its causes came to monks from the last chapter of the *Lotus Sutra (Hokkekyō)*, "The Encouragement of the Bodhisattva Universally Worthy" *(Fugen Bosatsu Kanpotsu Hon)*:

> If one sees a person receiving and holding this scripture, then utters its faults and its evils, be they fact or not fact, that person in the present age shall get white leprosy. If anyone makes light of it or laughs at it, from age to age his teeth shall be far apart and decayed, he shall have ugly lips and a flat nose, his arms and legs shall be crooked, his eyes shall be pointed and the pupils out of symmetry, his body shall stink, he shall have sores run-

ning pus and blood, his belly shall be watery and his breath short: in brief, he shall have all manner of evil and grave ailments.[32]

The identification of the cause of the outcasts' defilement with the Buddhist concept of karma allowed temples to cast the entire problem of the "other"—death/unknown/Shinto deities/evil spirits/outcasts—in a Buddhist framework, thus channeling the threatening flow of defilement in the familiar sea of rebirth and salvation. When the outcast was recognized to possess personal skills, he was employed to perform whatever act of cleansing the temple might require. When he was too sick to be part of the labor force, he was paraded in the temple's precincts as a *memento mori* for pilgrims. Not only were believers exposed to the inevitability of death; the presence of the outcasts was a lesson on the unfathomable occurrences in the afterlife, when the chain of retribution was back again in motion. At the same time they were reassured that salvation was available, since the benevolent grace of Amida was forgetting no one, not even the outcasts begging for alms in the temple.

Temples assimilated the symbolism of the bridge into their rituals by staging the last rite of passage—the soul's journey from the human world to the land of Amida Buddha, which was known as the "Amida Welcome Service" *(mukaekō)*—in the presence of the real "people of the bridges." Outcasts were a major presence in this rite, functioning at the same time as the performers of the cleansing act as well as the object that needed cleansing. The appearance of Amida exorcises and annihilates the treacherous power of the "other," depriving evil of its secret force and eventually transforming defilement into purity, the unknown and despised into the fixed meaning of the known and desired.

In the rituals of Taima Temple, Amida came to meet the souls of the dead on a long bridge connecting the Main Hall (Mandara-dō)—the symbol of Amida's Pure Land—to the Shaba-dō, a metaphorical reading of our defiled world. Each year, on the fourteenth day of the Fifth Month, a sacred representation of the coming of Amida was staged at this temple. According to the *Taima Mandara Sō*—a work in forty-eight volumes written in 1436 by Yūyo Seisō, the eighth patriarch of the Chinsei school of Jōdo—a statue of Chūjōhime was carried into the Shaba-dō, awaiting the arrival of Amida and his retinue. Twenty-five bodhisattvas leave the Main Hall—known as "Paradise Hall" (Gokuraku-dō)—followed by Amida's two companions Kannon and Seishi, and cross the bridge while playing sacred music. They all cross back over the bridge, carrying with them the statue of Chūjōhime who is finally brought to the Main Hall, Amida's paradise. By crossing the bridge the deceased is led to salvation and reborn in the Pure Land.[33]

Another medieval document, the *Suisaki,* records that a similar performance took place on the eighth day of the Tenth Month 1080 on the riverbank under the Kiyomizudera bridge—present-day Gojō bridge—in the vicinity of the burial ground of Toribeno.[34] Private citizens became increasingly dependent on the staging of these performances. Taking advantage of this situation, the enterprising monks of Daigoji Temple started fund-raising campaigns in which they assured rebirth to anyone who wished to cross the bridge and worship a mandala located at its extremity in exchange for a small admission fee—as the *Yamashina Ke Raiki* attests on the third day of the Eighth Month 1492.[35] The temples' exploitation of the symbolic implications of the "other" and the "unknown" provided them with new sources of financial reward.

An eloquent example of the role played by defilement within a sacred structure is the "Temple of the Four Guardians" (Shitennōji) in Naniwa, present-day Osaka, where the symbolism related to the liminal presence of nonhumans was assimilated into the rich web of Amidist meaning. The architectural layout of the complex was the social answer to the needs of homeless lepers, blind people, and beggars, who found shelter in the compound's subtemples. One building, the Hiden-in, was reserved for orphans and the elderly. Medicinal herbs were provided through the Seiyaku-in, adjacent to which was a free clinic for the poor, the Ryō-byō-in.[36]

The temple's Western Gate (Saidai-mon) is a monument to the concept of liminality and the direct relationship between the sacred and the "other." While providing nonhumans with shelter day and night, the colossal door represented the Eastern Gate of Amida's paradise and an entrance to the Pure Land. Its majestic presence made of a liminal, defiled area of impurity a cultic object for believers in Amida's grace. The following poem from the *Ryōjin Hishō* (Secret Selection of Songs)— an anthology of "modern-style" verses *(imayō)* collected by Emperor Go-Shirakawa in 1179—develops the symbolism of the gate:

Gokuraku Jōdo no tōmon wa	The Eastern Gate of the Pure Land
Naniwa no umi ni zo mukaetaru	Faces the sea of Naniwa Bay.
Tenbō rinsho no saimon ni	At the Western Gate of this sacred place of the Buddha
Nenbutsu suru hito maire to te	Come, people, to worship Amida's name.[37]

Under this gate Emperor Go-Reizei witnessed a performance of the Amida Welcome Service in the Tenth Month of 1048.[38] A new layer of potent symbols was added to the occasion by the very site of the representation, which was also known to host a cult centered on the worship of the setting sun *(nissōkan)*. Crowds of believers—most of whom lived in the seven nonhuman settlements east of the temple's Southern Gate, the so-called Tennō Shichi Mura—gathered at sunset under the Western Gate to contemplate Amida's Pure Land. Thinkers of the Jōdo school interpreted the physical blindness of the carriers of defilement as an example of spiritual vision that salvaged outcasts from their threatening/defiling nature. They praised blindness as a condition for spiritual understanding and supernatural insight. However dangerous the contemplation of the sun might be to the worshiper's eyesight, a much higher vision was in store for those trusting in the benevolence of Amida. One of the scriptures of the Jōdo school, the *Kanmuryōjukyō,* lists the contemplation of the sun as the first step toward the attainment of rebirth in Amida's land: "All sentient beings possess the visual faculty and can see the setting sun. Focusing their attention and sitting properly, they should face west and clearly perceive the sun. Then, with their minds firmly fixed and their thoughts unwavering, they should gaze upon the sun which, as it is about to set, looks like a drum suspended in the open sky."[39]

The symbolism of the Temple of the Four Guardians transforms the defilement of the blind into a prerequisite for spiritual realization. The more deprived among the outcasts—those without particular skills, whose physical condition forced them to beg for a living—are socially recycled by temples that determine the role of the nonhumans as symbols of spiritual vision that are paraded in the temple's compound to enrich the symbolic language of the sacred area. Defilement is domesticated in a process of spiritual purification that cannot take place without the "threatening" presence of the "other" to be cleansed.

The *nō* writer Motomasa—a son of Zeami—portrayed this process in a play entitled "The Tottering Priest" *(Yoroboshi)*. The victim of slander, Shuntokumaru is driven from his house and forced to become a beggar at the Temple of the Four Guardians. After losing his eyesight, he shares with his nonhuman companions a daily life of deprivation. He regularly venerates the setting sun through the temple's Western Gate, visualizing in his mind what he can no longer see with his eyes. His spiritual realization eventually leads him to perceive a superior reality to which people with clear vision are usually blind. In the following section the sightless Shuntokumaru *(shite)* guides his father Michitoshi *(waki)* through the rich symbolism of the temple:

WAKI: Now it is time to venerate the setting sun; please, do it!
SHITE: Indeed, now it's time. Since I am blind I only feel that I must turn in this direction to worship the Eastern Gate: Sacred the name of Amida!

WAKI: What? Why do you say the Eastern Gate? This is the *torii* of the Western Gate.

SHITE: Oh, what a foolish thing to say! Is it wrong to say that by going out from the Western Gate of Tennōji we face the Eastern Gate of Amida's paradise?

WAKI: No, you are absolutely right! By leaving from the Western Gate of Naniwa Temple . . .

SHITE: You enter the most important gate.

WAKI: By leaving from the most important gate of this temple . . .

SHITE: You face the sacred land of Amida . . .

WAKI: The Eastern Gate.

SHITE: Into the western sea of Naniwa facing the Eastern Gate . . .

CHORUS: The sun is setting, while dancing with joy.[40]

THE ANNEXED AREA: *SANJO*

Confronted by the difficulty of classifying the various categories of outcasts in medieval Japan, Niunoya Tetsuichi has drawn a clear line between the paupers populating slopes *(saka hinin),* shelters *(shuku hinin),* and temple gates *(sanzai hinin),* on the one hand, and those with personal skills that made them useful in acts of purification *(kiyome)*—the inhabitants of tax-free areas managed by major landowners *(sanjo hinin)* on the other.[41] The previous examples of actors coming from the boundary zones of the most deprived among the outcasts show that we cannot exclude the presence of a skilled labor force in the riverbank areas of which the artisans are just one example, nor can we ignore the presence of beggars in the tax-free annexed areas. This does not weaken Niunoya's hypothesis indicating a historical development of the *sanjo* in more and more specialized pools of skilled labor that came to be perceived as less and less defiled.

The *Kennaiki* reports on the fourth day of the Second Month 1435 that the riverbank people *(kawaramono)* in charge of maintaining gardens at the imperial palace were replaced by members of annexed areas *(sanjomono)* "because of the latter's lack of impurities."[42] Although this is undoubtedly a later development in the history of liminal areas, it supports Niunoya's distinction between different kinds of outcasts. He describes the actors of *sarugaku* as essentially belonging to the less defiled group *(sanjo hinin),* whose members performed at major shrines on the occasion of Shinto festivals. The actor—a typical name would be Sarumaru (Monkey Boy)—was in charge of the lion dances *(shishimai),* as well as juggling, acrobatics, and the like *(dengaku).*[43]

The confinement of actors to the annexed areas may sound too schematic and restrictive, particularly in light of the evidence to the contrary provided by the *Shin Sarugaku Ki*. When we consider that three or four centuries separate this Heian document from the records of late Kamakura and early Muromachi times, we may speculate that an increasing specialization and professionalization on the part of *sarugaku* actors led to their escape from the more "defiled," poverty-stricken areas and to their assimilation in the annexed areas in which they were more easily employable by the officials of shrines and temples. The actor's migration did not change his status, however. He continued to be perceived as an outcast and to share the same space with other outcasts.

The direct relationship between the actors *(sanjo hinin)* and the outcasts of the first group *(sanzai hinin)*—beggars and lepers—was reinforced at the time of their public appearances. Medieval records tend to group actors together with the most defiled elements of society. The "Illustrated Record of the Suwa Daimyōjin Shrine" *(Suwa Daimyōjin Ekotoba)* lists the animators of the shrine's festival on the sixth day of the Fifth Month 1356 as follows: "dancers *(shirabyōshi)*, *dengaku* performers, magicians, *sarugaku* actors, beggar outcasts *(kojiki hinin)*, blind and sick people."[44]

The *Myōgoki,* a mid-Kamakura dictionary, mentions a group of entertainers known as *Senzu Manzai* ("Wishing a Thousand, Ten Thousand, Years"), which was composed of "begging priests from the annexed areas" *(sanjo no kojiki hōshi)*. On New Year's Day, these beggars put on the garment of hermits *(sennin)* and went with a small pine tree in their hands from house to house to deliver congratulatory poems that wished people a long life, receiving alms in return.[45] Scholars believe that the so-called *Senzu Manzai*, whose name appears in the *Shin Sarugaku Ki*,[46] are a filiation of an eighth-century type of beggars who gathered alms in exchange for congratulatory words.[47]

Two poems by these entertainers appear in the *Man'yōshū* (Ten Thousand Leaves; 759), both examples of total submission to the ruler. In the first a stag swears obedience to the emperor by offering "my horn for his majesty's umbrella, my ears for his ink bottle, my eyes for his mirror, my nails for his bowstring, my hair for his brush, my skin for covering his box, my meat for filling his stomach."[48] The second follows the same drift: A crab living among the reeds of Naniwa Bay encourages the ruler "to put some salt in my eye, and praise me as a delicious salty pickle."[49]

The beggars play the role of local deities—deities of a lower order—who swear their submission to the heavenly gods of the Yamato clan and to their human manifestation, the emperor. The symbolic role assigned to the beggars was the same as the one later played by the actors of *sarugaku.* They were the intermediaries between the present ordered reality, represented by the emperor and the Buddhist cosmology, and a threatening "other"—local deities, Shinto gods—whose submission had to be secured in order to escape disruption of the social/political/religious world.

Several medieval documents mention the activities of *sanjo* outcasts in the precincts of temples and shrines. Two records kept by monks of Daigoji Temple, the *Daigoji Zōjiki* and the *Daigo Nenjū Gyōji*, refer to them with regard to the planning of the temple's garden, the building of the "sacred road" for transporting the portable shrine, and the presentation of congratulatory greetings on the occasion of festivals for the New Year *(shūshōe)*.[50]

Outcasts with a knowledge of the history of the temples to which their annexed area was attached would recite the temple's legends, making use of picture scrolls that provided listeners with an immediate visualization of the story. When similar groups of reciters *(etoki hōshi)* organized themselves in guilds, clashes erupted between different groups of outcasts who were charged with infringing upon the monopolistic rights of their rivals. In 1330 the lay priest Fujitsugu (Fujitsugu Nyūdō), a liminal "priest" belonging to Tōji Temple, created a controversy with the guild of lute-player/priests for using a lute *(biwa)* to accompany his narration of the temple's legends.[51] The use of the lute was, in fact, restricted to a group of blind musicians who sang passages from the *Tales of the Heike (Heike Monogatari)* and recited tongue twisters *(haya monogatari)*.[52] Although both picture-scroll storytellers *(etoki hōshi)* and lute-player/priests *(biwa hōshi)* were outcasts from a liminal area *(sanjo hōshi)*, their professional pride attests to the high degree of specialization achieved.

Other *"sanjo* priests" specialized in the staging of puppet plays. The *Kitanosha Hikitsuke* states that on the tenth day of the Tenth Month 1461, the shogun Ashikaga Yoshimasa stopped at Ichijō on his way back from Kitano Shrine in order to participate in a puppet show *(ayatsuri-mono)*. The artists were from an area annexed to the Hirata Shrine of Nishinomiya in Settsu province.[53]

Liminal areas produced the performers of an amateur type of *sarugaku* known as *tesarugaku*, who also practiced divination. Mobilized for fund-raising purposes, these actors/diviners—who were called *shōmonji* —organized themselves in groups as a result of the constant pressure from professional performers attempting to silence competition. The *Inryōken Nichiroku* mentions an actor/diviner of the Kitabatake group who performed a congratulatory dance on the second day of 1488.[54] In his diary, the *Kanmon Gyoki*, Retired Emperor Go-Sukō praises two famous *shōmonji*: "Young Dog" (Inuwaka) and "Small Dog" (Koinu). Inuwaka performed for the emperor in Fushimi Palace in 1420, while Koinu gave a similar performance in 1431.[55]

The *shōmonji* were eventually crushed by the professional troupes who lobbied with the shogun to deny them access to the shogunal palace. The shogun's guards restrained Koinu from giving his congratulatory performance on New Year's Day of 1337. This took place at the time when the Yamato troupe of Kan'ami (1333–1384) and Zeami was enjoying the patronage of shogun Yoshimitsu. In 1450, seven years after Zeami's death, the police, answering a request from the Kanze and Konparu troupes, stopped Koinu in the middle of his act while he was holding a fund-raising performance at Rokudō Chinkōji Temple in the capital. He was eventually arrested in 1466 for appearing on stage with a mask—apparently a prop reserved for the guilds of professional actors.[56]

The Marketing of Defilement

The ritual domestication of the defiling forces of the unknown translated into solid cash in the middle of the Kamakura period when, due to the thirteenth-century development of a monetary economy as well as the erosion of their proprietary rights on lands *(shōen)*, temples became increasingly dependent on the ability to gather money from external sources. Religious institutions launched fund-raising campaigns employing an array of "fund-raising saints" *(kanjin hijiri)*, an anonymous crowd of fund-raisers endowed with the most diverse expertise: monks preaching the Buddhist teachings in exchange for alms; storytellers and actors who were sent by temples to instruct villagers in the history of their institutions while informing their audiences of the temple's need of a new bell or some repair work on a leaking roof; and construction workers who could easily market their sought-after skills in designing and building roads and bridges.[57]

From around the middle of the thirteenth century, temples looked for new avenues of income by charging their customers to listen to a Buddhist sermon or to pray in front of a statue that was credited with healing power. Sacred representations on the topic of the sermon followed the monk's oratorical performance with the aim of instructing and entertaining a paying audience. "The Record of the Kagen Era" *(Kagenki)* states that "Eight Lectures on the *Lotus Sutra*" *(Hokke Hakkō)*, delivered at the Kokawadera in 1339, ended with a performance of *sarugaku* by the actor Kesadayū.[58] The same name appears in conjunction with a fund-raising campaign at the Hōryūji on the sixth day of the Eleventh Month 1317 and in 1320, the year in which, according to the *Ōdai Nenjū Gyōji* (1511), an actor named "Kesadayū from Sakato was asked by [Hōryūji] Temple to head the performances of *dengaku* because of his fame."[59]

The increasing involvement of temples in the arena of play followed their successful monopolization of rights over the performance of rituals dealing with death and defilement. A study of the mechanism of memorial services indicates a direct relationship between religious ritual and theatrical performance, as well as informing us on the dynamics of the economic gains made by temples in domesticating and silencing the threatening power of an impure "other." We know from texts such as the *Kanmon Gyoki* (9/23/1421) and the *Dajōin Jisha Zōjiki* (2/26/1497) that one of the main reasons why commoners and aristocrats provided temples with offerings was the sponsorship of memorial services. People needed to have rituals performed that would extinguish evil karma and guarantee rebirth in Amida's paradise.[60]

The medieval monk was not the first to master the art of convincing people that services held in memory of the dead were highly beneficial both to the destiny of the departed and to the karma of his generous relatives. The ninth-century *Nihon Ryōiki* by monk Kyōkai mentions the story of monk Jakurin who freed a dead woman from the sin of abandoning her babies without food by persuading those babies—now responsible adults—to sponsor a memorial service on the woman's behalf. The narrator argues that only the generosity of her filial children can spare the woman from the pains of hell:

> Thereupon, all the children grieved and said, "We don't bear her a grudge. Why does our loving mother suffer for this sin?" They made Buddhist images and copied scriptures in order to atone for her sin. After the ceremony was over, she appeared to Jakurin once more in a dream, saying, "I am now released from my sin."[61]

Frightening sermons on hell and karmic retribution were an eloquent exhortation to generosity. Fund-raisers of the Daianji—a temple in Yamato province—who solicited funds by performing memorial services for the dead used a popular legend for this purpose. In 1199, one of their monks, Keikō, wrote a document with the intention of raising money for the casting of a new bell. He justified the temple's fund-raising technique by mentioning a famous precedent dating back to the Heian period, when Emperor Uda (r. 887–897) entrusted seven temples with the recitation of sutras in order to save the spirit of Tōru from hell. Keikō was referring to a popular legend involving the figure of the minister Minamoto no Tōru (822–895), a patron of the arts, whose gorgeous villa—the Kawara no In—was in early Heian times the spatial symbol of courtliness *(miyabi)*.[62] According to the *Konjaku Monogatari,* after Tōru's death the villa went from his son Noboru to Retired Emperor Uda, who in turn left it to his own son, Emperor Daigo (r. 897–930). The spirit of Tōru used to appear to Uda complaining that the emperor was illegally occupying his dwelling. Eventually the evil spirit disappears—the legend continues —persuaded to do so by Uda's rhetorical skills.[63]

In another version that appeared in an eleventh-century anthology in Chinese, the *Honchō Monzui* (Choice Literature of This Realm; ca. 1040),[64] the spirit of Tōru confesses to the emperor that his fall into hell was due to his sinful habit of killing living beings. Since he had no descendants—Tōru argues—he cannot hope to have a memorial service performed that would release him from his sins. Therefore, on the fourth day of the Seventh Month 926, Emperor Uda—who was then living at the Kawara no In together with his consort Kyōgoku no Miya—sponsored sutra recitations in seven temples as a requiem for the repose of Tōru's soul. Ki no Arimasa wrote an oath *(fujumon)* soliciting the recitation of Buddhist scriptures.[65]

Other medieval collections, such as the *Jikkinshō* and the *Zoku Kojidan,* describe the emperor's pacification of Tōru's spirit. According to the latter document, in addition to the recitation of holy scriptures, Uda, following the advice of monk Hitoyasu, gave the order to build a statue of the Buddha to be worshiped at Daianji Temple.[66]

Keikō exhorts his parishioners to follow the example of Emperor Uda by providing themselves and their dead relatives with proper afterlife insurance. He argues that by remembering the meaning of the famous words, "the bell of the Gion temple tolls into every man's heart to warn him that all is vanity and evanescence,"[67] and by giving generous alms for the casting of the temple's bell, the ordinary man can escape "the kettles of hell" and be reborn in Amida's paradise. Monk Keikō put the textual bells of the *Tale of the Heike (Heike Monogatari)* to a practical end, a practice that became quite common during the Muromachi period. According to the *Moromori Ki,* the recitation of episodes from the *Tale of the Heike* often followed the delivery of sermons.[68] Moreover, the view of traveling holy men carrying signs with the image of a bell was widespread among donors who grew increasingly accustomed to the fund-rasing tactics of temples.

The activity of fund-raisers intensified with the approach of the Seventh Month and the Urabon Festival commemorating the spirits of the dead. The *Rakuchū Rakugaizu* (Scenes from Inside and Outside the Capital) portrays a group of monks, carrying a board with a bell on it, in the act of collecting money while narrating legends of their temple.[69] An offering for the casting of the temple's bell was publicized as the price of guaranteeing spiritual relief both to the donor and to his dead relatives suffering from the pains of the lower circles of the Six Realms *(rokudō).*

Accounts of the sinners' pains in hell such as the one about Minamoto no Tōru were eloquent devices in fund-raising campaigns. Actors provided the monks with even more graphic portrayals of "reality" in the afterworld, eventually developing a repertoire of *nō* that staged the victimization of the dead at the hands of angry demons—a form known as "demon-*nō*" *(oni-nō)*.[70] The playwright Kan'ami (1333–1384) transformed the legend of Tōru in a demon-*nō* entitled "Minister Tōru" *(Tōru no Otodo)*. The play was probably commissioned by a preacher who wanted his sermon on the minister followed by a staged account of the events. Kan'ami's play introduces the theme of a demon torturing Tōru in hell.[71]

The fourteenth century witnessed a substantial increase in the number of temples sponsoring *sarugaku* performances for fund-raising purposes. Before Zeami's accomplishments of the 1400s, we have records indicating eight major examples of *sarugaku*. They were staged in "defiled" zones whose association with the impurity of death made the geography of ludization a central element in the religious politics of domestication against the threat of the unknown and the "other." The following list records the sites where these performances took place, as well as the performers and the sponsoring temples:[72]

Date	Place	Actor	Source
1317	Hōryūji	Kesadayū	*Kagenki*
1339	Kokawadera (Kii)	Unknown	Temple records
1364	Yakuōji (Kyoto)	Yamato troupe	*Moromori Ki*
1371	Fukujōji (Settsu)	Kan'ami	Temple records
1372	Daigoji	Kan'ami	*Ryūgen Sōjō Nikki*
1380	Aya no Kōji Kawara	Inuō	*Gōyōki*
1383	Takakura Jizō-dō	Unknown	*Yoshidake Hinamiki*
1399	Ichijō Takenohana	Zeami	*Gōyōki*

Representations of Defilement

The reconstruction of the contextual elements in which a performance of *sarugaku* originally took place helps to clarify the role played by actors within a larger ritualistic performance. The presentation to the public of a religious drama was a small portion of a much larger play in which the professionals of the holy channeled defiling non-Buddhist components of the *mysterium tremendum* on a stage—the smaller text—on which impurities were transferred to a representative of the most "defiled" elements of society: the outcast actor. The performer of *sarugaku* exorcised on stage the elements that demanded expulsion from the frame of the social order—a threatening presence exemplified by the beggars and lepers auditing the play. By taking upon themselves the negative ingredients of defilement, actors played the role of scapegoats, which the medieval Japanese called the "dolls of pollution," that shrines' officials consigned to the river after transferring to them the impurities of the community.

The performance of the minor drama *(sarugaku)* was the temple's prerequisite for the success of the major drama, a ritual whose actors—the paupers of riverbanks—were paraded to remind commoners and aristocrats, the members of the ordered society, of the risks of an unsuccessful ritualistic performance. Outcasts were the protagonists of both the textual play and the play of reality. While providing audiences with concrete examples of defilement, they also owned the key to escape from their own personal defilement. Audiences were reminded that, because of the continuous threat posed by the nonresident groups, they could not shelter themselves from the attacks of the "other" unless they mobilized the forces of defilement to their advantage. Actors who played the role of scapegoats mitigated the harshness of the commoners' reaction to the presence of outcasts, who as "professional scapegoats" and restorers of order were sometimes given a chance to climb from the very bottom of a long and complex social ladder. This was made possible mainly by the actor's identification on stage with a deity *(kami)* in its peaceful and benign nature *(nigitama)* that recovered cosmic order after the same deity's violent aspect *(aratama)* had threatened to destroy it. The final restoration of order won the audience's respect for the actor—a pattern recurring in the staging of *nō* regardless of the community to which the play was addressed.

The Japanese anthropologist Yamaguchi Masao has devised a scheme for the interpretation of *nō* that—although originally applied to *Semimaru,* the story of Emperor Daigo's blind son—provides a thorough explanation of the plays that are most closely related to the problem of outcasts' defilement. The actor/character shelters the positive elements of society—such as centers of power, normality, organized settlements, the law, and the capital—from the negative factors—margins of power, abnormality, vagrancy, liminality, and the countryside—that challenge social stability. The process aims at either the avoidance of disorder or the restoration of order to any community that patronizes this theatrical ritual, be it a temple, a village, the court, or the shogun's palace. Because of the alleged ability of actors to free the community from "evil," troupes of outcasts were invited, put on stage, and then discarded after the "other" had been completely absorbed by the performers who, like "dolls of pollution" were then floated down the river to their new location, a temple or a neighboring village.[73]

The exorcising nature of the ritual was further strengthened by the actor's unveiling of his social status onstage in an act of self-representation showing the presence of outcasts among the characters of the play. Here I will mention a few examples whose topic was thought by temples to be congenial to the role played by *nō* within a Buddhist ritual of purification and pacification.

SLAVES

Three outcasts appear in the *nō* drama *Jinen Koji:* a fund-raiser, a slave trader, and a girl who sells herself in order to pay for a memorial service for her dead parents. The title of the play derives from the name of the main character *(shite)*—a man "naturally endowed *(jinen)* with the virtues of a lay priest *(koji)*." A translation of the Sanskrit word *gṛhapati,* "*koji*" indicates a paterfamilias who embraces the Buddhist faith and acts like a monk, although officially he does not take the tonsure.[74] An employee of Ungoji Temple in the Higashiyama area of the capital, Jinen Koji is likely to be the portrait of an articulate outcast from an annexed area *(sanjo)* whose rhetorical skills guaranteed his employability as preacher and fund-raiser. The fact that in medieval Japan "natural lay priests" *(jinen koji)* were often laughed at as "natural beggars" *(jinen kojiki)* unmasks a reality that is much closer to the historical circumstances of the social status of lay priests than to a simple play on words.[75]

The *Mii Zokutōki* mentions that a representation of a play with the same title took place on the fifteenth day of the Eighth Month 1313 at the Jōgyōdō of Miidera Temple.[76] The detail of the Jōgyōdō hall where the play was allegedly performed links *Jinen Koji* to the repertoire of "backstage *sarugaku*" of which we know so little. The records of the Miidera state that *Jinen Koji* was the fifth piece in a series of performances sponsored by the temple on the occasion of a "longevity display" *(ennen furyū),* a ritual aimed at the extension of the believers' life by dispelling evil spirits and summoning benign deities on stage. This performance occurred sixteen years before the birth of Kan'ami, who is credited with the authorship of the present play, but not without the revising hand of his son Zeami.[77]

Jinen Koji is in charge of the performance of a double ritual: The textual and fictional performance—the delivery of a series of sermons lasting seventeen days in order to raise funds for reconstruction of the temple—becomes the basic framework sustaining the larger and to the temple more central rite—the sheltering of the community from the danger of defilement that may occur if the larger ritual suffers any kind of disruption. The fund-raiser battles against the intrusion of disturbing elements that may jeopardize the results expected to benefit the two communities meeting in the temple: the fictional group of worshipers that has gathered in order to listen to the preacher's sermons, and the historical community that is witnessing the performance of the play.

The preacher's first concern is the proper execution of the ritual, a respect for the binding rules of the profession that, if improperly followed, may lead to a result opposite from the one desired—a summoning of evil spirits bringing misfortune to the community. The expertise of Jinen Koji in the basic matter of rules is emphasized by the fact that he faithfully reproduces on stage the norms collected in a medieval manual for preachers, "Essays on the Clear Vision of Sermons" *(Seppō Myōgen Ron)*. Jinen begins with preliminary arrangements such as putting on the proper garments, entering the sacred area, worshiping the Three Treasures, burning incense, and mounting the platform. Then he proceeds to the ritual—recitation of hymns, offering of flowers to the Buddha, striking the bell, reading of the supplication. These actions customarily preceded the delivery of the sermon.[78]

> SHITE: Seeking solace while awaiting the moon at the temple surrounded by clouds—Ungoji—in the evening sky, I said that I would give a sermon. Therefore, the preacher got on the platform and, before starting to read the written supplication, he struck the bell and said: "I respectfully address Śākyamuni, for whose teachings I shall be grateful all my life, and all the buddhas of the Three Worlds, together with all the bodhisattvas. I will recite the *Hannyakyō* in order to ask for the coming of all deities to protect the Buddhist Law.[79]

The ritual is disrupted when a girl appears on stage, offering a garment to the preacher in exchange for a memorial service for her dead parents. The girl's offering to the temple is, in fact, the result of a defiling action: She had to sell herself *(minoshiro)* to a slave trader in order to purchase a straw-coat-like cloth *(minoshiro goromo)* that might pay for the requiem. As the two Japanese words—*minoshiro*—indicate, the girl was making a human sacrifice to the Buddha by providing the temple with a symbolic item displaying the real nature of the sacrifice—the life of a human being forced to become an outcast in order to fulfill the duty of filial piety and assure her parents of a safe life in the afterworld.

Jinen Koji is faced with the hard choice of whether to address the problem of the girl—and, thereby, disrupt the order of his ritual—or to continue the rites undisturbed while exposing them to the potential defilement coming from the offering. He is so upset by the sight of the girl's proprietor, who has come to the temple to claim her, that he ignores a believer's complaint that, by interrupting his sermons on the last of the seventeen days, the preacher is preventing his audience from forming a tie with the Buddha. Arguing that rules must be broken and the sacrifice must be exposed to danger in order to escape a deeper defilement that would inevitably unleash its ruinous power against the sacred area, Jinen Koji decides to stop the rites. There is no point—Jinen says—in struggling to keep intact an order that has already fallen into disorder. Looking for a justification in the same manual which codified the rules he was breaking, Jinen Koji applies to himself a well-known argument from the *Seppō Myōgen Ron* according to which "a preacher must make his listeners achieve the principle *(dōri)* of understanding white and black, forcing them to distinguish good from evil."[80]

> AI: If you do so, all the sermons that you have delivered so far will be of no avail to me.
>
> SHITE: No, that's not the case. Although you may be listening to sermons one hundred or a thousand days, those words won't be of any help to you unless you learn how to distinguish good from evil. Now, the girl happens to be a good person, while the slave trader is clearly bad. Aren't these two paths straightforwardly laid in front of you?[81]

Defilement is removed and the restoration of order achieved through an act of ludization. The preacher shows his ability to exorcise the defiling presence of the "other" by staging a play within the play—three times removed from the temple's original ritual—in which he appeals to his rhetorical and performing abilities to persuade the slave trader to free the girl.[82] Jinen Koji puts his philological dexterity to the task of healing the hurt pride of the merchant whose boat the preacher inadvertently calls "a slave boat" *(hitokaibune)*. The same expression appears in a popular poem collected in the *Kangin Shū* (A Collection of Private Music) that attests to the practice, quite common in medieval Japan, of buying human beings and reselling them in the eastern or northern provinces. The poem says:

> Hitokaibune wa oki   A row of *slave galleys* goes offshore.
>   o kogu
> Totemo uraruru mi o,   Captain, at least row quietly the
>   tada   *first boat* carrying
> Shizuka ni koge yo   This body of mine which is waiting
>   Sendōdono.   to be sold.[83]

Incensed that he has been publicly exposed as a seller of human flesh, the man threatens to increase the temple's exposure to defilement through his anger. Jinen Koji calms the merchant and avoids the further accumulation of impurities by improvising an ingenious play on words that is based on the two meanings of the expression *hitokaibune* italicized in the poem. His rhetorical skills win the preacher the temporary admiration of the merchant who is almost persuaded to set his captive free:

> SHITE: Let me address that man in his boat.
>
> WAKI: Why should you call me, since this is not a boat meant for passengers?
>
> SHITE: As a matter of fact, I am not a passenger, and I am not looking for a boat to cross Lake Biwa. I have something to tell you.
>
> WAKI: What kind of boat do you think this is?
>
> SHITE: Well, this is a slave boat *(hitokaibune)*.
>
> WAKI: Not so loud! What are you driving at?
>
> SHITE: I am not surprised you are so upset; after all, people may be listening! I was referring to the oar of the boat.
>
> WAKIZURE (a dealer's colleague): You don't refer to an oar that way. If you had meant what you say, you would have used the word "sculling oar" *(kararo)*. There is no oar called *hitokai*.
>
> SHITE: Well, you say first layer of mist *(hitokasumi)* and second layer of mist *(futakasumi)* when you talk about mist on the water's surface. By the same token, you say first dyeing *(hitoshio)* and second dyeing *(futashio)* when you dye cloth. Why should it be wrong to say that your boat is the first oar *(hitokai)* or the first boat in a series of galleys?
>
> WAKI: Your reasoning is quite interesting, preacher![84]

Appealing to the written code of his guild that forbids the restitution of purchased slaves, the trader refuses to free the girl, transforming the object of the priest's philological performance—the oar—into a weapon of physical torture. With the oar he repeatedly hits the girl, filling her mouth with cotton in order to silence her cries.

The monk challenges the professional code of the merchant with the Buddhist rule of bodhisattvic action, according to which no person of the Law can neglect human suffering without being exposed to shame and disgrace. Looking for a psychological reversal that may transfer his own embarrassment to the trader, Jinen Koji offers to change places with the girl and be sold as a slave in the northern provinces. He knows that, should the trader arrive home with a priest on the boat, people would think that, unable to find any slave, the merchant had finally settled on a preacher, thus becoming the laughingstock of his town.[85] The preacher is successful, but on one condition: that a ritual be performed by Jinen Koji on behalf of the defiled slave trader.

The merchant's request gives Jinen Koji an opportunity to exorcise the serious defilement with an act of ludization. The fame of the preacher as a performer was well known to the people of the northern provinces who had once seen him dancing, after a sermon, "in order to get the attention of a sleepy audience."[86] The ingenuity of Jinen Koji's act—a mixture of narration,[87] music, and mimicry—battles against the threatening elements of the "other," leading to the staging of a civil war in which an outcast is asked to fight against his peers in order to legitimize his "acceptable" social function. The preacher summons the forces of nature to help him perform his professional act of purification. While rubbing his rosary on the frame of his fan in order to reproduce the sound of the instrument known as *sasara,* he uses as musical background the waves hitting the shore and the roar of the thunderstorm. After freeing the girl and exposing the merchant to the sinfulness of his trade, Jinen Koji finally leads the metaphorical boat of defilement "through Lake Biwa into the land of enlightenment."[88]

The symbolic mechanism that allows the preacher to restore order to the Buddhist community, shielding the temple from further disruption, is put in motion by the skills of a *sarugaku/nō* actor. His mastery of verbal as well as nonverbal languages—dance, music, and mime—is a central ingredient in the successful performance of a ritual that actualizes the ideal, "so that what ought to have been prevails over what was, permanent good intention prevails over temporary aberration."[89]

The outcast's mastery of the means of production—rhetoric, music, and dance—provided by the orderly hierarchical center brings about an act of pacification. The investment of temples and commoners in the skills of an outcast helps them to shelter their ordered world from the defiling forces of the disordered "other" that the outcast/actor channels to himself. The act of miming is central to the actor's achievement of control over the forces of defilement. Clarifying the meaning of the symbolism of confrontations, the anthropologist R. G. Lienhardt has eloquently explained the role played by nonverbal action in the context of peacemaking ceremonies among members of the African Dinka tribe:

> It seems that gesture without speech was enough to confirm, in the external physical universe, an intention conceived interiorly in the moral. . . . The symbolic action, in fact, mimes the total situation in which the parties in the feud know themselves to be including both their hostility and their disposition towards peace without which the ceremony could not be held. In this symbolic representation of their situation they control it, according to their will to peace, by transcending in symbolic action the only type of practical action (that is, continued hostilities) which for the Dinka follows from the situation of homicide.[90]

MURDERERS

The act of ludization that makes the actor/outcast the scapegoat upon whom all defilements are channeled becomes the central part of two plays that deal with the taking of animal life: "The Cormorant Fisher" *(Ukai)* and "Birds of Sorrow" *(Utō).*[91] Because of the belief in the idea of rebirth along the Six Paths *(rokudō)* and the possibility of a human being reborn as an animal, Buddhists condemned the killing of fishes and birds by anglers and hunters as a criminal activity no less sinful and defiling than manslaughter. This view explains the reason for the confinement of hunters to the settlements of nonresidents on riverbanks and other liminal areas, as we see from the pictures of the *Tengu Zōshi* mentioned earlier. The association established by Buddhist monks between the practice of fishing with the help of a cormorant and the maturation of a negative destiny (karma) leading to rebirth in hell is the topic of an eleventh-century poem addressed to coastal villagers:

Ukai wa itohoshi ya	How wretched for me to be a cormorant fisher!
Mangō toshi furu kame koroshi	I kill the ten-thousand-kalpas-old tortoise,
Mata u no kubi o yui	And tie the cormorant's neck.
Genze wa kakute mo arinubeshi	Somehow I will manage to go on with this life,
Goshō wagami o ikani sen	But what will become of me in the next?[92]

The subject undoubtedly appealed to Buddhist monks who employed Enami no Saemongorō, the leader of a *sarugaku* troupe that was active in the province of Settsu before Zeami, to perform his play "The Cormorant Fisher."[93] The presence of Nichiren Shōnin (1222–1282), as well as the way in which salvation is brought to the sinful protagonist, indicate a strict relationship between this play and the followers of the Buddhist saint. The deuteragonist *(waki)* is a monk from Kiyosumi Temple in Awa—Chiba prefecture—who appears as a pilgrim on his way to Isawa in Kai province—today's Yamanashi prefecture. The geographical setting is a variation on the biography of Nichiren, who took the tonsure at Kiyosumi Temple and spent his last years in Kai province at Kuonji Temple on Mt. Minobu. The holy man's teaching on the spiritual benefits deriving from the recitation of the sacred title—"Praise to the *Lotus Sutra*" *(Namu Myōhō Rengekyō)*—plays a central role in the ritual of ludization that the fisherman *(shite)* must perform in order to erase his ties in life with the impurity of death, as well as to put an end to the law of retribution that is confining him to the sufferings of hell.

The achievement of spiritual forgiveness requires the fisherman to stage an act of mimicry in which he restates the past with a major variation: He must experience the suffering of his prey by disguising himself as a cormorant and miming the action until the appearance of the moon eventually brings his anguish to an end. After becoming a vehicle of defilement, the man must carefully dispose of its dangerous power. He gathers pebbles from the stream, writing upon each of them a character from the sacred title *(Hokkekyō),* and then throws them back in the river. The action suddenly stops with the announcement by a demon from hell of the fisherman's final salvation. The community/audience has been successfully sheltered once again from the forces of the unknown and the "other."[94]

The central rite of miming also appears in "Birds of Sorrow," in which the hunter stages the pain of his victims by accepting to be victimized by them. All the chicks that he killed in the past are now hawks feeding on the hunter's body. The chorus explains the symbolic meaning of the dance as a necessary step that the actor must take in order to become the sheltering carrier of defilement. "He has become a pheasant! How difficult to escape his destiny! He is attacked by hawks in the sky and by dogs on earth—oh, how painful! Please, monk, help the agony of this man, who does not know a moment of peace. Meanwhile, the ghost disappears."[95]

The Buddhist monk *(waki)* rescues the ghost from his fall from grace after being commissioned by the hunter's wife with the celebration of a memorial service and the construction of a tombstone (stupa). The woman's offerings are a potent argument persuading the holy man to intone the sacred formula: "Pray to the spirit, free him from the cycle of life and death, and let him quickly become a buddha."[96] They are so compelling that the monk finds the courage to confront the serious defilement embodied in the ghost, whose fearsome symbolism is reinforced by the play's geography—Mt. Tateyama of Etchū province (Toyama prefecture) —where the hunter makes his mysterious appearance.

Since the Heian period this mountain's peak was considered a liminal area where people believed it possible to meet with the dead. Mt. Tateyama was regarded as one of the three most sacred mountains in the country together with Mt. Fuji of Suruga province and Mt. Hakusan of Kaga. Its volcanic activity with sulfuric acid and boiling water gushing out from the earth unleashed the fantasy of the ancient Japanese who came to associate Mt. Tateyama with the sixth and last path of the *rokudō:* hell. After all, it was only natural to explain the reddish color of the mountain's water as pools of human blood. An eleventh-century collection of Buddhist tales, *The Miraculous Tales of the Lotus Sutra from Ancient Japan (Dainihonkoku Hokkekyō Kenki,* 1040–1044) by priest Chingen, describes the site as follows:

> Steaming geysers constantly erupted from hundreds and thousands of apertures in an extensive wild area called the Field of Hell in one of the mountain valleys. Even boulders covering some of the openings were moved by the force of the gushing hot water. The heated air was too hot to permit approach into that area. A gigantic jet of fire burned incessantly in the inner part of the field by the huge Summit of Taishaku where Deva Taishaku and his officials were said to gather to evaluate the good and bad deeds of sentient beings.[97]

The extensive literature on Mt. Tateyama that made this area an ideal spot for fund-raising purposes guaranteed the effectiveness of such a geographical setting for the rituals of temples sponsoring the performance of "Birds of Sorrow." A story follows the quotation cited above—a tale of the daughter of a carver of Buddhist statues whose fall into hell at the top of Mt. Tateyama was prompted by her defiling activity: the sale of sacred images. Her emancipation from the underworld is brought about by a memorial service sponsored by the girl's parents who have the entire *Lotus Sutra* copied, so that the monk can plead with Kannon and have the girl transferred to the heaven of Bishamonten (Tōriten) at the top of Mt. Sumeru.[98] *Tales of Past and Present (Konjaku Monogatari)* records a similar event in which a woman is rescued from the hell of Mt. Tateyama to the Tōriten heaven thanks to her family's decision to provide the temple with a copy of the *Lotus Sutra*.[99]

From the eleventh to the fifteenth centuries, memorial services for the souls resting in the Valley of Hell—Jigokudani—of Mt. Tateyama were a major source of income for the monks and fund-raisers of the Ashikura and Iwakura temples at the foot of the mountain.[100] During their annual campaigns they spread the legends of Mt. Tateyama with the help of pictorial devices such as scrolls, of which the most famous today is the *Tateyama Mandala*. The monks of the Ashikuraji used to leave their quarters around the Tenth Month, starting a journey that would last approximately five months. They traveled carrying good-luck charms *(o-mamori)*, pictures of Mt. Tateyama, printed scrolls narrating the origin of their institution *(engi)*, and medicines to be distributed to almsgivers. Beside providing the temple with instant cash and produce, these campaigns helped to scout pilgrims and invite them to ascend the mountain during the summer. Since this was an activity forbidden to women, rituals were held at the bottom of the mountain to secure with salvation from the pains of hell those who, unable to climb the mountain, could not perform the symbolic journey in the afterworld.

The Ashikuraji developed a ritual known as the "Great Ceremony of the Cloth Bridge" *(Nunohashi Daikanjō)* that was modeled after the Amida Welcome Services previously described. The pilgrims—most of whom were women—were required to repent of their sins in the Emma Hall (Emma-dō) and then to cross a bridge of white cloth leading to the Uba Hall (Uba-dō). The common belief was that carriers of defilement would fall from the bridge into the river, where they died after being rolled up by snakes. Only those who had their defilements properly treated by monks could expect to reach the Uba Hall and enjoy the vision of Amida's paradise.[101]

The geographical setting of *Utō* highlights the play's major concerns with death, defilement, and outcasts, as well as relating the centrality of these elements to theatrical performances and Buddhist rituals. Although we do not have exact data on settlements of nonresident groups at the foot of Mt. Tateyama, the presence of outcasts in this liminal area would be far from surprising. The geography of death characterizing the mountain makes it an ideal spot for such settlements. We know, in fact, that villages of outcasts were scattered on Mt. Haku—the mountain of Shirayamabime, goddess of purity—where the ritual of the bridge was a common practice. Mt. Haku shares with Mt. Tateyama a very similar symbolism. According to the "Great Mirror of Mt. Haku" *(Hakusan Ōkagami),* the three roads leading to the mountain from Kaga, Mino, and Echizen provinces were a symbolic representation of the Sanzu ("Three Paths") River of the underworld. Like Mt. Tateyama, Mt. Haku was thought to be the site of hell: Shide no Yama. Believers were encouraged to purify themselves on the top of the mountain by going through a ritual death and to experience thereby the bliss of the Pure Land.[102]

A picture scroll *(emaki)* of the early Edo period, the *Chōri Yurai Ki,* states that the outcasts in charge of burial on Mt. Haku had at their disposal a machine called the "White Mountain Dragon of the Sky" *(Ryūten Hakusan),* a purification device used during the performance of sacred dances *(kagura).* It was a structure in the shape of a tower, the entrance of which could be reached only by crossing a bridge. On the second day of the performance, men and women in white clothes crossed the bridge, entered the tower, and, after simulating a symbolic death, were believed to be reborn in Amida's paradise.[103]

The potent symbols of liminal areas were all present in the performance of *Utō,* whose audience was reminded that "those who look at the mountain [as well as its defilements] without being terrified must be more ferocious than the demons of hell."[104] Temples made sure that people would constantly look at the mountain, translating the fear of the threatening "other" into the stability of economic gain. The maintenance of an off-limit presence within the sacred area by Buddhist authorities reinvented the process of fear to which commoners were daily subjected. The preservation of social and spiritual discrimination was a requirement if temples were to sustain one of their major arguments of self-legitimation: the need to shelter the hierarchical society from the disruptive attacks of "potentially powerful" margins.

COURTESANS

Buddhist institutions secured their political survival by waging wars against elements that they constructed as "potentially threatening" to social stability. They made sure that political authorities had to depend upon the services that only religious institutions could deliver. The Buddhist staging of a battle against defilements indicates the pragmatic and secular orientation of religious decision makers. While engaging in the control of an "order" that allowed the maintenance and increase of power, political centers—the court, the shogunate, local governments—could only welcome the Buddhist message against "desire" that was conductive to "social and political evil."

Thanks to the increasing penetration of the Buddhist presence among the common people through the zealous activity of preachers and "religious entertainers," governments could supplement their official policing policies with a shrewd program of socialization that temples promptly provided. The large crowds gathering in the holy precincts were given interpretive keys of a symbolic world that came to be perceived as a "natural" explanation of reality, a notion that was shared by a widening portion of the population. The believers' exposure to symbols led them to "acquire the restraint, the collective representations," of the large group to which they belonged.[105]

Thus efforts at socialization empowered temples to disseminate several cultural paradigms that people began to accept as "natural" constructs. An example is the acceptance of the assimilation of the defiled "other" into the mainstream social structure, as well as the conviction among members of the hierarchical society that the temples' efficacy could shield them from the threat of defilement. The ritual of theatrical representation was essential to the communication of these basic paradigms to the viewers, provided that each of them was given interpretive keys that made the stage production understandable. Temples were major players in the spreading of common paradigms to be shared by aristocrats and commoners alike. The increasing evangelical activities during the Kamakura and Muromachi periods led monks and temple affiliates to approach their customers with metaphorical readings of popular legends that were eventually assimilated into the web of Buddhist epistemology. Once the believer was exposed to Buddhist interpretations of well-known topics, the decoding of the story along Buddhist lines was easily achieved.

The temples' effort to provide interpretive keys by fashioning new legends and reinterpreting old ones becomes the focus of our analysis of yet another representative of defilement: the courtesan. This process required Buddhist thinkers to do more than simply exorcise a member of the nonresident group or stage/represent a courtesan as a scapegoat to be sacrificed for the safety of the community. Besides restoring the courtesan to the dignity of respected society by transforming her into a symbol of enlightenment—a buddha-to-be (bodhisattva)—they challenged and assimilated non-Buddhist popular beliefs involving the cults of female shamans. In order to insulate the community from the potential assault of religious competitors—either shamanistic, Shintoist, or Taoist, Buddhist mythographers first represented these "pagan" priestesses as courtesans, eventually transforming them into manifestations of a bodhisattva.

When we consider a religious complex preaching the eradication of cravings (Skt. *tṛṣṇā*) and complete freedom from desire and worldly attachments, a reading of the female body as an expression of defilement comes as no particular surprise. Even within the Mahāyāna stream of Buddhism, which provides compassionate representations of the feminine,[106] the association of women with the evil of defilement is not altogether absent. In *The Collections of Jewels (Mahāratnakūṭa)*—an anthology of Buddhist tales translated into Chinese by Bodhiruci between 706 and 713—Ānanda advises King Udayana to abstain from close relationships with women who, as symbols of sexual desire, keep men chained to the eternal cycle of birth and death:

> Like the overflow from a toilet
> Or the corpse of a dog
> Or that of a fox
> In the Śītavana cemetery
> Pollution flows everywhere.
> The evils of desire
> Are contemptible like these.
> Fools
> Lust women
> Like dogs in heat.[107]

With an increase in the amount of pollution following the commercialization of the female body, the nature of the feminine came to be considered no less defiling than the disposal of animals and the consumption of meat. Moreover, as we have noted, the association of the woman's body with blood through menstruation and birth was a source of deep concern for people confronted with the taboos of medieval Japan. The *Lotus Sutra*'s warning against worldly pleasures includes the sale of female flesh, and it is addressed to the prostitute as well as to her clients:

> If there is anyone who can receive and keep, read and recite, recall properly, cultivate and practice, and copy the Scripture of the Dharma Blossom, be it known that that person has been covered with Śākyamunibuddha's cloak. Such a person as this shall never again crave worldly pleasures, shall never again be fond of the classical books or the manuscripts of the external paths, shall also take no pleasure in approaching with familiarity persons [associated with these things] or the other wicked ones, be they butchers, or those who raise pigs, sheep, fowl, and dogs, or hunters, or those who advertise and sell female flesh.[108]

Prior to the Edo period, the major Japanese concentration of brothels was confined to two villages along the Kanzaki River: Kanzaki and Eguchi. Eguchi was located at the point where the Kanzaki departs from the Yodo River, eventually reaching into Osaka Bay. The village of Kanzaki stood at the estuary of the river. The eleventh-century litterateur Ōe no Masafusa (1041–1111) immortalized the place, calling it "the best recreational area under the sky" *(tenka daiichi no rakuchi)*.[109]

The brothels were conveniently located on one of the major maritime thoroughfares linking the capital to Osaka Bay. Travelers journeying to the island of Kyūshū descended the Yodo River by boat, transferring at Eguchi to the Kanzaki River, and then following the route of the Inland Sea. Since it took about one day to cover the distance between Kyoto and Eguchi, travelers to western Japan often spent the night at the village enjoying the local entertainments. The location of Eguchi at the point where the route to western Japan (San'yōdō) crossed the one to southern Wakayama prefecture (Nankaidō) made this area the most popular red-light district in the country for about four hundred years, until it was eventually displaced by the pleasure quarters of Edo. Harbingers of the late medieval courtesan/entertainer of the Yoshiwara district, the prostitutes of Eguchi engaged in a fierce competition in which their skills in pleasantly entertaining the customer with songs and dances were no less important than their looks. Even before seeing the women's faces, the traveler was, in fact, lured by their voices coming from small boats among the reeds singing modern songs of the time known as *imayō*.[110]

Buddhist thinkers assimilated the courtesan's performing act into their dialectic of skillful devices *(hōben)*, interpreting the woman's locutions as an expression aimed at realization of the supreme truth. The doctrine justified the courtesan's song as an expedient provided by the Buddha for the enlightenment of common people.[111] Retired Emperor Go-Shira-kawa (r. 1155–1158) expounded this Buddhist tradition in the notes that he added to his selection of *imayō:* the *Ryōjin Hishō Kudenshū* (The Oral Transmission of the Secret Selection of Songs). He credits the masters of modern songs such as courtesans *(yūjo)* and puppeteers *(kugutsu)* with special powers derived from their expertise that proved essential to the performers' spiritual salvation and to their birth in the Pure Land. The emperor states: "Having met with war, the courtesan Tonekuro sang in her last moment 'Now Toward the Western Paradise' and thus was born in Amida's land. Shirogimi of Takasago reached the Pure Land after singing the tune entitled 'Shōtoku Taishi.'"[112]

The *Jikkinshō,* a collection of legendary tales compiled in 1252, sheds some light on Tonekuro, a prostitute from Kanzaki who, while accompanying a customer to Kyūshū, was captured by pirates and killed. The song whose title is quoted by Go-Shirakawa was meant to lure her last patron, Amida, to whom she now must entrust her soul to reach Amida's land. A voice from the western part of an overcast sky assures the reader of the woman's birth in the Pure Land in spite of her sinful life. The lyrics of "Now Toward the Western Paradise" are as follows:

Warera wa nani shite oinuran	What have I been doing all this time while growing old?
Omoeba ito koso aware nare	How sad to think about it!
Ima wa saihō gokuraku no	Now it is time to contemplate Amida's vow
Mida no chikai o nenzubeshi	About the Western Paradise.[113]

Although we do not have any concrete information on Shirogimi of Takasago, her name links her to an area along the coast of Hyōgo prefecture that the *Ryōjin Hishō* mentions in connection with other prostitutes from Takasago, Eguchi, and Yodo, who are praised for their skills in the chanting of holy scriptures.[114] Shirogimi's last modern song, "Shōtoku Taishi," refers to the legend of the Chinese monk Xuan-zang (600–664) who, during a visit to India, found a statue of Kannon almost totally buried in the sand except for the face. The monk, therefore, pitied future believers who would be deprived of the view of Kannon's shining halo. The poem sung by Shirogimi is a Japanese version of the Chinese legend according to which, although the statue may eventually disappear, a manifestation of Kannon will shine eternally, day and night, in the nine halos surrounding the face of Shōtoku Taishi (573–621). The words of the modern song are:

Bisharikoku no	Now we will probably never see
Kannon wa	the topknot of Kannon
Ima wa ushitsu mo	Of Bishara Castle buried in the sand.
miejikashi irinuran	
Shōtoku Taishi no	And yet the light shining from the
kurin wa	nine halos of Shōtoku Taishi
Hikari mo kawarade	Does not change even after sunset.[115]
ima hi otsu ari	

The transformation of the courtesan's song into a medium for enlightenment was the Buddhist version of a more ancient religious practice in which female priests were believed to lend their voices to a deity to convey sacred messages to the common people who were unable to communicate with the god. However complicated the history of Japanese shamanism may be, scholars such as Carmen Blacker have argued that "by the late prehistoric period, the fifth or sixth century A.D., shortly before the coming of Buddhism, Chinese ethics and institutions and the system of writing by which they were recorded, Japanese shamanism was already a complex intermingling of two broadly different streams—northern and vertical [the Siberian stream] with southern and horizontal [the Melanesian and South Chinese streams]."[116]

Japanese authors of medieval anecdotal collections *(setsuwa)* played a major role in the assimilation of shamanistic beliefs into Buddhist symbolism. They portrayed the oracles transmitted by the inspired female shaman *(miko)* as words of Buddhist truth coming directly from the mouth of Amida. Modern songs *(imayō)* took the place of oracles in this new Buddhist rendition of supernatural communication. Recycling a potent shamanistic symbol, Buddhist mythographers interpreted Amida as a spiritual being who possesses the medium during her ecstatic journey.

The *Kojidan,* a collection of tales compiled around 1212–1215 by Minamoto no Akikane, portrays Genshin (942–1017), one of the most influential philosophers and monks of the Heian period, in the act of consulting a female shaman on Mt. Kinpu in order to know his future. The woman voices her answer in a modern song that reassures Genshin that Amida is waiting for his arrival in paradise. The shaman's *imayō* says:

Jūman'oku no	Although the myriad countries of Amida
kuniguni wa	
Kaisan hedate	Lie far beyond the southern mountains,
tōkeredo	
Kokoro no michi	I hear that, if your heart is pure,
dani naokereba	
Tsutomete itaru to	You will reach them swiftly.[117]
koso kike	

In the assimilation of shamanic elements into the Buddhist episteme, the shamaness becomes the intermediary between the Buddha and the monk. A problem remained, however, as to the subordination of the Buddhist clergy to shamans, a threat to the special function of the monk who, like all other lay members of society, was reduced to the role of beneficiary of the supernatural powers of a priest who did not belong to the Buddhist hierarchy. A solution to the problem of the shaman's dispossession of the monks' sacred prerogatives was found by lending the shaman's supernatural characteristics to the monk and by making the shamaness a female tutelary spirit—a "celestial wife"—that in shamanic practices led the priest to communicate with the deity through a sexually ecstatic experience. Analyzing the role played by mystical and carnal love between Siberian shamans and their female tutelary spirits *(ayami)*, the historian of religions Mircea Eliade has described the process as follows: "It should be noted that the *ayami* does not make her 'husband' able to shamanize simply by maintaining sexual relations with him; it is the secret teaching that she gives him over the years, and his ecstatic journeys, that change the 'husband's' religious practice, gradually preparing him for his shamanistic function."[118]

The role played in Siberia by female tutelary spirits in activating the shaman's ecstatic journey was assigned in Japan to female carriers of defilement—the courtesans—who, owing to the outcast's special relation with threatening supernatural forces, were well positioned to shield monks from the violent aspect of the god and to train them in the complicated rules empowering them to communicate with the deity. Buddhist mythographers resorted once again to outcasts as filters between the deity and the people—scapegoats of exclusion without whom monks could not engage in their dialogue with the sacred. The paradigm of the shaman/courtesan/bodhisattva became a common topic in one strain of anecdotal literature of the Japanese Middle Ages that asked the courtesan to play the role of mouthpiece for the Buddha. Here I will consider two examples of the Buddhist appropriation of shamanic concepts and the metaphorical reading of courtesans, both involving famous holy men whose enlightenment is described as the result of female intervention: the saint of Mt. Shosha, Shōkū Shōnin, and the celebrated monk and poet Saigyō (1118–1190).

Hagiographical literature portrays Shōkū as a famous preacher of the *Lotus Sutra* whose supernatural powers put him in communication with bodhisattva Samantabhadra (Jpns. Fugen Bosatsu). The *Heike Nōkyō,* a picture scroll commissioned in the twelfth century by Taira no Kiyomori (1118–1181) for the Itsukushima Shrine, contains a picture of the holy man having a vision of Fugen during the reading of the *Lotus Sutra* under a pine.[119] This is the theme of the following poem from the *Ryōjin Hishō:*

Kusa no iori no shizukeki ni	No matter how many times he is reborn,
Jikyō hōshi no mae ni koso	Fugen Bosatsu appears
Shōjō seze ni mo aigataki	In front of the holy man reading the *Lotus Sutra*
Fugen Satta wa mietamae	In the stillness of his hut.[120]

An image of Fugen was enshrined in a temple on Mt. Gabi in Murozumi that was named Fugendō after the bodhisattva. The temple's chronicler credits Shōkū with its foundation. In a poem collected in the *Honchō Mudaishi*—an anthology of Chinese verses compiled during the late Heian period—one of its compilers, Renzen (d. 1130), refers to the presence in the Fugendō of an old shaman who spent her days divining at the beat of a drum the destiny of the ships leaving from the port of Kanzaki.[121] The association between the holy man, the shaman/courtesan, and Fugen Bosatsu took place in the anecdotal literature of the thirteenth century, mainly the *Kojidan* and the *Senjūshō,* which report a slightly different version of the story.

As the shaman, they introduce the chief courtesan of Kanzaki whose appearance changes according to Shōkū's state of mind. When he looks at the woman with his human eyes, the holy man sees an appealing lady striking a drum and singing a modern song *(imayō).* Whenever he closes his eyes and joins his palms in prayer, however, Shōkū has a vision of Fugen Bosatsu riding on a white elephant, a ray of light springing from between his eyebrows. This transformation is accompanied by a change in the woman's song that becomes the sermon of the bodhisattva promising universal salvation. The sinful ripples of the sea of Murozumi taking clients to the courtesan's boat are transformed into the waves of the Absolute *(tathatā)* that purify "the wind of the five senses and six cravings" blowing onto the impure world. Whenever the holy man reopens his eyes, the courtesan appears again singing her luring song, until suddenly she dies and a fragrance spreads through the sky to indicate her arrival in the Pure Land. The death of the defiled scapegoat assures the holy man with a perfect Buddhist realization as well as protecting Shōkū and the common people from the threat of defilement.[122]

Figures of the Japanese cultural tradition who are known to us today for their accomplishments in religion or the literary arts were known to the Japanese of the Middle Ages as fictional heroes of Buddhist tales *(set-*

suwa) who, like the holy man Shōkū Shōnin, were idealized for their alleged possession of transcendental powers. In the popular imagination, the recluse Saigyō was certainly known less for his poetic production than for his encounter at Eguchi with a courtesan who denied him a night's shelter during a storm. Legends appealed to the popularity of Saigyō as a folk hero whose travels around the country spread his fame as a wanderer and singer of the natural world, whose deeds were recounted in a well-known biography, *The Story of Saigyō (Saigyō Monogatari)*.

The poet associated himself with the Eguchi courtesan in a poetic exchange which he included in his private collection, the *Sankashū*. This allegedly autobiographical poem portrays the woman in the act of reminding Saigyō that his religious robe must not be exposed to the impurity of her house, "an inn of brief, bought, stays."[123] In the fictional version of the *Senjūshō,* the exchange is followed by the woman's confession of repentance that makes possible her awakening to the Buddhist truth of impermanence as well as to the final rejection of her profession. The woman is transformed from a courtesan to a religious guide who helps monk Saigyō to experience "the seed of enlightenment." Once the pleasant entertainment of paying customers, her songs are now hymns asking the Buddha to shield the community from the impurities of which the courtesan was an example.[124]

The exposure of popular audiences to the fictional world of Shōkū Shōnin and Saigyō by storytellers, preachers, and fund-raisers—at times combined in a single person—provided pilgrims and temple-visitors with a commonly shared knowledge that enabled them to interpret the fourteenth-century *nō* play *Eguchi,* a piece currently attributed to the brush of Kan'ami, along similar lines. The symbolism of the courtesan playing the role of the bodhisattva suited the Buddhist attempt to domesticate "alien" shamanic practices for the purpose of making Buddhist philosophy the central episteme of medieval Japan.

In the play, the ghost of Lady Eguchi *(shite)* appears to a monk *(waki)* who, together with two attendants, was visiting Tennō Temple. An outcast courtesan takes the stage to justify her behavior in begrudging shelter to Saigyō during the storm. The play's interlude—a recounting of Eguchi's biography by a villager *(ai)*—introduces the theme of Shōkū Shōnin's ecstatic visions. Once known as Shunshōhime, the woman used to meet her clients on a boat at Murozumi. After moving to Eguchi, she encountered the holy man of Mt. Shosha, Shōkū Shōnin, who was told in a dream to visit Eguchi's boat in order to experience a vision of Fugen Bosatsu. The account continues with the episode of the holy man witnessing the transformation of the courtesan into Fugen, who appears surrounded by twenty-five bodhisattvas, exactly like Amida coming to welcome the dead to the Pure Land.

The play continues with the monks preparing to hold a memorial service for the spirit of Eguchi when a pleasure boat is seen floating in the moonlight. On it they see the ghost of the courtesan in the act of entertaining her customers. The reenactment of the scene of defilement lets the monks exorcise "the forces of evil" that threaten the safety of the community, so that "the boundless ocean of Reality and Truth *(jissō muro no daikai)* will never be ruffled again by the winds of the Five Defilements *(gojin)* and the Six Desires *(rokuyoku).*"[125]

A dialogue between Eguchi and the chorus argues that the waves of "reality subject to causation *(zuien shinnyo)* always rise" because of people's attachment to this impermanent world. The courtesan's final epiphany presents in a clear and straightforward way the sophisticated Buddhist move to assimilate shamanic symbols, transforming them into a figure of the Buddhist pantheon: Eguchi, the "celestial wife" who has trained the monk on the path to enlightenment, finally displays herself as Fugen Bosatsu riding a white elephant, "borne by snow-white clouds, across the western sky," the Western Paradise of Amida.[126]

Kan'ami combines the threads developed by Buddhist mythographers in a theatrical unity that perfectly answers the Buddhist need for an exorcising performance in which the threat of defilement is domesticated and assimilated into the structure of the sacred. Members of the nonresident groups such as slave traders, hunters, and courtesans replied to the Buddhist call for ritual scapegoats, channeling defilements upon themselves and becoming privileged characters in medieval theatrical representations. Because of the alleged "impurity" of the female nature, women especially—no matter whether outcasts by birth or not—provided religious institutions with a valuable ingredient in the fashioning of images of defilement. We may think of the Buddhist representations of famous female poets whose passions and worldly attachments made them appealing targets to the preachers of order and restraint.

FEMALE POETS

That an icon which traditionally belonged to the top of the hierarchical structure, the world of the aristocracy, should be included in the population of defilement is not as surprising as it might appear. Since the end of the Heian period Buddhist interpreters had leveled fierce attacks against the practitioners of literary arts that were not immediately translatable into Buddhist fable. As early as the twelfth century, monk Chōken (1126–1203) accused Murasaki Shikibu, the venerated author of the

Tale of Genji (Genji Monogatari), of immorality in a pamphlet titled *Genji Ippon Kyō* (*The One-Volume Sutra on Genji,* 1168), condemning her to suffer the pains of hell because of the corruptive nature of her literary work.[127]

One reason for the strong religious reaction to secular writing may be seen in the fact that the manipulation of language and its hidden/dangerous symbolism exposed the poet to a world that priests wished to keep to themselves. The act of writing made the poet a medium between the object of representation—the Absolute—and its consumer—the reader. A female poet added the defilement of her body to the list of potentially threatening elements that Buddhist thinkers constructed in order to continue exercising their power in the field of purificatory practices. The employment of famous poetesses of the Heian period strengthened the newly conceived paradigm of the courtesan/bodhisattva. The fact that these women belonged to the highest echelons of the social structure made them suitable candidates for the mythical creation of a fictional beginning for the courtesan/singers of low status. The poem *(uta)* of the famous poetess came to be considered the progenitor of the modern song *(imayō),* both manifestations of a music coming from a higher source: the sacred mouth of the Buddha.

The Japanese Middle Ages thus witnessed an explosion of legends on famous female poets of the Heian period. In the mind of the producers and consumers of written anecdotal literature *(setsuwa)* and its oral by-products—sermons, stories, songs, and the like—the representation of ideal love made these women poets; the fictional biographicalization of their lives—carnal love and sexual relationships—made them courtesans; their production of metaphors for the sake of the reader's enlightenment made them compassionate bodhisattvas; their continuous dialogue with the "other" made them mouthpieces of the Buddha. Two examples should suffice to clarify this process, both taken from among the most revered poetic voices of any time: Izumi Shikibu (ca. 970–1030) and Ono no Komachi (fl. 850).

Izumi Shikibu

When Buddhist mythmakers constructed the image of Izumi Shikibu as a courtesan obsessed by love, they developed a representation promoted by Izumi herself in her diary, the *Izumi Shikibu Nikki,* in which she records her romantic adventures with the two sons of Emperor Reizei (r. 967–969), Princes Tametaka and Atsumichi. Twice married, to Tachibana no Michisada and Fujiwara no Yasumasa, Izumi allegedly had an affair with the most powerful statesman of the Heian period, Fujiwara no Michinaga. The preface to one of Izumi's poems portrays Michinaga in the act of teasing her after recognizing Izumi's fan in the hands of a courtier—no doubt a pledge on the woman's part. Michinaga scribbles the word "courtesan" *(ukareme)* on the fan, eliciting an unexpected reply by the poet, who teases him back by coquettishly accusing the man of indecisiveness:

Koe mo sen	How can the man
Kosazu mo aran	Who is not the guardian
Ōsaka no	Of the Meeting Barrier
Sekimori naranu	Blame me, if he does not decide
Hito na togame so	Whether to cross it or not?[128]

During the Muromachi period, Izumi came to be portrayed as an attractive thirteen-year-old courtesan in a story *(otogizōshi)* entitled *Izumi Shikibu* that attempts to pull several fictional threads into a single narrative. The story relates that during the reign of Emperor Ichijō (r. 986–1011) Izumi bore a baby boy to a young courtier, Tachibana no Yasumasa. Abandoned at Gojō bridge, the boy was sheltered by the monks of Mt. Hiei, and eventually became the brilliant preacher Dōmyō Ajari. Commissioned by the court to deliver "Eight Lectures on the *Lotus Sutra*" *(Hokke Hakkō)*, the holy man notices in the audience a remarkably appealing lady-in-waiting *(nyōbo)*, who happens to be his mother Izumi Shikibu. Unaware of the woman's identity, he spends a night with her. After realizing the sinfulness of her incestuous relationship, Izumi withdraws from the capital in a rage of madness, looking for refuge on Mt. Shosha where she becomes a disciple of the holy man Shōkū Shōnin.[129]

The association of Izumi with Shōkū's temple, the Engyōji on Mt. Shosha, underscores the stereotypical treatment of the female poet as courtesan. Much of the literature on the holy man focuses on the fundamental role played by courtesans in the process of Shōkū's enlightenment. The chief courtesan of Kanzaki, who appears to him as Fugen Bosatsu, is certainly the best but not the only example. A poem from the *Go Shūi Waka Shū* introduces Miyaki, a courtesan who guides Shōkū through the complex philosophy of nondifferentiation.[130] The connection of a female presence with the holy man Shōkū automatically implies a characterization of the woman as a courtesan. The same mechanism compelled Minamoto no Akikane—the compiler of the *Kojidan*—to have the story of the meeting between Shōkū and the Kanzaki prostitute preceded by a similar encounter between Izumi Shikibu and the mid-Heian Buddhist saint Kūya. Izumi responds to Kūya's warnings to abstain from lascivious behavior by entrusting herself to the holy man in order to reach the Pure Land.[131]

Izumi's alleged lover and son, Dōmyō Ajari, provides another reason for Izumi's association with the holy man of Mt. Shosha.[132] An attendant *(bettō)* of Tennōji Temple in 1016, Dōmyō (972–1020), like Shōkū Shōnin, was an accomplished preacher and reciter of the *Lotus Sutra*. The section of Buddhist tales from the twelfth-century *Konjaku Monogatari* portrays the two holy men together in an episode in which Dōmyō climbs Mt. Shosha in the hope of meeting the mountain's holy man. While listening to Dōmyō's recitation of the *Lotus Sutra*, Shōkū is so impressed by the warmth of Dōmyō's voice that he is unable to restrain his tears or to emerge from hiding under the temple's eaves.[133] Another collection of Buddhist tales, the *Hōbutsushū*, credits Dōmyō's birth in Amida's land to his uncommon skill as a reciter "in spite of being an impure monk who had fallen in love with Izumi Shikibu."[134]

Overlapping Shōkū's biography with the fiction of Dōmyō's life was a necessary step in transforming the courtesan/client relationship that originally bound Izumi to the holy man into a more religious union such as the one between the shaman and his celestial wife. The *Konjaku Monogatari* describes Dōmyō as a kind of shaman whose pleasant voice had the power to summon the god of Mt. Kinpu, Kumano Gongen, Sumiyoshi Daimyōjin, and Matsuo Daimyōjin, all of whom took pleasure in listening to Dōmyō's sermons.[135]

The Guardian of the Fifth Ward (Gojō no Dōsojin), a minor deity of a liminal area who protected people from epidemics and other evil influences, narrates his ordeal in being admitted to Dōmyō's presence in a story from the twelfth-century *Collection of Tales from Uji (Uji Shūi Monogatari)*. The god had to wait for Dōmyō to spend a night at the house of Izumi Shikibu before he was able to hear the preacher's voice reciting the *Lotus Sutra*. Paradoxically, he can fulfill his desire to be admitted to Dōmyō's presence only because Dōmyō has acquired an impure state of mind by breaking the precepts and lying with a woman. The Guardian of the Fifth Ward argues that when Dōmyō recited the sutra after cleansing body and mind, all the major deities such as Brahmā and Indra would come, occupying the entire available space and excluding from the audience minor deities such as himself.[136]

The story reveals the compiler's effort to reconcile the "alien" worldview of popular beliefs into a Buddhist ethical framework. An exorcising ritual had to be performed on the sexual symbolism of shamanic practices that is so strongly present in the relationship between Izumi and Dōmyō, whose sexual proclivity is underscored at the very beginning of the *Tales from Uji*—"a man much given to amorous pursuits."[137] The supernatural powers of his partner Izumi Shikibu were no secret to medieval audiences. Her private collection of poetry, the *Izumi Shikibu Shū*, contains an exchange between the poet and the god of Kibune whose voice—"a male voice"[138]—only Izumi can hear.[139]

Dōmyō's sexual encounter with his celestial wife Izumi enables the preacher to communicate with the Guardian of the Fifth Ward who, besides protecting the village from evil spirits, was also a symbol of fecundity, the patron of reproduction, and the deity worshiped as a cure against impotence. Even today, statuary representations of the deity in the shape of a phallus or a mushroom are objects of worship in shrines and temples, sacred icons to which medieval courtesans offered their prayers.[140] The sexual power devolving upon Dōmyō from his celestial wife elevates him to the level of the major deities of the Indian pantheon such as Indra and Brahmā, the "pagan" gods that the Buddhist system struggled to assimilate into its basic structure of belief. Dōmyō's association with these gods obliges such a minor deity as the Guardian of the Fifth Ward to look up to the shaman in the hope of being graciously admitted to his presence.

Unless properly channeled, this excrescence of sexual power summoning heretic gods and evil spirits may endanger the order of the settled and hierarchical society. The Buddhist institution attempts to rationalize a disruptive dionysian cult of fertility that they simultaneously condemn as a sinful practice and uphold as an accomplishment leading to spiritual enlightenment. The compiler of the *Tales from Uji* must conclude with an admonition to the reciters of holy scriptures to avoid impure behavior and the breaking of precepts. The spokesman for moral conduct is the Buddhist monk and philosopher Genshin, the major Tendai theorist of the concept of birth in Amida's land.[141] An alternative admonition directly refers to the alleged danger from phallic exertion and warns preachers who lead impure lives that they may be reborn as mushrooms in their next existence.[142]

To bring the process of assimilation full cycle, the shaman is transformed into a devout monk while his celestial wife is transmogrified into a carrier of Buddhist truth. Izumi's escape to Mt. Shosha and her meeting with Shōkū Shōnin enlighten her to the meaning of a famous passage from the "Parable of the Conjured City" of the *Lotus Sutra,* a passage in which the sixteen sons of the Buddha discard their precious playthings—the false consciousness of reality—as soon as their father reaches enlightenment. The holy scripture says:

> The living beings, ever tormented by pain,
> Blind and without a guide,
> Do not recognize the Path wherein pain is terminated,
> Nor do they know enough to seek deliverance.
> Throughout the long night of time they gain in evil destinies

And reduce the ranks of the gods.
From darkness proceeding to darkness,
They never hear the Buddha's name.[143]

Izumi's Buddhist biographer made this quotation the source for one of the poet's most venerated compositions—one that, he argues, Izumi inscribed on a pillar of Shōkū's temple. Following his concern with assimilating the "other" into the Buddhist structure of pacification, the mythmaker suggests a metaphorical reading of Izumi's poetry that makes the woman the mouthpiece of Buddhist truth. The poem is famous:

Kuraki yori	From darkness
Kuraki michi ni zo	Into the path of darkness
Irinubeki	Must I enter:
Haruka ni terase	Shine off into the distance,
Yama no ha no tsuki	O moon above the mountain crest.[144]

The monks of the Seiganji, a temple of the Jishū school located in the capital, carried over the process of Izumi's beatification. The record of the temple's origin, the *Seigan Engi*, relates the events of Izumi's life after the composition of her famous poem on Mt. Shosha. She is said to have followed Shōkū's advice to worship the bodhisattva Hachiman, and to retire at Seiganji, where she took the tonsure with the name of Izumi-nun (Senni). The record mentions the date of Izumi's death, the twenty-second day of the Third Month 1014, and her blissful arrival in the Pure Land. A reference is made to the meeting between Izumi's ghost and the monk Ippen (1239–1289), who was allegedly required by Izumi to write the Six-Character Holy Name *(Namu Amida Butsu)* on the temple's gate.[145]

The meeting of Izumi and Ippen was staged in a *nō* play entitled *Seiganji,* attributed to Zeami, which was first performed in 1464.[146] In the play Izumi finally achieves the state of bodhisattvahood, bringing to closure the rites of passage that took Izumi from the stage of courtesan to the level of shaman and celestial wife. The ghost of the unknown is pacified and cleansed of impurities by the sacred waters of the Buddhist ocean of nondifferentiation:

> KYŌGEN: Now, Izumi Shikibu was a native of Inaba province and served Empress Jōtōmon-in. Knowing that a woman is deep in the evils of five hindrances and three subordinations, she came to this Seiganji night and day. Finally, she fulfilled her desire for rebirth, and was revealed as a Bodhisattva of Singing and Dancing (Kabu no Bosatsu). Accordingly, this is the monument to Izumi Shikibu.[147]

The subsumption of the famous poetess/courtesan under the rubric of Buddhist enlightenment created a historical precedent for the assimilation of "defiled" courtesans into the structure of Buddhist thought. The symbolic paradigm that was built around Izumi constituted a classificatory device by means of which courtesans were cleansed of their impurities, accepted into the mercy of Amida, and constructed as bodhisattvas. It also provided authors of anecdotal literature with a scheme applicable to episodes involving the presence of courtesans.

The model was already available in the thirteenth century when Kamo no Chōmei (1155–1216) included in his *Awakening of Faith (Hosshinshū)* the story of the arrival of the holy man Minor Captain (Shōshō Hijiri) at the port of Muro. A monk and the founder in 1013 of the Ōhara Shōrin'in, the captain was originally born a warrior by the name of Minamoto no Tokinobu. Noticing that the boat of a prostitute is approaching the monk's boat, the oarsman urges the woman to avoid defiling the robe of a priest. She defends herself by arguing that, far from planning to distract the holy man, she is seeking forgiveness and enlightenment. To prove her good faith she strikes a drum and sings Izumi's poem, "from darkness into the path of darkness," as if chanting a sacred scripture.[148]

Chōmei cast his narrative in the framework supplied by Izumi's mythographers. Casting the Heian poetess in a fable of spiritual legitimation by interpreting the "impure" courtesan as an achiever of bodhisattvahood, provided monks with a further means to silence the feminine threat of defilement. The fabrication of the model of legitimation required the refashioning of several legends that were all subsumed under the Buddhist agenda of social stability demanding a successful domestication of conflicting epistemological constructs. The exorcising of female defilement put an end to the fear of the unknown, thanks to the mythographer's power to prove that—to use the words of a female Buddhist believer—Izumi "obtained salvation in the next world *in spite of* the depth of her sins."[149]

Ono no Komachi

Several renditions of an oral legend of the Muromachi period that developed from temples venerating the healing buddha Yakushi Nyorai (Bhaiṣajyaguru) have as their main character a courtesan variously called either Izumi Shikibu or Ono no Komachi according to the version consulted. The explanation for this variation is mainly geographical, due to the diversity of the locales in which the legend became popular. The ambiguity of the story's character indicates that the biographical detail was less important than the central paradigm of the courtesan who achieves bodhisattvahood in spite of her original defilement. Be it Izumi or Komachi, the ritualization of impurity occurs unaltered.

The legend introduces the poet Komachi—Izumi in the versions from Kyūshū—addressing Yakushi Nyorai with a poem that begs the Buddha for a cure against her major illness, syphilis:

Namu Yakushi	Praise to Yakushi
Shobyō heiyu no	Who has vowed to cure
Gan tatete	All kinds of illnesses:
Mi yori hotoke no	More than my own body
Na koso oshikere	The name of the Buddha is dear to me.

The deity's communication with the woman takes place in the form of a poetic exchange that liberates the courtesan from her disease:

Murasame wa	The passing shower
Tada hitotoki no	Will be gone
Mono zo kashi	In a second:
Soko ni nugioke	Take off your straw coat and umbrella,
Onoga minokasa	And leave them there.[150]

The meaning of Yakushi's poem is contained in the ambiguity of the expression *minokasa,* which indicates the customary attire during the rainy season ("straw coat and umbrella") as well as "a body covered by syphilis." The deity cures the courtesan of her professional ailment, allowing her to "take off" her skin and replace it with a new one. The intervention of the Buddha restores Komachi with the physical attributes that in the tenth century were sung at the imperial court—an incomparable beauty "belonging to the same line as Sotoorihime of old."[151] A lover of Emperor Ingyō (r. 412–453), Sotoorihime was named for her legendary beauty, which the eighth-century *Chronicles of Japan (Nihongi)* describes as so "brilliant that it shone out through her clothes *(sotoori),* so that the men of that time gave her the designation of Sotoori Iratsume (Clothing-Pass-Maiden)."[152]

By the thirteenth century the representations of Komachi's beauty focused on its decline and perishability, portraying the poet's skull lying on the ground in the northern provinces, with pampas grass growing through its eye sockets. The *Kojidan* and Kamo no Chōmei's *Nameless Treatise (Mumyōshō)* record the story of Komachi's loneliness in her old years as an example of the transience of beauty and appearances.[153] One hundred years later Kan'ami began a play, *Sotoba Komachi,* with a portrayal that heals in a single narrative the fracture of a double representation by contrasting the object of lascivious desires—the court tradition—with the forlorn and aged beggar that suited the purposes of Buddhist preachers:

SHITE: Long ago I was full of pride;
   Crowned with nodding tresses, halcyon locks,
   I walked like a young willow delicately wafted
   By the wind of Spring.
   I spoke with the voice of a nightingale that has
   sipped the dew.
   I was lovelier than the petals of the wild-rose
   open-stretched
   In the hour before its fall.
   But now I am grown loathsome even to sluts,
   Poor girls of the people, and they and all men
   Turn scornful from me.
   Unhappy months and days pile up their score;
   I am old; old by a hundred years.[154]

As the title "Komachi of the Buddha's Tombstone" *(Sotoba Komachi)* implies, the central idea of the play is the relationship between the poet and the Buddha, whose body is symbolized by the cylindrical tombstone (Skt. *stūpa;* Jpns. *sotoba)* on which Komachi lies. Unlike Izumi Shikibu whose partner was a man of the Buddhist Law, Komachi addresses her sexual power to the Law itself: the Enlightened One. To become the celestial wife of the highest Buddhist symbol was no common endeavor. The monk *(waki)* confronting Komachi severely rebukes her for lying on "the body of the Buddha" *(buttai shikishō)* as if she were having an affair with him. His anxiety goes well beyond a natural repugnance at witnessing the profanation of a sacred icon. It also expresses the man's fear at the subjection of the Buddhist system to the shamanic power of a rival religious structure. The monk argues that the phallic image which Komachi is profaning is an emanation of Mahāvairocana Buddha (Jpns. Dainichi Nyorai), the original foundation of the process of creation and reproduction. The woman's—shamanic—appropriation of the act of production through a sexual union with the Buddha appears to a man of the Law pure folly and blasphemy.

WAKI: This stupa is the temporary incarnation in this world of
   Kongosatta, an emanation of Dainichi Nyorai.
SHITE: What is this emanation made of?
WAKI: Earth, water, wind, fire, and space.[155]

Like the courtesan approaching the monk's boat at the port of Muro, Komachi professes her innocence, displaying the positive aspect of defilement. She argues that, far from coming with the mind of a prostitute as the monk would like the audience to believe, she aims at becoming the enlightened consort of the Buddha—the "celestial wife" of shamanism or the śakti of Hinduism—thanks to whom the stupa that has fallen to the ground can finally regain its erection and recommence the process of creation. She casually remarks that, "Since the stupa was lying down, I thought to have a rest on it. What's wrong with that?"[156]

The monk experiences the same realization as the holy man Shōkū Shōnin when he recognized Fugen Bosatsu in the Kanzaki courtesan. He admits that what he thought to be a "decrepit outcast" *(hinin)* who had lost her mind is instead an example of perfect enlightenment. He must therefore bow his head and pay her homage. When in the final scene Komachi "offers the flower *(hana)* to the Buddha," the monk interprets the woman's freely giving herself to her holy client as an act of pious entrusting of the sinful body to the mercy of the Enlightened One. Once deflowered as a courtesan, the woman who was "a bright flower, whose dark brows / Linked like young moons,"[157] is finally accepted into the garden of enlightenment:

> Piling high the sands
> Till I be burnished as gold.
> See, I offer my flower to Buddha,
> I hold it in both hands.
> Oh may He lead me into the Path of Truth,
> Into the Path of Truth.[158]

The completion of Komachi's process of Buddhist beatification took place during the Muromachi period, when the legend of the poet's forlorn wandering in the northern provinces became the topic of the story *Komachi Sōshi*. After years of loneliness and despair in the Michinoku region, the old woman dies alone and only her white bones are found, the bones of one who in the past was the object of the court's utmost admiration. The author credits Komachi's poetic act with the power of leading the woman to eternal salvation. Superimposing his own hermeneutics upon Komachi's persona, the poet's mythographer engages in a brilliant discussion of a poem by Hitomaro, creating a masterpiece of Buddhist hermeneutics that he attributes to the woman's learned brush. The philological tour de force brings to closure the Buddhist paradigm that made of the poet/courtesan/shaman a buddha-to-be.

The poem by Hitomaro,

Honobono to	In dawn's first dim light,
Akashi no ura no	My thoughts follow a small boat
Asagiri ni	Going island-hid
Shimagakureyuku	Through the morning fog and mist
Fune o shi zo omou	At Akashi-no-ura[159]

was conceived for the salvation of all living creatures. "Akashi-no-ura" symbolizes the illusions of which all suffer. The "going island-hid" stands for the three worlds of the samsaric cycle through which people transmigrate. "My thoughts follow a small boat" shows the compassionate nature of the Buddha, his unbounded benevolence.[160]

The Buddhist appropriation of the Japanese poetic tradition transformed the image of leading female poets who became metaphors for the "polluting" nature of the female body. The staging of grand rituals that were officially aimed at the purification, pacification, domestication of the disruptive forces of defilement obliged Buddhist mythmakers to fashion a large number of lesser rites—the exposure of the carriers of "impurities," the dissemination of common paradigms, the sponsorship of theatrical performances, the creation and reinterpretation of legends—that made Buddhist institutions a major player in the advantageous game of discrimination.

Nō *and Shoguns: Patronage*

We have examined the relationship of *nō* and Buddhist institutions, as well as the development from the secret ritual of "backstage *sarugaku*" to public performances that played a major role in the grand Buddhist rites of pacification. However, the sponsorship of *nō* was not limited to temples and shrines for which the staging of a play was a proclamation of their monopolistic right to deal with the world of the supernatural. Were it not for the patronage of military leaders of the Muromachi and Edo periods, *nō* would hardly have survived as an independent art form.

Secular authorities found in the symbolism of *nō* as developed by religious authorities a potent means of representation that they turned to their advantage. By following a similar but reversed route, *nō* became a source for the mutual legitimation of religious as well as worldly powers. The ritualization of *nō* in religious environments played a policing role that shielded the shogun's subjects from violent confrontation with the victims of marginalization and their sacred supporters. At the same time, military leaders adopted the symbolism pointing to a supernatural order in order to promote the creation of images of power proving the "natural" relationship between the shogun and that superior order.

In the fourteenth and fifteenth centuries the search for employment by professional actors extended from temples to the shogun's palace—with an obvious preference for the latter, given the lavish economic treatment that only secular leaders could afford. A study of the biographies of the major figures of the time—Kan'ami, Zeami, and On'ami—indicates the presence of a severe competition for patronage among members of the same as well as rival troupes. Actors aimed at gaining the shogun's favor, well knowing that, should that support waver, they would have to go back to looking for religious aid. Lack of endorsement by major temples meant exile in the provinces where only actors with a good reputation could secure a job in a religious institution. Political disfavor—such as rejection from shogunal circles—could jeopardize the actor's career even among Buddhist communities, forcing the performer to wander and beg in search of daily sustenance.

When Kan'ami formed the Yūzaki troupe in Yamato—today's Kanze school—he competed with rival groups performing in the same area, such as the Tobi, Sakato (Kongō), and Enman'i (Konparu) companies, as well as with the troupe that Inuo Dōami led outside the capital. Although competition for sponsorship was already fierce when a temple was at stake, it could not be compared to the difficulty of eliciting the shogun's invitation to perform in his palace. Kan'ami's performance of 1374 at the Imagumano Shrine convinced the third Ashikaga shogun Yoshimitsu of the potential that *nō* offered to be exploited for political ends.

The fact that the symbolism of the religious act could be easily applied to the creation of military representations transformed victims of Buddhist mythographers into the writers of shogunal myths: the mythographers of the shogun. With the increased politicization of the performance, the chief actor *(tayū)* developed a more precise role in the planning, writing, and recitation of the play. He was responsible for the act of representation in a way unknown in previous religious performances, when the ritual itself held more weight than the performer.

The novelty of the shogun's exposure to a representation of *nō* was underscored in 1374 by Ebina no Naami (d. 1381), a cultural advisor to Yoshimitsu, who helped Kan'ami to win the shogun's approval by urging him to show the full potential of his performance. Ebina suggested a change in the order of the actors' appearance on stage. Because of the nature of the opening dance preceding each performance—known as the dance of the "old man" *(okina)*—the first performer to appear on stage was customarily the senior member of the troupe. Ebina, however, required the chief Kan'ami to wear a mask and perform the part of the old man. The opening dance held such a privileged position in the entire play owing to the metaphorical reading of the dance—the descent of a god to earth—that was crucially central to the symbolism with which the shogun wanted to be identified.[161] The assignment of the role to a secondary actor, however senior he might be, underplayed the magnitude of the moment that marked the beginning of a process which put the shogun in direct communication with the deity and equated the military leader with the active principle of creation.

The power of imagination that actors/authors lent to their military sponsors provided rulers with ideal classifications of an ordered reality. The shogun's new ideologues applied the paradigm of Buddhist enlightenment to valorous warriors and obedient subjects, using the ritual of representation to portray their employer as a primary actor in the acts of pacification and purification that guaranteed and maintained social and political stability. The *nō* actor played a major role in the fabrication of images of power projecting the political center in all its majesty to peers and subjects alike.

With the shogun's appropriation of *nō,* actors came to be seen less as objects of defilement than as creators of mythologies, the singers of political power. Apart from seeing their economic capital substantially increased, they enjoyed the benefits deriving from their new status. Like their European counterparts during the Renaissance, performers who were "traditionally considered itinerants, a step above beggars and highwaymen, became Gentlemen, the King's Servants, or the Queen's Men."[162] This radical improvement was a direct effect of the new role played by outcasts who provided political authorities with additional cultural capital and new fictions of legitimation. Following the examples of the famous warrior Hosokawa Yoriyuki (1329–1392) and the aristocrat Nijō Yoshimoto (1320–1388), who introduced the shogun to the courtly arts of poetry, kickball, and music, Kan'ami and especially his son Zeami put the grammar, syntax, and tropes of the Heian period—the aulic language of the nobility—at Yoshimitsu's disposal.

Despite undeniable improvements in the life-style of skilled outcasts, the issue of status remained a major problem in their acceptance by members of higher social classes. Warriors—not to mention aristocrats—opposed the shogun's association with the inhabitants of liminal areas, as Oshikōji Kintada (1324–1383)—a warrior in the service of Lord Hamuro Nagamune—lamented in his diary, the *Gogumaiki*. He blamed Yoshimitsu's patronage of *nō* and his favor to a boy of such undistinguished birth as Zeami on the ground that "*sarugaku* was the occupation of beggars" *(sarugaku wa kotsujiki no shogyō ari),* an entertainment unbefitting a warrior who instead should struggle to join the highest echelons of society and associate with "the people above the clouds."[163] Kintada neglected the fact that, however deprived of a proper pedigree, Zeami's mastery of the language of the nobility made him a perfect carrier of courtly culture. Yoshimitsu who, according to the *Shogun's Pilgrimage to the Kasuga Shrine (Kasuga Onmōde no Ki),* again saw Zeami in 1394 performing at the Ichijōin of the Kōfuku Temple in Nara, opened the doors of his palace to the young actor whenever a performer was needed. When in 1408 Yoshimitsu entertained Emperor Go-Komatsu with a series of *nō* plays in his Kitayama villa, a person of Zeami's status —perhaps Zeami himself—organized the event.[164]

The death of Yoshimitsu in 1408 led to a profound change in the history of patronage. The instability of the actor's status forced the king's servant to become a beggar again. The new shogun Yoshimochi dismantled the system created by his father in revenge for Yoshimitsu's plan to have his other son Yoshitsugu adopted by Emperor Go-Komatsu in an attempt to make Yoshitsugu emperor and himself a retired emperor (Daijō Tennō). Yoshimochi revoked all the titles held by his father and ordered the imprisonment of Yoshitsugu. Zeami became the scapegoat of cultural politics when the new shogun decided to patronize the actor Zōami instead. This sudden change compelled Zeami to look for new sponsors among religious institutions, treading once again the path previously walked by his father.

The *Reflections on Art (Sarugaku Dangi)* by Zeami's second son Motoyoshi states that in 1412 the Kanze group performed ten plays at the Inari Shrine in the capital.[165] Most of Zeami's performances took place at the Daigo Kiyotaki Shrine, which, for a long time, had entrusted the annual celebration of the shrine's festival to Enami's troupe of Kawachi province. In 1424 the Kanze troupe had definitely replaced Enami who was now concentrating on more lucrative fund-raising campaigns in the provinces.

While the Kanze performance of 1425 at the Kiyotaki Shrine yielded a total of three thousand rolls of silk equivalent to 30 *kan* of cash, an analogous performance held ten years later for fund-raising purposes at the Nagahama Hachimangū of Ōmi province brought the troupe a total of 101 *kan* and 200 *mon* out of the 440 *kan* earned that day by the shrine. However large, these figures are trivial when compared to the fifty thousand rolls of silk or 500 *kan* received by On'ami (1398–1467)—the son of one of Zeami's brothers—as the fee for his performance at the shogun's Muromachi Palace on the fifth day of the Fourth Month 1428.[166] In the same year Zeami's son Motomasa (1394?–1432) obtained five thousand rolls of silk for a performance at Daigoji Temple.[167]

In one of his treatises, *Style and Flower (Fūshikaden)*, Zeami mentions his search for new patrons in the provinces while hoping to regain the favor of the political center. He stresses the need for a performer to keep his skills polished, no matter what the audience, in order to capture the attention of a refined audience again when the time comes to return to the capital. He contends that the actor "can perform in the countryside and in the far provinces, be appreciated there, and thereby retain his Flower, so that his art will not suddenly disappear. And if he can maintain his art, then there will come a time when he will meet with approbation [read political approbation = shogun's] again."[168]

Zeami never regained the favor of later shoguns. Yoshitsugu died in prison in 1418, most probably a victim of Yoshimochi. After the premature death in 1425 of Yoshikazu, in 1428 Yoshinori—a brother of Yoshimochi—became the sixth Ashikaga leader and the sponsor of Zeami's relative and rival On'ami. The new star took the headship of the Kanze troupe from Zeami's sons after Motoyoshi took the tonsure in 1430 and Motomasa died in 1432, probably a victim of his relationship with the anti-Ashikaga forces of the Southern court. Zeami's exile to Sado indicates the total unreliability of patronage that is not sustained by solid birth credentials.[169] Nō continued to be sponsored by the shoguns Yoshikatsu and Yoshimasa who favored On'ami and his son Nobumitsu. The function of the actor was so basic to the formation of representations of power that the beneficiaries of this new breed of mythography could hardly discard the performative act.

THE AESTHETIC PROGRAM

The Renaissance ruler was staged in the West as an exemplary figure, an embodiment of virtuous behavior, and a model for an audience witnessing a proclamation of absolute and benevolent kingship. Playwrights portrayed the sovereign in the act of bringing order to a wild nature that only its creator—God and his human counterpart, the king—could control and keep free of destructive elements. As supreme powers on earth, kings and queens brought harmony to a society in tension, transforming "the powerlessness and compulsory physical labor of the peasant into a paradoxical experience of power, freedom, and ease."[170]

In the sixteenth century Queen Elizabeth created her own pastoral of power by having herself represented as the earthly manifestation of the Virgin Mary. She promoted a liturgy of state that attempted through pastoral mystifications "to subordinate the wills of all subjects to the will of their Queen."[171] Actors and authors presented absolute monarchy in its most benign aspect, creating an illusion of the sanctity of political power. The chastity of the virgin empress towered over the vices of pagan deities and ruled over "a terrorized and exploited peasantry presented as happy shepherds and shepherdesses at play."[172]

The imagination of the mythographer was the real force behind this celebration of power in which the ruler "transforms winter to spring, renders the savage wilderness benign, makes earth fruitful, restores the golden age."[173] The creators of representations were central to the establishment and maintenance of power since "the truth of the royal productions was the truth of appearances."[174] The employment of actors, more-over, required the creation of architectonic structures that would host the theatrical representation, doubling the main ritual on stage with a no less impressive spectacle—the arrival of the king/shogun at the place of representation, so that what the ruler offered "was not simply an image of his power, but the power of himself as image."[175] By taking the seat of honor during the performance, the ruler produced a second stage in the theatre which was reserved for the god witnessing his own epiphany.

The first step for Yoshimitsu to establish himself at the center of the cosmological process was to prove to his subjects and neighbors that the shogun and not the emperor sustained the structure of Japanese kingship. Yoshimitsu's patronage of the emerging Zen sect and its carefully planned structuring in the system of the "Five Mountains" *(gozan)* provided him with an ideological basis for the creation of a pyramid at whose top the military ruler replaced the emperor. If not totally displaced, the framework of imperial power was joined by an alternative construct that recognized a commoner at the center of authority.[176] The Zen monks employed as advisors to the shogun became Yoshimitsu's mythographers, fashioning him into the king of Japan. In a famous letter compiled in 1403 by monk Zekkai Chūshin (1336–1405) and addressed to the Chinese emperor, Yoshimitsu signed as "the vassal Minamoto, King of Japan" (Nihon no Kokuō).[177] Probably noticing the Chinese emperor's reluctance to deal with any foreigner who was in a subordinate position in his own country, Yoshimitsu denied the submission of the shogun to the Japanese emperor, recognizing the superiority of the Ming sovereign alone for obvious diplomatic purposes. The commerce with China in 1407 yielded to Japan a profit of 200,000 *kan,* of which 1,000 *kan* was offered to the court with thanks to the emperor for going along with shogunal politics.[178]

A theatricalization of Yoshimitsu's usurpation of kingship took place on the occasion of the shogun's progress to the port of Hyōgo prefecture, when he paraded his consorts and children to review the Chinese ships carrying the ambassadors from the Forbidden City. The nobleman Yamashina Noritoki records in his diary the majestic impression made by Yoshimitsu on the crowds that gathered to see him dressed in Chinese garments in the act of accompanying his foreign guests along the streets of the capital to view the maples at their best.[179] By the beginning of the fifteenth century Yoshimitsu was recognized by his countrymen, and by Chinese and Koreans alike, as the unsurpassed sovereign of Japan.

The producers of *nō* provided pastoral representations of the "king" by combining Taoist, Shinto, and Buddhist motives in the creation of a new mythology that aimed at legitimizing the presence of the military ruler, as solar myths successfully sustained the imperial system. As Zeami points out in a passage from *Takasago,* the shogun had dispossessed the emperor of the prerogatives reserved for a sovereign *(kimi).* By allegedly pacifying the country, he had brought harmony to a world that Zeami describes in its most pastoral moments in a scene of love between the deities of Sumiyoshi and Takasago symbolized on stage by twin pines, a metaphorical reading of longevity and conjugal fidelity. All social fractures heal in the shogun's utopian land in which commoners witness the materialization of their dreams, escaping the trap of life and death that human time puts in motion. The two Shinto gods introduce the Taoist theme of immortality as expressed by the evergreen pine tree that erases the Buddhist notion of the samsaric or constantly flowing cycle of human life:

> Calm lies over the Four Seas,
> The world's at peace,
> The soft wind scarcely moves the boughs;
> In such a reign as this
> Happy are the pines born at one time
> And growing old together.
> In vain words strive to tell
> The happiness of those whose days are lived
> Under our Sovereign's blessed rule,
> Under our Sovereign's blessed rule . . .

> Straight is the way of the Gods and the Sovereign
> *(kami to kimi to no michi)*
> And straight the road to Miyako
> By which the traveler "Returns to the Imperial City."
> Clad in auspicious
> Omi robe—,
> Dread spirits quelling, arms are stretched out,
> Life and treasure gathering, arms are inwards drawn.
> "A Thousand Autumns"
> Rejoices the people's hearts;
> And "Ten Thousand Years"
> Endows them with new life.
> The soughing of wind in the Twin Pines
> With gladness fills each heart,
> With gladness fills each heart![180]

The success of the act of ideological erasure, however, was not complete unless the negative effect of actions or Buddhist destiny (karma) was neutralized. This was made particularly difficult by the violent nature of the military society that the shogun wanted portrayed in utopian terms. Yoshimitsu's mythographers created a new category of *nō* that was centered on the mythologization of heroic types—the so-called *shura mono* or martial figures *(asura)* plays. The character of a valorous warrior replaced on stage the deity that was the protagonist of the first category, the *waki-nō* or *kami-nō* (god plays). The thirteenth-century *Tales of the Heike (Heike Monogatari)* provided plenty of examples of courage and endurance drawn from the historical events of the clashes between the rival Taira and Minamoto clans. A problem remained of how to convince the audience of the sacredness of bravery when valor inevitably put in motion a chain of causes and effects leading to conflict, wounds, death, and the unending reproduction of negative karma. The shepherd failed to protect his flock unless he ruled over the law of retribution in order to shelter them from the defilements of evil. Therefore, besides being courageous, the warrior had to be portrayed as detached from his action and pacified in his heart; he must become a buddha.

The *nō* play works as a ritual—the process of the actor's deification— that transforms the carrier of defilement into a symbol of enlightenment. *Sanemori,* a piece by Zeami named after the protagonist, deals with the ambiguities that are inherent in the virtues of a soldier. This monument to the military code of honor is a sublimation of the defiling nature of killing into the spiritual glory of detachment and inner realization. Unconcerned with old age—he was seventy at the time—Sanemori dyes his white hair in order to hide his identity, which would prevent him from dying in battle the honorable death of the warrior. In spite of the aulic and eulogic words of the panegyrist, the Buddhist mythographer highlights the fact that Sanemori cannot escape the destiny of those who make murder their trade:

> The snows of yester-year still linger
> Upon the locks and beard of the old warrior,
> Attired in splendid robes.
> In the unclouded light
> Of the setting moon,
> In the light of the tapers,
> Shimmers his rich brocade,
> Shimmers his rich brocade.
> His armour is joined by green silk braid,
> His sword and dagger are enchased with gold.
> But little does this grandeur profit one,
> Who rather craves a Lotus-Seat
> In the Lake of Treasure.
> In truth, the Way in which we trust,
> Like gold untarnished, will endure forever.

"If I, a man of more than sixty years,
Again should go to war,
'Twould ill become my age
To vie with younger warriors
And be the first to charge the foe;
Yet I would not be an age-worn warrior
Despised of all.
So dyeing black my locks and beard,
In youthful guise I'll fight and die!"[181]

No matter how both enemies and friends might acclaim Sanemori as "the bravest warrior in the land" *(Nippon ichi no kō no mono)*,[182] his pacification cannot take place without the participation of a monk whose prayers lead the warrior to his real moment of glory: the transformation of physical might into spiritual and mental power. The epiphany of the military ruler produces Sanemori's beatification, putting him in the center of a sacred order. This transformation could not be accomplished without the efforts made by Buddhist institutions to inject the theatrical performance with ritual meaning. The shogun's appropriation of religious symbolism applied a Buddhist ritual to a secular process serving his political plans: the legitimation of the position enjoyed by the military class at the top of the social hierarchy, and the justification of Ashikaga power as a representative of a supernatural order. Temples put the story of Sanemori in the well-known framework of defilement/purification/sheltering/shielding.

The *Mansai Jugō Nikki* states that on the fourteenth day of the Fifth Month 1414 the spirit of Sanemori appeared at Shinohara, the site where the warrior died. Yūgyō Shōnin, a holy man of the Jishū sect, performed a memorial ceremony and erected a tombstone (stupa) to honor him. Fearing that the unpacified spirit of Sanemori might cause epidemics and bring other misfortunes to their village, the inhabitants of Shinohara solicited Yūgyō's services to deal with the wandering ghost's threats and bring Sanemori to salvation.[183] West of the Kinki area the ritual straw dolls that were used to gather the village's defilements before being discarded in a river were known as Mr. Sanemori (Sanemori-san). The name was also applied to dolls made by peasants after the planting of rice as an exhortation to the parasites to gather on the doll rather than destroying the crops.[184]

No matter whether it was the symbol of shogunal might, the carrier of the temple's defilements, or the designated victim of worried peasants, the object of the actor's representation played in medieval Japan a fundamental role in the creation of rituals and myths that became basic components in the formation and maintenance of political power. The bipolar fragmentation of the practice of *nō* between Buddhist temples and the shogun's palace led to a fracture that made possible the aestheticization of *nō* through the linguistic sophistication of its major representative, Zeami. The symbolic structure of the world of *nō* remained essentially the same, however, providing competing centers of power with legitimating images of representation.

CHAPTER THREE

Fables of Power: The Freezing of Social Mobility

I n the previous chapter we discussed the central role played by temples in the creation and diffusion of cognitive paradigms that provided the medieval Japanese with common interpretative devices to explain both apparent and invisible realities. The multiple means employed by temples to this end included the staging of theatrical performances, the delivery of sermons, the narration of legends on the origin of temples for fund-raising purposes, and similar activities on the part of monks and laymen working under the auspices of a Buddhist institution. The constant need for new material to be used in the act of proselytism forced the monks in charge of public relations to gather from all over the country stories legitimating the claim to authenticity of even the most obscure temples and shrines. This explains the growth in the thirteenth and four-teenth centuries of collections of Buddhist anecdotal literature *(setsuwa)* that became the source material for narratives of the late Muromachi *(otogizōshi)* as well as early Tokugawa sermon-ballads *(sekkyō-bushi)*.[1]

Social Fluidity

We now turn our attention to the social impact that some of these stories were meant to produce on the common people whose acquaintance with local and popular beliefs—what we may label Shintoism for the sake of classification—led Buddhist mythographers to the appropriation of these creeds, their translation into the language of Buddhist philosophy, and their transformation in a moralizing message aimed at containing the tendency toward social fluidity that characterized the society of the time.[2] The unsettled political situation following Go-Daigo's failed Kenmu Restoration and the establishment of the Northern and Southern courts was accompanied by unrest that shook the social structure's traditional order.

The metamorphosis of the emperor's loyal vassal into the mighty and independent Ashikaga shogun not only threatened the legitimacy of imperial and aristocratic prerogatives, but it also sent a message to the lower classes that saw in the act of military usurpation a precedent that could be applied to their social condition and to their advantage. The disruption of hierarchies deriving from the displacement of loyalty loomed high in the mind of the Muromachi ideologues who, like the historian Kitabatake Chikafusa, considered the first Ashikaga shogun, Takauji, "a thief without merit or virtue, [who] rose in the world and for some four years distressed the imperial mind and now has caused [Go-Daigo's] death."[3]

This situation of social unrest became the target of political satire on the part of an anonymous group of people from the capital whom the documents of the time refer to as the "Kyoto Boys" *(kyō warabe)*. They attacked in a series of lampoons *(rakusho)* all centers of power—the court, the shogunate, and Buddhist temples.[4] A favorite spot for the posting of these satirical masterpieces was along the banks *(kawara)* of the Kamo River mentioned earlier in relation to the settlements of outcasts *(hinin)*. The concealment of the identity of an author who operated in a liminal area belonging to no one with the exception of its nonhuman inhabitants highlights the anonymity of the subversive act. One of these lampoons, the *Lampoon at Nijō Kawara (Nijō Kawara Rakusho)*, appeared in 1334 along the Kamo River in the Second Ward of the capital. The anonymous author introduces the word *gekokujō* or "turned-upside-down" to describe a reality of "free disorder" *(jiyū rōzeki)* that he said was eroding the stability of the social structure in spite of Go-Daigo and Takauji's claims to have the situation under firm control.

The lampoon argues that the lack of leadership makes the streets of the capital unsafe because of the threatening presence of robbers and murderers who regularly go unpunished. Monks are suspected of betraying their orders and returning to lay life, while jobless soldiers are felt to be a destabilizing force in the capital. The city has become the center of legal suits for landowners whose properties have been confiscated and who put their trust in unskilled officials. Members of the military class wear the garb of aristocrats and freely enter the imperial palace, a place traditionally reserved to the highest echelons of the aristocracy. This newly acquired right empowers soldiers to share company with the noblemen's wives, whose disloyalty the author regards as a reflection of a much broader trend. Here is a complete translation of this satirical portrayal of social fluidity:

> Recently in the capital the most popular sights are nightly attacks, burglaries, false imperial orders, criminals, empty disturbances, freshly severed heads, monks who have returned to secular life, unordained holy men,

people who have suddenly become lords, wanderers, confirmations of land ownership, rewards, skirmishes, people who have lost their domains, plaintiffs, thin arrowroot binding up legal documents, flattery, slanderers, monks, people who have met with success by building an up-side-down society *(gekokujō suru naridemono)* with no relation whatsoever to their personal ability.

How strange to see people enter the imperial palace holding scepters and wearing headdresses and clothes that they were never allowed to wear! How foolish to see the so-called wise men fighting over the right to deliver a message to the emperor, men who compete in the skillful concoction of lies! We cannot even count the number of soldiers from the capital who keep their caps crooked on their heads like country bumpkins, falling victim to their sexual desire as soon as dusk approaches. The spouses of allegedly respected "lords" behave like prostitutes in their own palaces; a glimpse of them makes you feel sick. These soldiers sport with small hawks whose tail feathers are bent, forever unable to capture a single bird. They wear big swords made of lead which hang with their hilts in the wrong direction.

Lords from the Kantō plain come in their palanquins with poor fans made of only five bones and wearing thin garments and old armor from the pawnshop. Major and minor lords wearing beautiful garments and armor catch the dogs without even taking off their official costumes and without any skill at loosing their arrows. They fall from their horses more often than the number of arrows they shoot. Although they cannot count on the help of a master, they play archery games all over the place—a new and fashionable trend.

Both in the capital and in Kamakura people perform varieties of pseudo-linked poetry *(ese renga)* without even bothering to form a group. There is not a person who at present does not play the judge at *renga* parties. Lords and subjects live alike in this world of free confusion. Although they say that no dog nor *dengaku* performance can be seen in the Kantō plain, still *dengaku* remains very popular in the capital. Many are the tea and perfume gatherings in Kamakura, yet they are even more popular here in Kyoto. While lantern shops fall into decay, administrative offices prosper everywhere. Land properties are not clearly divided, and many houses are left unfinished. What last year was an empty plot ravished by fire this year may become a fortune. The surviving houses may be confiscated, forcing their owner to leave. Soldiers lose their jobs, good manners are forgotten. Everywhere it is wasteland. All you can see in the capital are cows and horses.

The soldiers that since the ruling of the family of the Major Minister of the Right *(Udaishō)* had prospered in Kamakura—the city that conquered the world—are now in a state of great decay. Those loyal retainers who in the morning take care of the cattle, proving their skills in the evening, do not get anywhere. On the contrary, those whose loyalty is frail receive exaggerated promotions. How strange this unified country whose people put their trust in what takes her to ruin! How sad to witness the present upheaval for those of us who were born in the present reign! This is but a fraction of what this capital's "boy" *(miyako warawa)* can say.[5]

The conservative subversion of medieval lampoons challenged people in power with a task of reconstruction: the reinstatement of order—the main victim of the clashes between the two antagonist courts and their supporters.[6] In order for the Confucian idea of "principle" to be an effective rule for government, the threatening elements of the "upside-down-society" had to be restored to their lower original place. Within this context of social structuring the Sui-dynasty scholar Xiao Ji introduced the expression *"gekokujō"* in the tenth chapter of the second volume of the *Wuxing Dayi,* a Chinese treatise of the Ying-Yang school, in which we read:

> Winners are the ruler, the husband, the official, and the devil. Losers are the subject, the wife, and the property. . . . If the upper overcomes the lower *(jōkokuge)* we have order; if the lower overcomes the upper *(gekokujō)* we have evil disorder. The law says that the ruler punishes the subject, but there is no principle saying that the subject overcomes the lord. A father trains his son, but no son teaches his father. Therefore, the upper overcoming the lower follows principle *(ri),* while the lower overcoming the upper acts contrary to principle.[7]

In an attempt to restore the values of social stratification, Buddhist institutions launched a program of social and political restoration. They secured their political survival by providing military leaders with an ideological apparatus legitimizing their power. Buddhist temples continued to forge ideological discourses by appropriating alternative modes of thought, such as shamanism, Confucianism, and Shintoism, to be assimilated into the framework of Buddhist philosophy. This cultural appropriation allowed the spread of the Buddhist restorationist message among the masses who were less familiar with the peaks of Buddhist speculation than with the superstitions handed down by their forefathers.

Unless Buddhist monks succeeded in infiltrating and appropriating the popular beliefs of the common people, they could hardly achieve the goal of providing them with common cognitive paradigms, as well as putting an end to the social fluidity that was threatening the maintenance of traditional prerogatives. The reaction of Buddhist institutions to the social mobility of medieval Japan urged this process of religious appropriation that we now examine as an introduction to our analysis of the theme of Buddhist conservative ideology.

Buddhist Appropriations: Mirrors and Symbols

Historians such as Kitabatake Chikafusa as well as the anonymous authors of medieval lampoons accused the fragmentation and usurpation of power as a major cause of political instability. Buddhist temples traditionally sponsored by members of the imperial family agreed on this basic assumption, realizing that a fragmentation of religious power was to the social order no less threatening than the disintegration of the political body. They felt that the disorder generated by the coexistence of separate unassimilated religious systems was the macrocosmic counterpart of social and political confusion. The Buddhist restorationist program aimed at reviving the utopian image conceived in the Nara period of the relationship between religious and secular worlds, according to which a mutually legitimating equilibrium between the Imperial Law *(ōbō)* and the Buddhist Law *(buppō)* guaranteed social harmony and righteousness.[8]

This ambitious religious program required the ideation of a multilayered structure that could justify the "natural" order of the imperial system, bypassing intermediary stages of power such as military might that had caused the equation to collapse. The idea of the emanation of imperial power from the Shinto deities to whom the emperor was allegedly related by blood was rechanneled into a Buddhist interpretive mold that explained the nature of the legitimizing deities as manifestations *(suijaku)* of a Buddhist Original Ground *(honji)* from which the Shinto gods and their human representation—the emperor—originally derived. By subsuming the legitimating pattern of imperial rule under the framework of Buddhist thought, Buddhist theorists conceived of power as a pyramidal structure with the Buddhist Law at the top followed by Shinto deities, the imperial family, and all their subjects.

The popularization of this complex process of assimilation was the result of the work of anonymous religious spokespersons. These included a most diverse population: nuns from the Kumano area *(Kumano bikunī)*, wandering female shamans *(aruki miko)*, holy men soliciting contributions *(kanjin hijiri)*, preachers *(sekkyō hijiri)*, mountain ascetics *(shugenja)*, and interpreters of painted scrolls *(etoki hōshi)*. They transmitted orally what eventually came to be recorded in collections of legendary tales *(setsuwa)*. An example is the *Shintōshū* (Shinto Stories), a ten-scroll collection of fifty narratives compiled in the period of the Northern and Southern courts, probably around the Bunna and Enbun eras (1352–1360), during the reign of Emperor Go-Kōgon.[9]

The fact that the *Shintōshū* includes legends from all parts of the country, with a particular concentration of stories from the Kantō region, attests to the compilers' massive effort to recast in Buddhist guise the most heterogeneous literary material. Scholars credit members of the so-called Agui school of preachers founded by Chōken (1126–1203) and his son Seikaku (1167–1235) with the authorship of this act of proselytism. The ethnographer Origuchi Shinobu argues that the Agui school originated within the tradition of Tendai Buddhism from which it departed at a fairly early stage in order to join the emerging Jōdo school, whose music they used for the accompaniment of their sermons.[10]

The Japanese scholars Kikuchi Ryōichi and Iwasaki Takeo have analyzed the policing role played by preachers in the diffusion of stories from the *Shintōshū,* stories that include the basics of Shinto philosophy as well as legends concerning the origin of deities *(kami),* temples, and shrines. They conclude that a motive for the collection's compilation was a need to restore order in villages in which wealthy farmers and ambitious soldiers usurped the rights of traditional authorities. Belief in the Buddhist pattern of assimilation provided local magnates with a spiritual and social cohesion that earned the villagers a new sense of community.[11] It also gained them a common interpretive framework that added a new layer of symbolic understanding to their reading of reality.

Buddhist mythographers fashioned common paradigms by assimilating alien symbolisms into the net of their ideological constructs. Their starting point for political purposes was the appropriation of the highest Japanese religious and political symbol—the mirror—which as a manifestation of Amaterasu was considered the most sacred of the imperial regalia. In an earlier chapter we examined the role played by the mirror as a poetic trope in the literary battles among the ideologues of the two courts who all sang the legitimacy of their ruler. An explanation in Buddhist terms of this Shinto motif was needed to link and subdue the cult of the sun goddess to the Buddhist creed, presenting the authority of the imperial line as an emanation of Buddhist power. The impression of Buddha's image over the Sacred Mirror was stamped in order for the emperor to see himself as a reflection of the Enlightened One who had taken the form of the sun in the eighth-century solar myth discussed in the *Chronicles of Ancient Matters (Kojiki, 712).*

This famous mythopoeic reading of a total eclipse narrates the concealment of Amaterasu in a cave, for fear of retaliation by her brother Susanoo, and the sudden darkening of the globe. Only an act of ludization, in which the mystery of the mirror deceives the deity out of her cave, restores brightness to the world. Buddhist authors of anecdotal literature exploited the incompleteness of the god's omniscience, for she fails to grasp the meaning of the Absolute, erroneously taking her own reflected image for the presence of another sun in the sky. The myth reads as follows:

> The Heaven Shining Deity was astonished. She opened the door of the heavenly rock cave a crack and said from inside it, "I thought that when I secluded myself the Plain of Heaven would be dark, and the Reed-Plain Land too: why then does Uzume make merry and why are the eight hundred myriad deities all laughing?" Then Uzume said, "We are laughing with joy because there is a deity more illustrious than you." Koyane and Futotama pushed the mirror toward the Heaven Shining Deity so that she would see it. At this, she was even more astonished, and little by little she ventured from the doorway to peer into it, whereupon the Hand Strength Male Deity, who had been standing concealed, grasped her hand and pulled her out. Then the deity Futotama drew a rope behind her and said, "Go no further back than this!" And when the Heaven Shining Deity had come out, both the Plain of High Heaven and the Central Land of Reed Plains naturally became light again.[12]

The mirror gave a concrete image to the Japanese politics of reflections that projected Amaterasu's power onto the first human emperor Jinmu and his descendants. The physical possession of the regalia at the time of the sovereign's enthronement was taken to guarantee the legitimacy of a human relationship with the sacred. In the *Jinnō Shōtōki,* Kitabatake Chikafusa gives a Confucian interpretation of this kingly symbol, arguing that from the mirror the emperor absorbs the virtue of honesty *(shō-jiki),* since "its virtue is to reveal all forms with perfect fidelity."[13] In a struggle to erase Amaterasu's comical misunderstanding of the qualities of mirrors, Chikafusa lingered on the "heroic" virtues of imperial symbolism by creating an epic of the mirror in which Jinmu is said to have "enshrined the regalia, which had been passed down by Amaterasu Ō-mikami, in the great hall of the palace at Kashiwara in Yamato, and kept them near his couch."[14]

The Buddhist exploitation of Amaterasu's comedy of mistakes and obfuscation of judgment surfaced at a popular level when Buddhist preachers pushed onto the masses their interpretation of the Sacred Mirror. *The Story of the Mirror Deity (Kagami no Miya no Koto)* from the *Shintōshū* develops the theme of the "marvelous" qualities of a common mirror that an old peasant from the northern village of Yamagata, on his way to the capital to pay the annual tax *(nengu),* believes to be the Sacred Mirror kept in the imperial palace. The narrator infuses "historical" credibility in the account by stating that the event took place in the nebulous past of Emperor Ankō (r. 29 B.C.–A.D. 70). The old peasant of medieval

Japan may not have been alone in believing that the Sacred Mirror reflected the image of Amaterasu and her human descendants, the emperors. After all, mirrors were not a widespread commodity in rural areas.

Problems arise after the man brings home his newly acquired treasure that no one had ever seen in the snowy regions of the deep north. His wife, whose knowledge of mirrors equals her husband's, misconceives her own reflection as the face of a mistress that she believes the man has taken from the capital. The peasant's three daughters-in-law feel the same jealousy, fearing that their father is planning to replace them with three other women in the affection of their respective husbands. A nun restores peace to the family by explaining the Buddhist qualities of the mirror that—she argues—helps people to realize the law of impermanence *(mujō)* by showing the ravage of time on one's face. The woman convinces the incredulous peasants that the mirror has the power to lead them to salvation by making them sensible to the problem of change. Her argument goes as follows:

> There is no reason to cry! This treasure, which is called mirror, has the power to reflect all forms. The 54 or 55-year-old gentleman that you have seen reflected in it is the master of this house. The 40-year-old lady is his wife. In the past the man was a good-looking lad as now are his sons. He has given way to the younger generation, becoming quite ugly. The man's wife was once as pretty as her daughters-in-law, and now she is old with white hair and a bent back. Many are those unaware of the inevitability of the law of time. This mirror is the messenger of the other world to which we eventually all go. By looking into it, we marvel at how much we change through the years. It is the virtue of the mirror that leads us to pray for our future life. We must be grateful for this treasure that works as a mediator between present and future.[15]

The metaphorical reading and assimilation of a basic Shinto symbol into the Buddhist concept of impermanence convinces the peasant that he should display the mirror in a portable shrine, take the tonsure, and secure his birth in the Pure Land by calling upon Amida's name. The narrator argues that the peasant was a manifestation of the mirror god— Kagami no Miya, whose body is customarily represented by a mirror in the secrecy of Shinto shrines.[16] Here a pattern emerges—to which we return later—in which a human being acts as the mediating intermediary between the Shinto manifestation and its Buddhist origin. The social delimitation of the human being between two moments of sacred/imperial history constructs a fixed social structure whose extremities are both related to the Buddhist definition of imperial power. The Buddhist production of assimilation appropriates the central symbol of Shintoism, placing the consumer in the middle of this religious/political process:

Original Ground (Honji):	Mediator:	Manifestation (Suijaku):
Amida	→ Old peasant →	Kagami no Miya (Amaterasu)

Another major story from the *Shintōshū,* "The Origin of the Kumano Deities" *(Kumano Gongen no Koto)*—which we will discuss in detail in the following section—deals with the Buddhist appropriation of imperial symbolism. According to the narrator, the three main deities of the Kumano Shrine (Kumano Sansho) originally came from India disguised as mirrors "in order to protect the Japanese emperor and his people."[17] They were found by Chiyokane, a hunter from Manago of the Muro district who was tracking a wounded wild boar when he noticed a sun-crow *(yatagarasu)* walking in front of him. The sudden change in the bird's color arouses Chiyokane's curiosity. He notices several luminous objects in the sky that he unsuccessfully attempts to strike with his arrows. The mysterious items turn out to be the Three Mirrors, which in the past were the Indian king of Magadha. The narrator identifies the king as a fifth-generation descendant of Amaterasu.

Ashamed of his blasphemous behavior, the hunter begs for forgiveness and builds three shelters at the bottom of a tree where he enshrines the mirrors. As soon as the emperor learns of the miraculous event, he orders three hundred households to cooperate in the construction of the three Kumano Shrines—Hongū, Shingū, and Nachi—in order to secure health and prosperity for themselves and their descendants. Chiyokane becomes the chief *(bettō)* of the Kumano complex during the reign of the mythical Emperor Kōrei (r. 290–215 B.C.).[18]

Japanese Buddhists argued that if the historical Buddha was born in the Indian continent, Japanese deities too must have come from the land of the Buddha. The detail of the Indian king of the state of Magadha provided them with the missing link by casting the story in the framework of the hagiography of the Buddha's previous lives *(jātaka).* Japanese imperial symbolism was subsumed under a larger structure in which the sacred images of the mirror and the sun-crow are interpreted as manifestations of an Indian ground. The use of the sun-crow is particularly eloquent since this mythical bird plays a fundamental role in the epic of Emperor Jinmu that Kitabatake Chikafusa was resurrecting in the third decade of the fourteenth century. *The Chronicles of Japan (Nihon Shoki,* 720) mentions the sun-crow as the bird sent by Amaterasu to guide Jinmu in his conquest of the land:

> Then Amaterasu no Ōkami instructed the Emperor in a dream of the night saying: "I will now send thee the Yatagarasu, make it thy guide through the Land." Then there did indeed appear the Yatagarasu flying down from the Void. The Emperor said: "The coming of this crow is in due accordance with my auspicious dream. How grand! How splendid! My Imperial Ancestor, Amaterasu no Ōkami, desires therewith to assist me in creating the hereditary institution."[19]

With the appropriation of imperial symbolism, temples also aimed at establishing a political superiority over rival religious institutions that were all advancing similar claims. When the compiler of the story of the Kumano Shrine faced the difficult challenge of justifying the high position of his temple on a hierarchical scale that traditionally recognized the imperial Ise Shrine at the very top of the list, he argued for the superiority of Kumano on the ground that "the Kumano deities were the first protectors of the Sacred Mirror."[20] This battle for supremacy and legitimation explains the efforts of mythographers in producing creation myths, as well as the medieval inflation of legends on the origin and traditions of temples *(engi)*. The reflections of the Japanese mirror were undoubtedly reflections of power.

The Mandalization of Sacred Space

The "Origin of the Kumano Deities" presents what is probably the most ambitious example of complete assimilation into the Buddhist system of an entire sacred area: the Kii peninsula. Buddhist mythographers made of this sacred space—traditionally associated with gods, the afterworld, and ascetic practices—a religious map of Buddhist beliefs (mandala) upon which pilgrims and viewers were asked to concentrate and meditate. The pattern of assimilation is the well-known concept of "provisional manifestation" *(gongen)* temporarily taken by buddhas and bodhisattvas in order to bring all sentient beings to salvation. The title itself, *Kumano Gongen no Koto,* refers to the central role that the concept of manifestation plays in the story—the representation of the epiphany of a buddha or bodhisattva *(honji)* who is provisionally born as a Shinto deity *(suijaku)*.

The story begins with the identification of the Kumano deity with a Chinese prince who lived on Mt. Ryōsan—the Mountain of Spirits— which scholars identify with Mt. T'ien-T'ai, the center of the Chinese Tendai school. Allegedly the prince left China and descended atop Mt. Hikone on Kyūshū in what is today Fukuoka prefecture, taking the form of an octagonal stone made of pure water approximately one and a half meters in height. The deity manifested himself as Kumano Gongen in the forty-third year of the reign of Emperor Jinmu (618 B.C.). The narrator argues that the god's Original Ground took in the seventh-century the human form of the ascetic En no Gyōja and in the eighth-century that of monk Baramon Sōjō, a holy man from southern India who reached Japan in 736 and supervised the dedication ceremony of Tōdaiji's Mahā-vairocana Buddha.

The following list records the details of Kumano's grandiose process of assimilation:[21]

Honji	*Suijaku*
(Original Ground)	*(Manifest Traces)*

The Three *Gongen (Sansho Gongen)*

Amida Nyorai	Shōjō Gongen
Yakushi Nyorai	Naka no Gozen
Kannon	Nishi no Gozen

The Five Princes *(Gosho Ōji)*

Jūichimen Kannon	Nyaku Ichi Ōji
Jūichimen Kannon	Zenji no Miya
Ryūju Bosatsu (Nāgārjuna)	Hijiri no Miya
Nyoirin Kannon	Chigo no Miya
Shō Kannon	Komori no Miya

The Four *Myōjin (Yosho Myōjin)*

Senju Kannon, Fugen, Monju	Ichiman, Jūman no Miya
Shaka Nyorai (historical Buddha)	Jūgosho
Aizen'ō, Bishamonten	Higyō Yasha
Senju Kannon	Hiryū Gongen

The reference to En no Gyōja as a human manifestation of the Kumano deity unveils the process of Buddhist appropriation of the cradle of Japanese popular beliefs. En no Gyōja, in fact, is considered the founder of the *shugendō* sect of mountain priests *(yamabushi),* whose endowment with magic powers made them a privileged target of the Buddhist process of assimilation immediately after the introduction of Buddhism to Japan in the sixth century. The holy man played a major role in the hierarchization of religious systems that secured Buddhism with a position of superiority over non-Buddhist popular beliefs. The Heian scholar Ōe no Masafusa (1041–1111) helped to shape this Buddhist vision of religious supremacy by portraying En no Gyōja in the act of chaining to the mountain the Shinto deity Hitokoto-nushi whose slanders had led to En no Gyōja's arrest.[22]

The Record of the Manifestations of Kumano Gongen (Kumano

Gongen Go Suijaku Engi)—which partially survives in a few excerpts preserved in the *Prayer of the Chōkan Era (Chōkan Kanmon)* of about 1163—attests to the association of mountain priests with the Kumano area. By mid-Heian times, Kumano had replaced Mt. Kinpu and other mountains of the Yoshino region as the center of *shugendō* practices. Ascetics aimed at the realization of enlightenment by exposing their bodies to danger, be it the climbing of high mountains, the practice of confession on steep cliffs with their head hung down, the stepping over hot coals, or the recitation of Amida's name while standing naked under a freezing waterfall.[23] The symbolic death of the mountain priests and their awakening to Buddhist enlightenment was another kind of assimilation of popular beliefs, inasmuch as it reinterpreted an ancient symbolism that made Kumano a vast sacred area for burials.

In the initial chapter on the Age of the Gods, the *Nihon Shoki* states that when Izanami died at the hand of her own son, the fire god, she was buried "in the village of Arima in Kumano, in the province of Kii."[24] Kumano was believed to be the entrance to the Japanese underworld—known as either "Yomi no Kuni" or "Tokoyo"—as the *Nihon Shoki* mentions on the occasion of the arrival at Kumano of Emperor Jinmu's army. The imperial vessel was tossed about by a fierce storm, causing the indignation of Ina-ihi no Mikoto, who curses his ancestors—the gods of the sea—for badgering them during their journey. The same frustration is felt by the deity Mike Irino no Mikoto, who, "treading upon the waves, went to the Eternal Land."[25]

This account implies the reader's familiarity with the ancient Japanese custom of tossing corpses into the sea at Kumano, since this was believed to be the entrance to the otherworld, a passage leading the dead to the final destination. Buddhist mythographers transformed the defilement of the polluted realm of Yellow Springs ("Yomi no Kuni"), which not even a major deity such as Izanami could escape,[26] into a world of eternal bliss whose inhabitants satisfied their dream of immortality. They located this utopian realm in the southern part of the Kii peninsula, near the present Nachi Shrine, identifying it with the Southern Mountain of bodhisattva Kannon (Skt. Potalaka; Jpns. Fudaraku) as described in the "Entering into the Dharma Realm" chapter of the *Flower Garland Scripture* (Skt. *Avataṅsaka Sūtra;* Jpns. *Kegon Sūtra).*[27] The zealous activities of mountain priests gradually transformed the land of the dead into the realm of spiritual realization that swarms of pilgrims—from emperors to commoners—visited in order to achieve Buddhist enlightenment. By the tenth century Mt. Yoshino and Mt. Kinpu had become the cultic centers of the Buddha of the future Miroku, while Nachi was the sacred place for the worship of Kannon.

By the end of the Heian period, the process of Buddhist appropriation of the Kumano area was complete. When, with the development of *mappō* thought, the cult of Amida replaced the faith in Miroku and Kannon, this sacred space came to be represented as a Pure Land free of worldly corruptions. With the aid of the *honji-suijaku* theory, Buddhist scholars made Amida the Original Ground *(honji)* of the foremost deity at Kumano, Shōjō Gongen, worshiping this combination of Buddhist/Shinto power at the central shrine, the Hongū. At the same time Yakushi Nyorai, Senju Kannon, Jizō Bosatsu, Fugen Bosatsu, Monju Bosatsu, and the historical Buddha were all presented as the Original Grounds of the Twelve Manifestations at the main Kumano Shrine (Hongū Jūnisho Gongen).

By assimilating Shinto elements into the Buddhist hierarchy, Buddhist mythographers introduced local deities as compassionate bodhisattvas attending to people's needs. No matter how complex the philosophical implications might have been to their unaware audiences, preachers wanted the believers to continue to feel the reassuring presence of local deities. We know from the *Enkyū Kimon* (1071) that the popular cult of Shōjō Daibosatsu was addressed to the request for health and food; Nishi no Miya was worshiped as a protector of children and their families; Naka no Miya was credited with the power to restore health to the sick, securing peace in this world and salvation in the next.[28] Following their assimilation into the Buddhist ethical system, the three deities of Kumano became known as the "*Kami* of Substance," the "*Kami* of Health," and the "*Kami* of Filial Piety."

Although no immediately perceptible visual change was ever brought to the cultic experience of the worshiping crowds, the source of legitimation of religious practices was drastically transformed by having the entire sacred area assimilated into a map of Buddhist signs. A mass of holy men and women made this symbolism available to pilgrims, convincing them that Shōjō Daibosatsu's supernatural power was the result of a buddha's benevolence. The sacred water of Kumano that people believed to restore health to the sick and prosperity to the needy was much less a stream of Shinto purity than an ocean of Buddhist enlightenment.

Buddhist mythographers faced a crucial dilemma whenever confronted with a contradictory epistemology that resisted assimilation. The widely developed ethical norms of the Buddhist faith clashed with cultic practices that did not find justification in the Buddhist ethical system. The need for Buddhist philosophers to provide explanations and legitimations for common practices whose eradication threatened the entire process of assimilation trained them to develop argumentative techniques that proved essential to the unfolding of a conservative discourse. An example of the Buddhist attempt to solve the contradictions of conflicting epistemologies is the Buddhist explanation of the popular practice of offering slaughtered animals to deities such as Suwa Daimyōjin, the protector of hunters. If sacred mirrors could be safely explained as manifestations of a superior spiritual power, the rationalization and justification for religious purposes of an act of murder—one of the Buddhist capital sins—required a much stronger leap of the imagination. The "Story of the Origin of the Suwa Deity" *(Suwa Engi no Koto)*—a narrative from the *Shintōshū* that discloses the Original Ground of the god of Suwa—proposes to transform a sinful practice into an act of spiritual realization.

After an account of the god's deeds in a previous human life, the holy man Kandai Shōjō asks how it was possible for a god such as Suwa Daimyōjin—a direct manifestation of a buddha—to accept as offerings the victims of hunting.[29] The deity appears in a dream to the holy man, explaining that sinful animals can only reach Buddhist enlightenment by becoming the victim of a god and by being presented as an offering to him. The animal's acceptance into the belly of a deity who is a manifestation of a buddha prompts the victim to establish a deep tie *(kechien)* with the Enlightened One so as to secure spiritual salvation in the next life. The Buddhist appropriation of the Shinto voice legitimizes the act of killing as follows: "Sentient beings are hindered by a deep karma: however free they may be, they cannot live. Therefore, by living inside myself, they are assured of enjoying the fruits of Buddhist enlightenment."[30]

Buddhists grounded their justification on the fact that the killer gives his victim the only available chance for enlightenment. This line of thought contributed to the maintenance of a conservative ideology inasmuch as it defended a system of social injustice by legitimizing the victimization of the subject. Audiences at religious institutions—mainly farmers and laborers—were told that the fulfillment and realization of holiness was the result of a trajectory of hardship that even buddhas had to endure before manifesting themselves as Shinto gods. The condition for partaking of the divine required commoners to accept and welcome the social, economic, and political exploitation that the deities themselves had allegedly withstood during their experience as humans. The eliciting of total resignation was voiced by the very structure of anecdotal literature that dilated the traditional pattern of Buddhist/Shinto assimilation *(honji-suijaku)* by adding a third stage in which the Buddha incarnates as a suffering human being before developing into an object of popular worship. This pattern, which became very popular in narratives of the Muromachi period, unfolds as follows:

Buddha → Human Being → *Kami*

Only after overcoming the inevitability of discrimination is the deified human qualified to bring common people to salvation by "softening the light" of their wisdom and "identifying with the dust" of human passions *(wakō dōjin)*.[31] This theme reduces the actions of Shinto gods to the salvific activity of buddhas-to-be (bodhisattvas). A non-Buddhist god performs an act of Buddhist salvation by mastering the art of complete resignation.

In the late Muromachi period the anonymous authors of *otogizōshi* came to perceive the central phase in the process of assimilation—the recounting of the god's experience as a human being—as its more meaningful part. Two sixteenth-century compilers took these central sections from the stories of Kumano Gongen and Suwa Daimyōjin mentioned above, reworking them into the popular narratives *(otogizōshi)* of *The Original Ground of Kumano (Kumano no Go Honji no Sōshi)* and *The Original Ground of Suwa: The Story of Kōka Saburō (Suwa no Honji: Kōka Saburō Monogatari)*. The result was a total exposure of the conservatism of the Buddhist politics of assimilation.

Resistance to Change

The first story portrays the Indian king of Magadha, Zenzai, in a moment of intimacy with Gosuiden, the less favored among his one thousand queens. She had, in fact, succeeded in conceiving the king's only son. In a fit of jealousy, the rival 999 queens, afraid of being displaced from Zenzai's attention and demoted from their privileged position, wage war against Gosuiden in an attempt to remove her from the palace. They first resort to bribery, hiring a physiognomist who must convince the king that, seven days after his birth, the boy will turn into a demon, burn the entire country, and take the life of his father. Because of the king's indifference, his consorts proceed to stage the diviner's oracle in the streets of the capital, disguising themselves as demons, beating drums, and spreading the rumor that wolves and tigers have gathered at the news of the prince's imminent birth. An order is eventually issued to exile and murder Queen Gosuiden. The hardships of the pregnant woman last seven days before the escorting soldiers try to cut her throat, and discover that the presence of the little boy in her womb prevents the blade from penetrating the woman's skin. They must wait for the delivery before being able to carry out the imperial command.

The misfortunes of the woman engender a reversal in the destiny of the baby boy whose survival is brought about by the miraculous flowing of milk from the breast of his dead mother. He enjoys the protection of tigers from the attacks of wild animals and finds shelter with a holy man who attends to the boy's education. The tale eventually discloses the moment of truth that leads to the sacralization of the concept of misfortune and to its representation in the form of divine epiphany. After the final reunion, prince and king abandon the state of Magadha on a flying chariot that takes them to Japan's Kii peninsula, where they appear as divine presences: the gods of Kumano.[32]

As we can see from the following list, human suffering and endurance are prerogatives for godliness, the central step—both spatially and symbolically—in the process of Buddhist assimilation:

Original Ground		Human Being		Manifest Trace
Amida Nyorai	→	King Zenzai	→	Shōjōden
Kannon	→	Queen Gosuiden	→	Ryōsho Gongen
Yakushi Nyorai	→	The Holy Man	→	Nachi no Gongen
Jūichimen Kannon	→	The Boy	→	Nyaku Ōji

Among the several codes embedded in the story, the religious/political interpretation is central to our discussion. The cult of Kannon, the goddess of mercy, figures prominently as the Buddhist origin of Gosuiden, the heroine of tribulations. It is because of Kannon's compassion that the king is finally granted a son, Gosuiden fulfills her dream by becoming the focus of the king's attention, and the prince is delivered in spite of dramatic circumstances. In the version from the *Shintōshū*, an invocation to Thousand-Armed Kannon (Senju Kannon) transforms Gosuiden from an ugly and forgotten queen into the most appealing lady among the regal consorts. Moreover, the safe delivery of the prince follows his mother's recitation of the *Senjukyō*, a sutra addressed to Thousand-Armed Kannon.[33]

The Buddhist argument that, despite her perfection as a bodhisattva, Kannon suffered the most severe humiliations by incarnating herself in Gosuiden underscores the merciful nature of the buddha-to-be, whose final realization can be accomplished only through the endurance of suffering. Misfortune becomes a condition for spiritual realization and a prerequisite for the Shinto deity to come into being. If the justification for the existence of gods was found in the deity's strength to withstand adversity, the social and political implications of this cultic construct easily led to the realization that the sharper the pains to be suffered, the greater the benefits to be enjoyed. The cultic/religious experience could then provide people with solace, securing for them spiritual rewards in a process that required the silent acceptance and obedient maintenance of the present social situation, however hard and unjust it might be.

The same structure is apparent in—and the same conclusions may be drawn from—*Suwa no Honji* (ca. 1575), which portrays the god of the Suwa Shrine, Suwa no Daimyōjin, in the human form of Saburō Yorikata, youngest member of the Kōka clan. His wife Kasugahime mysteriously disappears during a hunt in which Saburō takes part together with his brothers Tarō Yorinori and Jirō Yoritada. After appealing to the Kasuga deity, Saburō starts his long search in the underworld to which he has access through a cave beneath Mt. Tadashina in Shinano province. With the help of a rope he lowers himself into the darkness of the unknown, where he sees Kasugahime reciting a sutra at a mansion located in the middle of a pond. The magical intervention of the Kasuga deity facilitates the woman's rescue. Saburō, instead, becomes the victim of Jirō who, wishing to take his brother's place in the affection of Kasugahime, cuts the rope that kept Saburō tied to the present world, forcing him into a long journey at the bottom of the earth and through the mythical land of Yuimankoku.

Saburō returns to his country after an absence of three hundred years, a marriage with Yuimanhime (the daughter of his new king), and a visit to Mt. Fudara, the sacred mountain of the bodhisattva of mercy Kannon. In the meantime Kasugahime has secluded herself at the Kasuga Shrine in order to escape the advances of her brother-in-law Jirō, for "the good vassal does not serve two lords, the faithful wife cannot have two masters."[34] Such a long time had passed since his departure that Saburō finds the entire village in ruin. His own appearance has changed, as well, and from human form he has been reborn as a snake. Three monks—the human representations of the god of the Ise Daijingū, Kumano Gongen, and Kamo no Daimyōjin—enable Saburō to regain his human features and to be reunited with Kasugahime, with whom he plans to sail for India. Only the intervention of the god of Ise persuades them to remain in Japan by enlightening them to "the Shinto truth" and making their misfortunes the basis for their enshrinement as the gods of Suwa (Suwa no Daimyōjin).[35]

The pattern of assimilation absorbs both victims and villains. The wicked Jirō is part of the same structure of sacred epiphany that brings sufferers a late but boundless reward: eternal enshrinement as a Shinto deity. A reason may be found in the Buddhist dialectic of justification and legitimation that we mentioned earlier. The oppressor—Jirō in this case—is not denied spiritual realization because of the Buddhist interpretation of negative action—either murder or attempted murder—as a seed for salvation of the victim's soul. Far from becoming the target of the mythographer's punitive justice, the moment of exploitation is rewarded as the first link of a chain that, although it momentarily produces pain and suffering, eventually leads to an experience of spiritual fulfillment.

The following list summarizes the process of assimilation and legitimation in the story of Kōka Saburō:

Original Ground	*Human Form*	*Manifest Trace*
Fugen Bosatsu	→ Saburō	→ Suwa no Daimyōjin (Kami no Miya)
Senju Kannon	→ Kasugahime	→ Suwa no Daimyōjin (Shimo no Miya)
	Saburō's father	→ Kōka no Daimyōjin (Ōmi province)
	Saburō's mother	→ Nikkōsan no Gongen (Shimozuke Province)
	Tarō	→ Uchita no Naka no Myōjin
	Jirō	→ Tanaka no Daimyōjin (Hitachi province)
	Yuimanhime	→ Sangen Daibosatsu (Shinano province)

The Buddhist rationalization of the problem of suffering and its legitimation of the structure of social injustice became a common theme in narratives of the Muromachi period. We can detect several examples from a genre known as sermon-ballads *(sekkyō-bushi),* an art form that was developed orally by independent preachers and was eventually recorded in printed form during the late Muromachi and early Tokugawa periods. These are variations on the theme of the Buddhist pattern of assimilation that voids human suffering of its most painful elements, making it the necessary trial leading to the achievement of holiness: Persecuted outcasts find their moment of glory by being recognized and worshiped as gods.

Scholars have highlighted the partially autobiographical nature of this lachrymose genre, relating the social position of the main characters to the low status of the storytellers—outcasts originally employed by temples who found themselves with a desperate need to market their skills after losing the sponsorship of their religious institution.[36] The litterateur Ichijō Kanera (1402–1481) made the same observation in the fifteenth century after witnessing a performance of sermon-ballads. As he records in the *Sekiso Ōrai,* he was struck by the humble origin of the performer, a man "without a fixed abode, who narrates stories of *kami* and buddhas among the people."[37]

A major example of sermon-ballads is "The Story of Sanshō-dayū" *(Sanshō-dayū),* which deals with the fall of Lord Iwaki Masauji's family following the man's exile to Kyūshū and the confiscation of his land. His wife, his son Tsushiōmaru, and his daughter Anju no Hime fall prey to a slave trader, Yamaoka no Tayū, who sells the old woman to a man from Hokkaidō and the siblings to Sanshō-dayū of the port of Yura in Tango province. Tsushiōmaru escapes, taking refuge in a temple, while his sister dies after being tortured by Sanshō-dayū and his wicked son Saburō. A felicitous conclusion is brought about by the discovery of Tsushiōmaru at Shitennō Temple in Osaka by an aristocrat—Mumezu no In—who was inspired by Kannon to look among the temple's little beggars for a boy to adopt. The emperor returns the land to Masauji and the surviving members of his family, while Saburō is ordered to decapitate his father with a saw.[38]

The Japanese cultural historian Hayashiya Tatsusaburō has interpreted this story as the dream of the inhabitants of liminal areas *(sanjo)* wishing to free themselves from the yoke of exploitation. He argues that the title, *Sanshō-dayū,* is the result of a copyist's error for *Sanjo-dayū,* meaning "The Boss of the Liminal Area." As the steward in charge of the *sanjo* at the port of Yura and the intermediary between the workers and the proprietor, Sanshō-dayū had complete control over the management of people such as Tsushiōmaru and Anju no Hime, who had no rights to which they could appeal for protection.[39]

The historian Anno Masaki has recently reproposed this theory, defining the story as a cry for freedom on the part of people living in a state of slavery—people whose first move toward ameliorating their social condition was, in the footsteps of Tsushiōmaru, to entrust themselves to the mercy of a temple.[40] If we accept this explanation, we may argue that the story of Sanshō-dayū is an attempt by outcasts to enjoy the social mobility that a few members of liminal areas were experiencing thanks to their personal skills, as indicated in the previous chapter.

Far from promoting social mobility, temples confronted the demands for freedom with a multiple politics of containment, assimilation, and epiphanic disclosure that resisted subversion. The actualization of Tsushiōmaru's escape from the grip of his torturers is confined by the particularity of the occasion to the realm of "channeled subversion," which, like the practice of carnivals, was strictly regulated by central authorities and planned as a safety valve that would hold social dissatisfaction at an acceptable level. Tsushiōmaru's choice of the sixteenth day of the First Month for his getaway was carefully planned, since on this day—as well as on the sixteenth day of the Seventh Month, the Japanese Day of All Souls (O-Bon)—servants and slaves were free to spend twenty-four hours in their homes. This practice came to be known in the Tokugawa period as "the entrance into the grove" *(yabuiri),* meaning that the object of exploitation was temporarily allowed to return to his native place. This suspension of customary rules allows the inhabitants of the mountains to help Tsushiōmaru with food and shelter despite Sanshō-dayū's order under threat of execution to report the fugitive to the authorities. Commands became ineffectual on the very rare occasions when the rules of the festival took precedence over local laws.

This does not imply that this process of provisional suspension empowered servants and slaves. Their place of refuge was nothing but another center of power—Buddhist temples—that were responsible for setting the regulations for the extraordinary days. Thus, the victims of exploitation were assimilated into the cognitive paradigms of religious institutions. The cults to which commoners were exposed through devotional practices became "the law" of the day, a rite of purification celebrating the glory of—and deliverance from—daily hardships. A human sacrifice was required in order to transform the sinner into a god.

Given the analogy between the role played by scapegoats in the structure of secular and religious powers alike, we have seen how, far from clashing, the centers of authority proceeded on parallel tracks of mutual confirmation and legitimation. The two extraordinary days were acceptable to temporal power because the laws of the temple reproduced the rules of the dominating structure. As noted in Chapter Two, religious rituals asked for a scapegoat to be burnt and destroyed in order to "renew" —meaning "maintain"—the social structure. The killing of Anju no Hime on the same day as her brother's escape to freedom exemplifies the adaptation of this process by secular authorities. The girl becomes Sanshō-dayū's sacrificial victim: an offering to the deities in an act of propitiation that aims at keeping unchallenged the "prosperity" and the closure of the status quo.

Temples vigorously defended the hierarchical classifications of authority. The appropriation of the highest secular power was a prerequisite for ascension to the state of godliness. The Shinto myth of the divine nature of the emperor eased the Buddhist process of imperial assimilation. As an emanation of the sacred and as its human representation, imperial power was the link reuniting god's children—the outcasts—to their divine father. The act of purification that takes place during the ritual removes defilement and discloses the "true" nature of reality. Tsushiōmaru's bathing at Shitennō Temple transforms a slave and outcast into the heir of an aristocratic family and a member of the exclusive imperial club. Misfortunes are deified, and Tsushiōmaru's Original Ground, the bodhisattva Kanayaki Jizō, is enshrined in a temple of Tango province.[41]

The presence of defilement, the intervention of the celestial wife *(miko)*, the process of purification in the sacred area, the final epiphany —all are elements resisting social mobility and enshrining a decapitated subversion in yet another sermon-ballad whose title, *Oguri,* comes from the protagonist's name. Oguri's refusal to play an assigned social role surfaces in his rebellion against his father Kaneie and in his union with an unsuitable bride who turns out to be the big snake of Mizorogaike. Oguri's association with the snake—the symbol of water and a constant threat to farmers—makes him a disrupter of social stability. In order to be domesticated, he must be recycled in the Buddhist pattern of assimilation. After his exile to Hitachi province, the father of Oguri's new bride Terute no Hime fights against him, finally killing him with poison.

The purificatory process that restores Oguri to human life after the painful experiences of hell and the realm of hungry ghosts *(gaki)* takes place in the sacred waters of Hongū Shrine at Kumano. His wife and spiritual guide Terute no Hime redefines Oguri's role in the social structure. Her sufferings—she ends up a slave in a brothel—is a precondition for the man's spiritual realization. Thanks to the unwavering efforts of his celestial wife, Oguri finally reaches the Pure Land where he manifests himself as the god of war Shōhachiman.[42]

Be it defilement, subversion, or any other threat to the stability of the social order, the Buddhist pattern of assimilation provided powerful arguments in favor of maintaining the status quo by resisting and neutralizing the process of change. The enshrinement of subversion was a potent silencing device that justified acts of exploitation with the promise of future rewards. This religious policy of containment was a powerful stratagem in the exercise of political power. Religious institutions were not alone in upholding conservative models of social order. Their opponents too—the "liberal" voices of the city—defended their newly developed sphere of authority, as we shall see, with a similar program of domestication.

CHAPTER FOUR

Politics of Appropriation: The Citizens and the Containment of Subversion

I n the fifteenth century a new center of power began to take definite shape among the scattered sources of authority that governed the capital during the Muromachi period. The result of a process of economic transformation, Kyoto witnessed the organization of its entrepreneurs in commercial and trade guilds *(za)* that made artisans and merchants the backbone of a new class striving for independence *(jiritsu),* autonomy *(jishu),* and self-government *(jichi).* These protagonists of economic success—who came to be known as "citizens" *(machishū)*—accumulated their capital through commercial enterprises such as the sale of rice and the brewing of *sake,* increasing their wealth to astounding proportions by engaging in usurious practices.

The Rise of the Urban Voice

The presence in the capital of the representatives of the entire field of power—from the traditional imperial/aristocratic system to Buddhist institutions competing for the favor of patrons, to military lords who found their legitimation in the shogunal structure—made all the more difficult the constitution of a new body politic claiming autonomous status in the process of decision making. Transformations in both the means and the modes of production created a political space to be filled by the *nouveau riche.* Yet the concomitant presence of traditional modes of production never allowed the capital the same degree of autonomy enjoyed by harbor cities such as Sakai, for example, whose major economic role in the fifteenth and sixteenth centuries gave merchants a privileged position in the running of local governments.[1]

The Citizens asserted their autonomy mainly in the field of internal affairs. They provided military authorities with independent corps of police whose formation resulted from the Citizens' need to defend their own storehouses from the attacks of starving peasants and debtors who urged the government to grant them remission from debts through the fashionable "acts of grace and benevolence" *(tokuseiryō)*. The cooperation with military forces won the Citizens the gratitude of *bakufu* officials, particularly in the unsettled political climate following the assassination of shogun Ashikaga Yoshinori in the so-called Kakitsu Incident of 1441. The leaders of a weakened professional army could only welcome the extra help received from the Citizens in quashing the increasing number of fifteenth-century revolts.[2]

The situation changed when this unsolicited aid to the military government began to threaten shogunal prerogatives by showing an uncontrollable economic and military growth. The power of the Citizens was a source of concern for the shogun's deputy *(kanrei)* Hosokawa Takakuni, who on the eleventh day of the Seventh Month 1506 forbade the performance of dances inside the city for fear that political criticism would arise from the gathering of the *machishū*.[3]

The physical act of gathering was not the only threat to the constituted order. Planning of the assembly was under the direct control and jurisdiction of the Citizens, who availed themselves of such occasions to display their economic and decisional power. The best example in this regard was undoubtedly the organization of the Gion Festival—Gion *matsuri*—that the wealthiest merchants financed each year, when hundreds of Citizens carried gigantic floats through the streets of the capital. Takakuni's concern about losing power to the Citizens was quite justified. By the years 1532–1536 the capital's most opulent families, which controlled major monopolistic interests in the country, were providing Kyoto with deputies *(sōdai)* who were totally unrelated to the shogunate. The Citizens were striving for independence under the leadership of well-known familial groups such as the Gotō (jewelers), Chaya (clothiers), Suminokura (doctors), and Hon'ami (sword makers).[4]

All these families patronized the Hokkeji-in, the center of the Hokke sect that Nichizō, a disciple of Nichiren Shōnin (1222–1282), founded around 1294. The Citizens were no exception in the process of ideological production. Following the same path trod by emperors and shoguns, their political distinction could only be warranted by the choice of an alternative religious structure that would justify with its novelty the beginning of a new ideological construct. The Citizens' acceptance of the exclusive nature of Nichiren's religious heritage—which rejected most Buddhist practices in favor of exclusive faith in the *Lotus Sutra* and its title—underscores their desire to constitute themselves as an autonomous center of power whose ideological legitimation they found in the epistemology of Nichiren's followers.

This explains the Citizens' generous patronage of Nisshin (1407–

1488)—a patriarch of the Hokke sect—whose most powerful parishioner was the merchant Hon'ami Motomitsu. When, during the Tenbun Hokke revolt of 1536, the monks of Mt. Hiei and the lord of Ōmi, Rokkaku Sadayori, attacked the Hokke sect, members of the Hon'ami family were at the head of the Hokke troops together with other famous Citizens from the Gotō and Chaya families. Uprooted from the capital, Nichiren's message was kept alive by the merchants of Sakai, a city that was better equipped to withstand the reaction of the shogun's troops.[5]

In the construction of their self-fashioned images the Citizens aimed at creating a strong sense of distinction that surfaces in religious and cultural choices alike. While the shogun turned his attention to the performers of *sarugaku* in an attempt to construct an alternative literary/cultural canon to replace the one traditionally associated with the center of cultural power—the court—the Citizens offered their patronage to actors like Koinu who, as a representative of the amateur type of *nō* known as *tesarugaku,* were marginalized by political authorities. The successful attacks by professional schools on Koinu and his colleagues could not be carried out without the intervention of military forces. Accepting the petitions of institutionalized troupes, the police intervened by canceling Koinu's scheduled appearances such as the one planned at the Rokudō Chinkōji in Higashiyama in February 1450, as well as arresting and punishing the actors of unauthorized performances.

The pressure of competition in winning the temples' bid for the right to perform in lucrative fund-raising campaigns was certainly a major reason for the Kanze and Konparu troupes to fight for the removal of competitors like Koinu. Yet it is hard to explain the intervention of the shogunate as a disinterested favor to the providers of cultural capital. The explanation of the shogun's resistance to amateur players must be related to his concern for the creation of a cultural identity by Citizens who were distinguishing themselves as a growing and threatening political competitor. They had to be crushed before the mechanism of replacement could deface the shogun's own cultural identity. The military attack on *tesarugaku* was waged much less against an individual actor than against his proud sponsors—the Citizens—whose enjoyment of an art form that ridiculed the values of aristocrats and powerful warriors was hardly shared by the carriers of traditional power. The parodying nature of *tesarugaku,* combined with the energy of a blooming urban society, was a perfect candidate for an act of silencing and erasure. But the declining power of the Ashikaga shogunate in the sixteenth century could not stop the process of *tesarugaku* production and consumption on the part of the *machishū* whose members, according to the *Awataguchi Sarugaku Ki* (1505), joined in large numbers to stage "forbidden" plays.[6] The Citizens even created their own troupes—such as the Toraya, which performed in the years 1530–1550, and the Sasaya, active in the 1570s.

We cannot consider the weakening of shogunal power as the only reason for the strengthening of a cultural structure whose subversive seeds could easily threaten the stability of traditional values. The structure itself secured its survival by containing the threat and modifying the rules of its own game. By the beginning of the sixteenth century the category of townsmen known as "Citizens" encompassed people from the most diverse income brackets and economic activities. What defined them as a cohesive group was a shared commonality in the means and modes of production. In the span of a century, from the fifteenth to the sixteenth, the Citizens grew into a new economic and cultural bourgeoisie that, like its later counterpart of the nineteenth century, constructed a cultural pattern of binary extremism. The initial stage of rejection and subversion was eventually silenced by its assimilation into the mainstream of traditional values that bourgeois revolutions inevitably pretend to erase.

An infusion of aristocratic awareness into the bloodstream of the Citizens took place after the long war fought by the barons of the Ōnin era (1467–1477),[7] when aristocrats dispossessed of their wealth came to live shoulder to shoulder with merchants and artisans. Unprotected by the impenetrable walls of their palaces, noblemen came to share the same space with the Citizens, while accepting the loathsome economic laws of the market. Besides selling valuable family property such as literary manuscripts and letters—as well as forged documents which the economically pressed descendants of famous poets and scholars did not hesitate to counterfeit—the impoverished nobility eked out a living by marketing their knowledge to wealthy merchants in search of cultural capital. The aristocrat Yamashina Tokitsugu records in his diary, the *Tokitsugu Gyōki,* his participation in the daily life of the commoner, including his effort to redeem a mosquito net, a halberd, a pleated skirt, and a ceremonial court robe that he had pledged to a pawnshop the previous year.[8]

The presence of a defeated nobility in the economic sphere of commercial power engendered in the Citizens an ambiguous and contradictory response. While laughing at the values of a social structure that they were turning upside-down, they also felt reverence for the providers of a tradition that, however dwarfed by the loss of economic legitimation, was extremely valuable to the formation of cultural capital. This ambiguity explains why the sponsorship of *tesarugaku* did not preclude talented Citizens such as Hon'ami Kōetsu (1558–1637) and Suminokura Soan from publishing illustrated versions of *nō* plays from the institutionalized Kanze repertoire—versions that, beginning in 1608, the sons of merchants used as textbooks for their education.

Members of the aristocracy *(kugeshū)* directly participated in the diffusion among commoners of their literary tradition by cooperating in the production of illustrated versions of the classics which are known today as the "Saga Books" *(Saga-bon)*. Chūin Michimasa—a renowned man of letters, a teacher of Emperor Go-Yōzei (r. 1586–1611), and the recipient of the secret poetic tradition of the *Kokinshū (Kokin Denjū)* from the general and poet Hosokawa Yūsai (1534–1610)—contributed to making widely available one of the basic texts of court tradition: the *Tales of Ise (Ise Monogatari)*. Michimasa worked on the production of an illustrated version, correcting doubtful passages from a manuscript of the poet Fujiwara Teika (1162–1241), the *Tenpuku-bon*.[9]

Narratives of the late Muromachi period, commonly known as *otogi-zōshi* ("narrative books"), voiced the ambiguity of the urban reaction to the decayed world of the aristocracy. We must clarify this relationship, and the process of the Citizens' appropriation of aristocratic values, in order to better understand the cultural politics of the *machishū*.[10]

Economic Success and Aristocratic Legitimation: "The Story of Bunshō"

In "The Story of Bunshō" *(Bunshō Sōshi)*, two economic codes come into collision that highlight the transition from a feudal economy based on the silent and respectful observation of hierarchies to an urban set of economic rules stressing the end—sheer profit—at the expense of traditionally "mannered" means. The medieval essayist and poet Kenkō (ca. 1280–1352) records in his "Jottings" *(Tsurezuregusa)* that in the fourteenth century the traditional mode of production symbolized by the glittering of gold competed with the sturdiness of an economic system in which iron was replacing its more valued rival.[11] Kenkō's plan of cultural restoration required the adoption of a traditional ethical code of honesty and devotion that—he argued—should be applied to the laws of the market. According to him, eagerness for profit was no excuse for neglecting the art of harmonious relationships that, far from limiting the amount of economic gain, improved the quality of business. Honesty, in fact, engendered good feelings in customers, persuading them to buy more and also more often.

Kenkō gave his economic advice through one of his characters, a millionaire *(daifuku chōja)*, who reminds the reader of the economic gain derived from being "honest *(shōjiki ni shite)* and abiding firmly by your promises."[12] By teaching an apprentice the rule that will make him a millionaire, the narrator shows that acceptance of a system which makes a subject even more subjected has the potential for economic accumulation. Kenkō's advice comes in *dan* 217, in which we read that "a man's first obligation is to *devote himself* with all his energies *(hitafuru)* to making a fortune."[13]

The aristocracy and the military class expounded an ideal formula for the accumulation of wealth that was a balanced mixture of honesty, respect, diligence, and obedience—a secret that the saltmaker Bunshō masters in his social and economic rebirth.[14] Born the servant *(zōshiki)* of the wealthy Grand Priest (Daigūji) of Kashima Shrine in the province of Hitachi, Bunda—alias Bunshō—climbs the social ladder, becoming an extremely wealthy merchant *(tokunin)* and a member of the highest aristocracy, by being appointed a major counselor *(dainagon)*. The narrator explains Bunshō's ascension to the top of the aristocratic hierarchy on the grounds of his professional ethos—honesty and loyalty toward employers, uncommon strength, and constant diligence. The beginning of this process of economic and social apotheosis is rooted in Bunshō's diligence as a worker. His natural skills win him the private ownership of his means of production—two kilns received as a reward from his employer for his good service through the years *(go-on)*. As the narrator states: "Although he was a lowly servant, he was honest *(kokoro wa shōjiki ni)* and held his master in high regard, serving him with diligence *(kokoro ni tagawaji)* day and night, taking care to obey his every wish."[15]

Through diligence and honesty—the engine driving Bunshō's cycle of economic production—a nonhuman and servant becomes the creator of a special salt which has the quasi-magical power of keeping the consumer in good health and in a state of perennial youth. In the effort to announce his new status publicly, the self-made millionaire *(chōja)* renames himself after the title of an era, the Bunshō period (1466–1467), reversing the imperial prerogative of designating the epoch of his rule. The choice of the name is revealing inasmuch as it indicates the start of a bloody civil war that aimed at erasing the aristocratic rules of precedent and tradition.

The transformation of the market led to a change in the way economy was traditionally perceived as a menial field of manual operations. Instead, the accumulation of wealth came to be seen as a rewarding and justifiable practice. The search for immediate profit challenged the values of those who prided themselves upon aloofness from commerce and exchange. The salt workers of Hitachi province voice this transformation of the merchant's ethical code by abandoning their employer in exchange for better wages, as soon as they become aware of the fortune accumulated by Bunshō. Their lively comments question the legitimacy of traditional rules: " 'It's not so much who you work for, but what you get paid that counts. Why worry about loyalties?' Such were the sentiments of the people of Hitachi, for times had changed and they all went to work for Bunshō."[16]

The fracture of the two ethical codes is resolved in the integration of the story into the traditionally "medieval" mode of court legitimation. The anonymous author adopts the scheme developed by Buddhist authorities and upheld by the aristocracy in which the reward for the victim's suffering is his disclosure as a nobleman and a god. The field of economic power still lacked the degree of autonomy required of an author to avoid the use of supernatural explanations for events grounded in the reality of the market. Not until the seventeenth century will an author be free from the need of metaphysical explanations, when the writer Ihara Saikaku, who lived in the commercial city of Osaka, was finally able to justify the literary act as yet another link in the economic chain of production and consumption.

The strong subordination of moneylending and commercial enterprise to higher forms of political and cultural powers precluded the "Story of Bunshō" from developing into an independent celebration of capitalistic ventures. The durability of Bunshō's fortune could only be guaranteed as long as his economic power was legitimized by the symbolic source of monopolies and privileges. Since the court was the only center of power whose symbols were never seriously threatened, the imperial system provided the necessary tools of legitimation. Although the ingredients of mercantile success—diligence, honesty, and trust—could transform a commoner into a millionaire, they failed to make him an aristocrat. The miraculous intervention of the deity—a convention accepted as "natural" by medieval readers—allowed this process to take place, providing the wealthy merchant with the additional capital of status.

The infusion of aristocratic values that fictionalizes this account of economic success begins with the birth of Bunshō's two baby daughters, Lotus Flower (Renge) and Lady Lotus (Hachisu Gozen), thanks to the merciful intervention of the god of Kashima.[17] This event upsets both Bunshō and the Muromachi reader who, as merchants and heads of commercial enterprises, put all their hopes in a male heir to whom they could entrust the family business. A daughter was certainly more an asset in the structure of the Heian court in which power was obtained and maintained through wise uxorial practices. Yet this fictional substitution of gender is a prerequisite for Bunshō's acquisition of status and, therefore, power, whose sphere encompassed much more than simple economic capital.[18] Although one must not downplay the economic growth that brought about the "economic revolution" of the late Muromachi period, one cannot deny that the issue of status still held enormous importance at the time in spite of the downfall of the aristocracy.

When the time comes for the daughters to marry, Bunshō's wealth allows them to ignore representatives of intermediary stages of power in their refusal of noble suitors. His economic capital appeases the rage of powerful lords *(daimyō)*, as well as the disappointment of the Grand Priest and the governor of Hitachi, who are all rejected, despite Bunshō's disapproval, because of the girls' determination to become imperial consorts. In less fictional circumstances disobedience to a parent was considered the utmost unfilial act and accordingly punished. Bunshō was in fact accountable to the authorities for the girls' unforgivable refusals. The accumulation of wealth shelters the merchant and his family from the harshness of feudal rule, leading to a further investment in status with the marriage of the first daughter to the son of the prime minister and the marriage of the second-born to an emperor. Bunshō's last investment transforms the saltmaker into a Minister of State *(saishō)* of the Second Rank, a Major Counselor *(dainagon)*, and very likely the grandfather of the next emperor, reminding the reader of the unlimited potential of labor.

The Marketing of Culture

The "Story of Bunshō" highlights a tension between the narrator's idea of what ought to be—the dignified world of the aristocracy—and a reality that pulls this "ideal" mode of life into the *anomia* of a social structure regulated by the laws of the market. The economic field's lack of autonomy requires an act of legitimation by a higher center of cultural/symbolic/status power. But the growth of the field and its preeminence in the sphere of immediate production challenges the hierarchical formation, fashioning a new structure of social distinction in which commercial wealth, although still calling for imperial legitimation, becomes a prerequisite to the creation and maintenance of power. The object of a process in which they derive their cultural capital from the penetration of aristocrats into the "lower" streets of Kyoto, while the accumulation of a more "plebeian" sort of wealth produces their mark of distinction, the Citizens must deal with the ambiguity of this new social formation. At the same time that the "lowering" of the aristocrat into the social texture of the *machishū* through the marketing of his knowledge guarantees the survival of an endangered species, the Citizen's investment in the culture of aristocratic men of letters becomes his act of empowerment.

Culture becomes a commodity at the mercy of the laws of the market, another item of merchandise to be publicized and commercialized. In the "Story of Bunshō" the son of the prime minister introduces himself to Bunshō's reluctant elder daughter as the ideal peddler from the capital who has mastered the aristocratic art of poetry—rather than showing his true identity, the holder of a captainship, which may raise the eyebrows of a merchant for whom status comes as an addition to wealth, not a replacement. This strategy allows the young man to be welcomed at Bunshō's house, for goods from the capital were in high demand in the provinces. Moreover, as an aristocrat educated at the court, he can count on formidable rhetorical skills shaping his remarkable selling technique.

Listing his goods according to their different uses in the four seasons, the captain casts his solicitation in the language of poetry. He organizes his merchandise as a poet would divide the seasonal songs of an imperial anthology. The insensitivity of the provincial folks *(yamagatsu)* employed in Bunshō's household adds a sense of distinction to this uncommon peddler whose wealth in cultural capital makes up for his staged lack of economic stability.

In this osmotic process warranted by the need for survival and legitimation, both parties proceed to erase the past and their origins. Like his historical counterparts—the aristocrats living in the space of Citizens—the captain must forget the source of his cultural power, accepting subordination to the new rich. The astonishment of the captain's companions at the sight of a provincial merchant who takes the place of honor and drinks before their lord, overturns the rules of precedent and etiquette, as we can see from the following passage: "The captain could not refuse, and he accepted the wine. His companions were astonished. 'Oh, the tragedy of love! Who beside the prime minister would dare drink before our lord does?' Thus did they lament as they shed tears. Although the captain was dismayed, he could not refuse and he drank the wine."[19]

Likewise a general amnesia on the part of Bunshō and his family erases their past as subordinate merchants, thus purposely blurring the source of their economic capital. The economic sphere's dependence upon traditional modes of thought leads to the repudiation of origins and to a display of new values recently absorbed from the aristocracy. The fact that the peddler, far from being a merchant, is a member of the highest nobility dispels the guilt and shame of Bunshō's daughter for rejecting "other men only to lie with a merchant *(akibito),*"[20] as well as reassuring her worried mother who fears that "she would reject *daimyō* and then sleep with a merchant!"[21] The effacement of origins becomes a necessity for the maintenance of power together with the accumulation of wealth and cultural capital.

The assimilation of the peddler into the structure of imperial/aristocratic symbolic power certainly appealed to the urban readers of *otogizōshi*. In the story *Izumi Shikibu* previously discussed, a Citizen *(machinin)* raises the boy abandoned by his mother at Gojō bridge. Besides receiving a strictly religious education and rising to fame as the eloquent preacher Dōmyō, the boy acquires from his experience in the city the skills of the cultured Citizen whose success depends on knowledge and its uses. Struck by the charm and beauty of a lady-in-waiting during a court performance of "Eight Lectures on the *Lotus Sutra*" *(Hokke Hakkō),* the holy man, unaware of the woman's identity and hence the consequent incestuous result, resorts to his urban upbringing to plan his amorous conquest. After returning to the court disguised as a peddler of citruses *(koji),* the preacher is allowed to approach the emperor and his lady-in-waiting Izumi, thanks to an unusual selling technique that unites the practical values of the merchant—numbers, the true figures of business—with the rhetorical figures developed by court poets through the ages. The peddler portrays his journey in the unfulfilled meadows of his heart by pairing each order of citrus to a poem. The twenty poems are translated here:

Hitotsu to ya	First,
Hitori marone no	I slept alone in my clothes
Kusamakura	On a grass pillow:
Tamoto shiboranu	There is no dawn that does not wet
Akatsuki mo nashi	My sleeve with tears.
Futatsu to ya	Second,
Futae byōbu no	When shall I see
Uchi ni nete	My beloved
Koishiki hito o	Who sleeps within
Itsu ka mirubeki	A twofold screen?
Mitsu to ka ya	Third,
Mite mo kokoro no	Although I see her
Nagusamade	I cannot be consoled:
Nado ukihito no	Why should I be in love
Koishikaruran	With such a heartless person?
Yotsu to ka ya	Fourth,
Yobuka ni kimi o	Is it because I long for you
Omouran	Deep in the night
Makura katashiku	That the only sleeve used as pillow
Sode zo tsuyukeki	Is wet with dew?
Itsutsu to ya	Fifth,
Ima ya ima ya to	While waiting, repeating to myself,
Matsu hodo ni	Now she will come,
Mi o kagerō ni	How sad to see her as fleeting
Nasu zo kanashiki	As a shimmering of air.
Mutsu to ka ya	Sixth,
Mukai no nobe ni	Even the deer
Sumu shika mo	Living in the field across the way

Tsuma yue ni koso
Nakiakashikere

Nanatsu to ya
Nakina no tatsu mo
  Tsurakaraji
Kimi yue nagasu
Waga na narikeri

Yatsu to ka ya
Yayoi no tsuki no
  Hikari oba
Omowanu kimi ga
Yado ni todomeyo

Kokonotsu ya
Koko de awazu wa
  Gokuraku no
Mida no jōdo de
Au yo arubeshi

Tō to ka ya
Toya o hanareshi
  Arataka o
Itsu ka wagate ni
Hikisuete min

Jūichi ya
Ichido makoto no
  Aru naraba
Hito no koto no ha
Ureshikaramashi

Jūni to ya
Nikushi to hito no
  Omouran
Kanawanu koto ni
Kokoro tsukuseba

Jūsan ya
Sanomi nasake o
  Furisute so
Nasake wa hito no
Tame ni araneba

Jūyon to ya
Shinan inochi mo
  Oshikarazu
Kimi yue nagasu
Waga mi nariseba

Spends all night crying
For his mate.

Seventh,
I won't mind
  Being called fickle
If such reputation comes
Because of you.

Eighth,
I wish the light of the moon
  Of the Third Month would stop
At the house of the person
Who never longs for me.

Ninth,
If we cannot meet here,
  There should be a time
When we will meet in the paradise
Of Amida Buddha.

Tenth,
When shall I see
  Standing on my hand
The young hawk that has just left
The aviary and changed his feathers?

Eleventh,
If she had been sincere
  Even only once,
Then I would be happy
To listen to her words.

Twelfth,
They must think
  Me detestable:
To work my head off
For something unachievable.

Thirteenth,
Don't throw away the chance
  To show pity to somebody:
Taking pity on people
Is not something you do for others.

Fourteenth,
Even should I die
  I won't have regrets:
My life wanders
Because of you.

Jūgo to ya	Fifteenth,
Gose no sawari to	It may become a hindrance
Nari ya sen	To my future life:
Mi no hakanaku mo	For this fleeting being
Awade hatenaba	To die without meeting you.
Jūroku ya	Sixteenth,
Rokuji no hodo o	Even when I pass by
Suguru ni mo	This land
Kimi ni kokoro o	My heart is always with you
Tsurete koso ike	Wherever I might go.
Jūnana ya	Seventeenth,
Shichido mōde no	Each time I make a pilgrimage—
Tabitabi mo	Seven in a day—
Kimi ni au yo to	I always pray that time comes
Inori koso sure	When I will meet with you.
Jūhachi ya	Eighteenth,
Hazukashinagara	Although I feel ashamed,
Iu koto o	Wouldn't you agree
Kokorotsuyoku mo	To meet me just to tell me
Awanu kimi kana	Heartless things?
Jūku to ya	Nineteenth,
Kurushi yo goto ni	I cannot wait every night
Machikanete	With such painful thoughts
Sode itazura ni	Lest my sleeves
Kuchi ya hatemashi	Rot in vain.
Nijū to ya	Twentieth,
Nikushi to hito no	They must think
Omouran	Me detestable:
Ware naranu mi o	To fall in love
Hito no koureba	With someone I do not know.[22]

The merchant's mastering of the poetic tradition affords him a double gain. As a businessman he is so convincing that Izumi's servant asks for an additional citrus just for the pleasure of listening to the peddler. As a lover, he gains the woman, with whom he spends the night. Far from being peripheral, the possession of cultural capital leads to the growth of economic power—not to mention the gain in status achieved by joining company with the mythical people "above the clouds." Although the story continues with the portrayal of Izumi's guilt and her last years of reclusion, for the Citizens the narrative has reached its closure and no further mention is made of the handsome preacher. Only the witty merchant remains in the mind of the reader, together with the last order of citruses:

Nijūichi to	Twenty-first,
Ichido no nasake	I tried to show all my love
Komen to te	At one time:
Ōku no kotoba	I have finally exhausted
Kataritsukushitsu	All my words.[23]

The Power of Parody: "The Story of Genji the Monkey"

The Citizens' penetration of the iron curtain of aristocratic culture that for centuries was jealously protected from the "contaminations" and "vulgarizations" of the uninitiated gave them access to the highly valuable commodity of the literary tradition, whose transformation could hardly be achieved without an act of appropriation. The fracture in the modes of production that gave priority to the wealth of means over the hierarchy of status led to a reshuffling of the notion of culture in which traditional elements were retained but only after being exposed to the blade of social criticism. The parodying mode of cultural interpretation allowed the retention of a traditional kind of knowledge whose new versions kept the rules of the game substantially unchanged, although its major player was now the unaristocratic urban voice.

The appropriation and reinterpretation of traditions provided commoners with an increased share of power, while the maintenance of previous traditions in an altered and parodied form established their legitimation. The perennial victims of cultural hegemony turned the structure of knowledge to their advantage with an ambiguous program of cultural appropriation. After adopting traditional canons, aestheticizing the "low" according to the traditional rules of a hierarchical society, they then reversed the cultural patterns by creating variations that would allow them to replace the aristocracy in ruling over cultural production. The marginalized victims of culture struggled to master the pattern of cultural domination by approaching traditions with the inquisitive eye of the skeptic whose laughter became his measure for interpreting reality.

In the Citizens' process of self-aestheticization the merchant appears as the spokesman of a culture that integrates the practicality of daily matters with the aristocratic heights of secret knowledge. Narratives of the Muromachi period represent peddlers in the moment of their ascension to the forbidden realm of culture that they challenge by envisioning alternative cultural models. Sarugenji, the hero of "The Story of Genji the Monkey" (*Sarugenji Sōshi,* 1474),[24] is a seller of sardines from Akogi Bay (Akogigaura) of Ise province who lives like a fisherman and speaks like an aristocrat. A few decades earlier, the anonymous brush of a *nō* writer accomplished the aestheticization of the inhabitants of this fishing area. He wrote a play, *Akogi,* about the guilt of a fisherman *(shite)* who loses his life for daring to fish in the waters reserved for the Ise Shrine and venturing to kill the deity's offerings. The impoverished aristocrat Yamashina Tokitsugu witnessed the popularity of this story well into the sixteenth century. He recorded in his diary, the *Tokitsugu Gyōki,* that a performance of *Akogi* took place on the first day of the Fifth Month 1532 at Ichijō Nishi no Tōin on the occasion of a fund-raising campaign.[25]

In his story about a sardine seller from Akogi, the anonymous author of "The Story of Genji the Monkey" based his account of the merchant's poetic accomplishments and cultural sensibility on a theme that was already well known to his readers. In the following scene from the *nō* play *Akogi* the fisherman invites the deuteragonist *(waki)*—a traveling monk leading him onto the path of spiritual salvation—to acknowledge his abundant share of cultural capital that will eventually spare the fisherman the tortures of hell:

WAKI: How can I address this fellow?
SHITE: Are you talking to me?
WAKI: In the province of Ise, what's the name of this bay?
SHITE: This is Akogi Bay.
WAKI: Oh, so I have reached Akogigaura, the bay mentioned in the ancient poem,

Ise no umi	If you keep on
Akogigaura ni	Pulling the nets
Hiku ami no	In Akogi Bay
Tabikasanareba	Of the Ise sea,
Arawarenikeri	You will soon be found out.

Oh, how interesting!
SHITE: Oh, what an accomplished traveler! How can I ignore the famous verses on this place,

Au koto mo	If you keep on
Akogigaura ni	Meeting and pulling the nets
Hiku ami mo	In Akogi Bay,
Tabikasanaraba	You will soon
Araware ya sen	Be found out.[26]

Since a fisherman composed this poem, you shouldn't despise the unrefined fisherman of Ise or think of him lightly.
WAKI: Indeed, the unrefined man who has spent his life in a famous place . . .

SHITE: The evening smoke of the seaweed that the fisherman burns . . .

WAKI: Although he does not need to burn himself with the passion for poetry . . .

SHITE: If you live in a famous place, even the waves . . .

WAKI: Will change their sound.

SHITE: Listen!

CHORUS: Even names change according to places: even winds blowing through the rushes of Naniwa change their sound when they reach the beach reeds of Ise.[27] Listen! How can a fisherman, of whom they sang,

Moshio yaku	Now the smoke of the burning
Kemuri mo ima wa	Seaweed for the fabrication
Taenikeri	Of salt has ceased:
Tsuki min to te no	This is the work of the fisherman
Ama no shiwaza ni	Wishing to see the moon,[28]

be excluded from being carried by waves to this land of poetry?[29]

When Genji the Monkey—Sarugenji—from Akogi Bay reaches the capital with a load of sardines on his shoulder, he brings the cultural capital that the writer of *Akogi* associated with the fishermen of Ise. Following the laws of the Muromachi market, however, the peddler turns his intellectual resources to the amorous conquest of Keiga, one of the capital's highest-ranking courtesans. Like the Shining Prince Genji, the hero of Heian readers, this plebeian version of worldly success addresses his cultural might to the accumulation of political assets. For Genji the assimilation of court traditions translated into the gathering of female figures to be placed as imperial consorts at the court.[30] For Sarugenji, as well as for his later colleagues of the Tokugawa period populating the pleasure quarters, the hiring of an unapproachable courtesan was a display of wealth that was central to the acquisition and maintenance of distinction within the business community. Merchants fought between themselves and against the hierarchically superior military lords for the favors of famous courtesans, and the quarrels were all resolved with the weapon of hard cash.

Although the fishmonger achieves his goal with the exploitation of the same cultural code employed by Genji, the technique used is different inasmuch as the merchant needs both to accept the tradition and to change it in order to establish his sense of distinction. He must appropriate for his own personal ends the hegemonic role played by culture, so as to sustain his economic capital with the power of knowledge. The merchant's move to dominate tradition makes him aware of the strength of cultural distance—the ability to subject the scrutinized object to the gaze of the viewer. This act of domestication eventually empowers the scrutinizing subject to laugh back at an object that otherwise would be laughing at him.

The very beginning of the story with the peddler's first glance at Keiga, passing in her palanquin over Gojō bridge, sets the parodying tone of the narrative. By starting with a quotation from the *Tales of Ise (Ise Monogatari)*, the narrator reverses the aesthetic code of courtly refinement *(miyabi)* developed in the Heian masterpiece.[31] He achieves this aesthetic inversion by changing the gender of a poem's persona. Sarugenji quotes a few famous lines from *Ise* expressing the sorrow of a lady being neglected by her lover. The scene takes place while the woman, who is washing her hands, gazes at the water in front of her. The weakness and vulnerability of the ignored woman are transferred to Sarugenji who, burning with passion for the courtesan, murmurs the poem to himself:

Ware bakari	No one else,
Mono omou hito wa	I had thought,
Mata mo araji	Could be so miserable as I—
[To] omoeba mizu no	Yet there is another
Shita ni mo arikeri	Under the water.[32]

The association of water with the business of the fishmonger vulgarizes the seriousness of the occasion, paving the way to the creation of the most famous parody of the Heian classic, *The Counterfeit Ise (Nise Monogatari)*, that became a bestseller at the beginning of the Edo period. To fully appreciate the irony of this reversal, the reader must know the answer given to the lady by the refined man who assures the woman that he, too, is suffering from the same pain of love. The purposely silenced reply says:

Minakuchi ni	You will see me
Ware ya miyuran	In that pool,
Kawazu sae	For even frogs
Mizu no shita nite	Cry in pairs
Morogoe ni naku	Under the water.[33]

Muromachi readers undoubtedly knew the exchange by heart. Although the author of Sarugenji's story omits this reply, since Keiga was no easy conquest, its presence in the reader's mind amplifies the ironic tone of the quotation by associating the metaphorical frogs *(kawazu)* of the *Ise* text with the plebeian sardines *(iwashi)*—and their smell—sold by Sarugenji. The aristocratic tone of the poem collides with the marine surroundings of Sarugenji, the inheritor of the business of his father-in-law Ebina no Rokurōzaemon.

The parodying tone continues with the deployment of another technique: indifference to textual matters and a tendency to dilate on the classics, adding whatever detail may prove the narrator's point. The mastering of the literary code is complete only when the user becomes part of the process of creation, a new voice in the intricacies of the act of narration. Arguing against Ebina's conviction that love at first sight is impossible, Sarugenji mentions a famous precedent from the *Tale of Genji (Genji Monogatari)* regarding Kashiwagi's enchantment with Genji's consort, the Third Princess (Onnasan no Miya), after a very furtive look. The traditionally deferential attitude toward the central work of the Japanese literary canon is lost to a recreation of the novel in contemporary idiom— the language of late Muromachi—in an attempt to erase its classical tone and give characters the vividness of the present. Sarugenji rewrites the literary canon by maintaining the centrality of Genji's story while preparing a new version suiting the linguistic and topical needs of the merchant.

Sarugenji argues that he "is not the only one to have fallen in love after a simple glimpse. Captain Genji deeply loved the Third Princess (Nyosan no Miya) but, after a while, he dumped her and turned his attention to Lady Aoi."[34] The narrator grounds his dispute on a textual mistake—by the time of the marriage between Genji and the Third Princess, Aoi had already been dead several years. Moreover, as a man of refinement, Genji never repudiated a consort, no matter how extensive her infidelity. The fabrication of details and the intentional amnesia of plot development empowers the Muromachi narrator to escape submission to the Heian text, imposing on it his hegemonic thrust.

Once in charge of the process of literary production, Sarugenji can replace even the most refined *daimyō* in the affection of Keiga, since he has acquired cultural capital that permits his disguise as a famous lord from the eastern provinces, Utsunomiya no Danjō. Sarugenji's ability to recreate the classics helps him to obtain and maintain the love of Keiga even after he almost reveals his true identity by unconsciously repeating in his sleep his sales pitch: "Hey, buy the sardines of Genji the Monkey from Akogi Bay!" *(Akogigaura no Sarugenji ga iwashi kō ei).*[35] Sarugenji's explanation of each word in order to justify his slip marks the apotheosis of the merchant's wit. The commercial slogan of the sardine seller provides him with an excuse to display his uncommon knowledge of anecdotes concerning major events of the poetic tradition.

The *nō* play *Akogi* saves Sarugenji from the embarrassment of admitting his place of origin in the bay of Ise. He pretends to have been invited by the shogun to a session of linked-poetry *(renga)* together with the most renowned masters of the land. He argues that, requested by the generalissimo to cap a verse, he keeps repeating in his dreams the famous poem from the *Kokin Rokujō* on the fisherman from Akogi Bay who drowned in the open sea for violating the ban against fishing in that sacred area.[36] Sarugenji finds further justification in a quotation from the medieval military tale *Genpei Seisuiki,* of which he gives a parodying reading. The passage in question is related to the medieval theme of the bodhisattvic role played by courtesans that made "women of pleasure" paradigms of Buddhist enlightenment. The narrator mentions the Heian poet Saigyō in connection with the Eguchi courtesan whose role as the poet's "celestial wife" Sarugenji ridicules by stressing the way in which the woman addressed the poet. She calls Saigyō "the man from Akogi Bay," implying that he was not allowed to fish in the woman's area.[37]

The narrator elucidates the puzzle "Sarugenji" with another complex exercise in textual fabrication over the narrative of *The Tale of Genji.* He explains the first part of the compound—*saru,* indicating both "monkey" and the name of the homonymous pond (Sarusawa)—in the light of an episode from a major literary work of the Heian period, *The Tales of Yamato (Yamato Monogatari).* Feeling abandoned by the sovereign, a female servant of the Nara emperor—either Monmu, Seimu, or Heizei—drowns herself in Sarusawa Pond. While sadly looking at the corpse, the emperor recites a poem that provides the peddler with half a way out of his predicament.[38] The second half of the explanation comes from Sarugenji's free recounting of the life of Prince Genji who allegedly stopped at this pond during a pilgrimage to the Kasuga Shrine, where he composed a poem as a memorial for the girl.[39] Therefore—the peddler alleges—the unconscious mentioning of the word *sarugenji* was the result of his obsession with Genji's poem at Sarusawa Pond.

Sarugenji's narration of a humorous anecdote on the life of the Heian poetess Izumi Shikibu concludes his poetic tour de force, putting an end to Keiga's doubts about her lover's social status. The narrator portrays Izumi in the act of being caught by her husband Hōshō—Fujiwara no Yasumasa—while eating sardines. Fearing the exposure of a private moment of domestic relaxation, the woman hides the fish, giving the wrongful impression that she is concealing a love letter from the preacher Dōmyō. Hōshō's forceful manners only unveil an embarrassing truth that induces Izumi to compose a poem indicating that in Japan no one can resist the inviting taste of sardines.[40] Izumi incorporates the unpoetic expression "sardines" *(iwashi)* in the name of one of the major shrines in the capital: the Iwashimizu. Her poetic refinement wins the approval of Hōshō who gladly comments that, "since they warm up the skin and are particularly good medicine for improving the color of a woman's face, there is no point in blaming you for eating sardines."[41]

Sarugenji's success is complete. The merchant's knowledge is so impressive that the foremost courtesan of the capital surrenders to his advances and decides to live with him even after she eventually discovers the man's true identity. The merchant's victory goes well beyond the gain of sexual gratification. He conquers the entire tradition, showing that victims of domination can play a dominant role by appropriating the means of production—economic, cultural, and status capital—that legitimize the act of subjugation. This change of leadership in the process of cultural production requires a reexamination of a tradition that scholars loosely call "medieval."

Debunking the Medieval Tradition: "The Story of the Lazy Fellow"

The use of the expression "medieval" in connection with a historical period of Western civilization has been the subject of heated debate among scholars who, in spite of understandable disagreements on a controversial topic, would hardly deny the didactic convenience of the word's etymology as a middle age between the declining glory of antiquity and the burgeoning prosperity of the Renaissance. No matter whether "medieval" conjures up a positive view of the age ("the good middle ages") or a negative one ("the dark middle ages"),[42] it bridges different cognitive structures, epistemological,[43] political,[44] economical,[45] or social.[46] The Foucaultian notion of "episteme"[47] to indicate historical transition—or, to be more faithful to Foucault's philosophy,[48] historical discontinuities, breaks, displacements, and gaps—has led to the definition of "the boundary line separating the historical 'period' of the 'Middle Ages' from the 'Renaissance' " as "the revolution of a new episteme,"[49] implying a philosophical move away from Scholastic logic.

Historians have used the Japanese translation of the word "middle ages" *(chūsei)* to create a fictional counterpart of the West in which an allegedly golden age of Japanese civilization—the Heian "empire" (794–1191)—was followed by two intermediary stages—the Kamakura (1192–1333) and the Muromachi (1334–1573) periods—leading to the blooming urban culture of the seventeenth century, the time for the "classical revival" of the Japanese Renaissance.[50] Others have located the Middle Ages between the time of the Japanese acceptance of Chinese culture ("the Ancient Age") and the moment of Western acculturation ("the Modern Age"), highlighting once again the transitional nature of the "years in between."[51] Those applying the notion of episteme to the definition of medieval Japan see in Buddhism the hegemonic framework of thought informing the epoch's "basic intellectual problems, the most authoritative texts and resources, and [its] central symbols."[52] Because of the centrality of Buddhism in the Japanese tradition, this approach has led to the expansion of the time borders of the period well beyond the traditional markers, stretching the Japanese Middle Ages from the ninth to the seventeenth century.[53]

Far from entering into the complexities of the issues supporting and questioning the validity of the application of the term "medieval" to the Japanese context, I will limit this discussion to a few structural elements that highlight the tension between two modes of production—agrarian and commercial—in which the latter challenges the former in the attempt to transform the rules of the medieval social and political game. In examining the Muromachi narrative known as "The Story of the Lazy Fellow" *(Monokusatarō),* we see how the world of the peasant with its values of loyalties and obedience to a static order of power—in which immutability is the prerequisite for the maintenance of order and the reproduction of the social system—is contrasted to the urban world of the capital's Citizens, whose behavioral code is molded less by tradition than by the witty use of newly accumulated cultural capital.

The geography of stasis that characterizes the life of the peasant from the Shinano region—the present-day Nagano prefecture—explains the situational rather than congenital laziness of Monokusatarō. The rural worker's lack of social mobility and hopes for improvement displaces the man's energy into the realm of the imagination, enabling the narrator to open the story with the fictitious house of Monokusatarō's dreams—the fruits of successful urbanization. The fact that he presents the dream as if it already were reality, relegating the truth to an incidental note at the end of the paragraph, emphasizes the gap between the reality of unrewarding labor that Monokusatarō marginalizes in his dream and the fictitious environment of social change in which dreams materialize, making utopia real. The marginalized reality that Monokusatarō struggles to silence by taking a totally passive attitude toward work and human relationships, speaks the language of "choppy hands and feet, fleas, lice, and dirt on his elbow"[54] that accumulate while the man spends his time reclining and dreaming. The narrator deals with the nature of dreams as follows:

> His name was Monokusatarō, and his house was far from being the usual dwelling. Made of four huge roofed mud-walls, the house had three entrances on three different sides. Ponds were dug in the east, west, south, and north corners, and in each of them floated an island. Pine trees and cedars had been planted, and an arched bridge connected the island to the garden. The ornamental tops of the bridge's railing were shining—a view unmatched in the entire world. The house was made of a twelve-pillar room for the guards, a nine-pillar corridor, a pavilion over the pond *(tsuri-*

dono), a connecting corridor *(hosodono)*, a Plum Court *(mumetsubo)*, a Paulownia Court *(kiritsubo)*, one hundred different kinds of flower planted all over, and a twelve-pillar main residence. All roofs were thatched with layers of cypress bark, and brocades hung from the ceilings. Beams and rafters were made of gold and silver, while the blinds were crafted with jewels. Everything was fine in this house, even the stables and the room for the guards. How he would have liked to live in a house like this!—Monokusatarō thought.

But since he was lacking the means, as a matter of fact, his house was made of four bamboo stalks and a straw mat hanging as a roof.[55]

Monokusatarō eventually fulfills his dream in the urban space of the capital to which the narrator must move him in order to show the reader the humanistic potential of an imagination fed with the food of incentive and economic/social/sexual stimulation. The spark igniting the transformation of laziness into productivity is Monokusatarō's desire to find an attractive wife in the capital. He agrees to work for the Nijō Major Counselor *(dainagon)* Narisue as part of the compulsory service due by his village to its absent lord in Kyoto. The active space of commerce and traditional culture starts a process of regeneration in a man whose meeting with a land of opportunity transforms him into a strong and diligent worker overstaying his contract by more than eight months.[56]

The initiation to the world of economic and cultural hegemony is undoubtedly painful for a country bumpkin whom the fair-skinned townsmen constantly mock for his dark complexion. The narrator emphasizes the distinguishing quality of the Citizens—witticism—by playing it against the simplemindedness of a peasant whose first step toward urbanization requires the repudiation of the qualities of honesty, loyalty, and obedience. Dependence on these traditional virtues in a context of commerce and wit leads to humorous exchanges such as the following, in which a shrewd citizen acts as Monokusatarō's love consultant:

Addressing the master of the inn, [Monokusatarō] said: "I am going back to Shinano. Could you find me a woman who you think would be a good match for me as a wife?"

The master laughed, and replied: "What kind of a woman would take a man like you as her husband? To get a woman is not that hard," he continued, "but getting married is a big step. You should look for a streetwalker *(irogonomi)!*"

"What's a streetwalker? What are you talking about?"

Unable to believe his ears, the man answered: "You go after a woman who has no husband. You pay her money and sleep with her. That's what I mean by streetwalker."

"If that is the case," said Monokusatarō, "get me one! Here are twelve or thirteen *mon* that I saved for my return to Shinano. Give them to the woman."

Hearing this, the master thought that he had never met a fool like Monokusatarō in his entire life, and he added: "Why don't you do crossroads stopping?"

"What's crossroads stopping?" Monokusatarō was surprised.

"Crossroads stopping means taking by force the girl that you like while she's walking alone with no palanquin behind her. That should make it a forgivable act."[57]

The tension between past and present, country and city, dullness and activity, ignorance and culture, diminishes with the unfolding of the story and Monokusatarō's disclosure of his mastery of the poetic tradition. His encounter with the girl of his dreams at the Kiyomizu Temple affects in the man the awakening of his dormant cultural capital. Monokusatarō's imitation of the aristocratic disposition for leisure and acculturation (what the Romans called *otium*) allowed him to accumulate his cultural assets during his lazy life in Shinano. The peripherality of the geographic area did not, however, provide him with any legitimation for his appropriation of "noble" means of production.

An ideally beautiful and educated girl from the capital affects this process of cultural resurrection. Monokusatarō notices her while standing in front of the temple with his arms outstretched in order to capture his prey. He "pushes his dirty head" under the girl's umbrella "so as to be face to face with her." In the same way that the view of the capital's layout and its bursting commercial activity inspired in the man a desire for capitalistic adventures, the exploration of feminine beauty displays to Monokusatarō the code of aesthetic refinement—of which a court lady was the most appropriate symbol. The narrator pairs the contrasting portraits of Monokusatarō and the lady in the following scene:

He wore the same old unlined summer clothes that he had worn since his arrival from Shinano. He used a straw rope as an obi on a kimono so worn-out that color and pattern were impossible to recognize. His short straw sandals were all in pieces, and he supported his body on a bamboo stick. . . .

She looked like a spring cherry blossom, her black hair as glossy as the feathers of the kingfisher. Her blue-black eyebrows were so flowery that they were no different from the cherry trees of the distant mountain. Her beautifully supple sidelocks looked like the wings of a cicada in autumn, and she had all the thirty-two marks and eighty indications of a buddha—she was just like a golden Nyorai. Everything in her bespoke of gracefulness, from the eyebrows to the tips of her toes. She wore several unlined kimonos of different colors, a deeply red pleated skirt which had been dyed several times, and a pair of unsoled sandals. Her hair, which was longer than her height, had the fragrance of plum blossoms.[58]

The narrator's response to this fractured portrayal of reality exposes the reader to the transformation of the cultural pattern from what is "in between"—the Middle Ages—to what comes after it. Far from replacing the practice of the game, the change occurs at the level of rules and players. The basic structure of the cultural paradigm—the tradition of court poetry—remains unchallenged, although it undertakes undeniable transformations in the uses to which the urban voice now puts it. A complete replacement cannot take place, since the assimilation of the cultural tradition is a prerequisite for the "aristocratization" of the rising bourgeoisie and its taking over the traditional game of power. Since cultural capital washes away the otherwise indelible traces of origin, and since the Citizens' movement along the hierarchic scale is upward toward the aristocratic values of the court, a displacement of the court tradition would annihilate the efforts of the social climbers. The maintenance and assimilation of the tradition is the first step to being accepted into a higher sphere of power. The second step, however, consists in transforming the rules regulating the exercise of power.

Monokusatarō's debut on the stage of the aristocracy takes place through a ritual which strips him of the marks of inferior status. It begins with a changing of clothes and the removal of "dust and lice"; soon he dons the nobleman's headgear *(eboshi)*. The awkwardness of a man "used to walking on mountains and peaks" makes him slip on the shining wooden floor of the villa and "fall down on a *koto* treasured by the lady, smashing it into little pieces."[59] A subsequent demonstration of poetic mastery—appropriate to a man who struggles for acceptance into the world "above the clouds"—makes up for the traces of rusticity that the narrator constructs as a natural heritage for the inhabitants of Shinano. By capping a verse by the lady expressing her deep sorrow for the loss of a dear musical instrument—a potent symbol of courtly aesthetics—he develops a play on words on the sound of his crime, "to break the *koto*" *(koto o waru)*, defining the woman's sorrow as an absolutely reasonable *(kotowari)* outcome.[60]

The comical effect of the episode involves much more than a boor smashing a musical instrument. It also underscores the dreamy nature of a peasant whose loyalty to a cultural tradition that keeps him subjected may falter, creating a secret desire for physical removal and erasure. The displacement of authority, however—the Oedipal killing of the father in the treacherous game of power—also requires the maintenance of that same symbolism that the murderous son challenges but cannot replace. Monokusatarō accomplishes the mending according to the very rule that he attempts to remove: He appeals to the courtly code of poetry that for centuries had availed aristocrats with easy solutions to social mistakes.

The application of a set of traditional knowledge to the plebeian circumstances of daily life redirects the use of culture toward the empowering of the excluded and marginalized. Although the social role played by poetry during the classical Heian period already allowed for a pragmatic definition of the poetic act, the Citizens' appropriation of the poetic tradition removed from the game of amorous exchange the veil of pretension that concealed beneath an intricate curtain of denials and excuses the main purpose of the game—the acquisition of political, social, and economic power. The Citizens took pride in their ability to restore life to a moribund tradition by applying it to a contemporary setting and turning it into immediate profit. The economic orientation of the urban bourgeoisie gives priority to the concrete result; the techniques employed in the process of gaining is relevant only in proportion to the degree of its success. No effort is made to conceal the presence of a practical objective in the cultural act, whose justification the Citizens found precisely in the suitability of culture to the reality of the here and now.

Monokusatarō mobilizes all his intellectual resources for the fulfillment of his immediate goal: the personal appropriation of a token from the cultural center. He exploits the classical narrative device of poetic enumeration for his immediate personal gain. Poets recorded in sequences names of geographic areas well known in the poetic and religious traditions in order to create a narrative of movement, taking the reader on a symbolic journey *(michiyuki)*. Monokusatarō's employment of this technique leads him to the creation of a list of the capital's historical spots that he pretends to have visited in the past with the girl. He fabricates a fictitious intellectual background that empowers the poor laborer with cultural wealth. His semantic journey around the capital becomes an amorous pilgrimage to the worship of the newly found goddess who is at a loss how to escape the man's passionate attacks.[61] Monokusatarō's philological expertise helps him to unravel the puzzles hiding the location of the woman's house, as well as convincing her and the reader of the marketability and practicality of the Citizens' witty use of cultural capital.[62]

The poetic form *(waka)* that for centuries had been in the mainstream of the court's process of cultural production was voided of its classical aspect at both semantic and topical levels. While dressing people's "vulgar" jokes in the acceptable aulic language of legitimation, the explicitness of images appealing to the sexual curiosity of urbanized readers treated the unreachable heights of aristocratic culture as an entertainment widely welcomed by commoners. In order for the process of courtship, which played a central role in the court's aesthetic game of love and power, to hold the interest of less aristocratic audiences, the rules of the game must change in order to please the new readership. The metaphorical reading of poetic images became more transparent, although a straightforward presentation of reality that would threaten the secretive nature of *waka,* and betray the "purity"/legitimacy of the aesthetic code of the upper classes, was carefully avoided.

The narrator's presentation of metaphorical readings of his characters' reproductive organs is indicative of the changes that the poetic tradition underwent at the time of urban growth. Instead of dispensing with descriptions of the human body—which, in classical times, was seldom mentioned and, if it was, was customarily presented in its closures and finish—the Citizens' view of the body corresponds to what the Russian literary critic Mikhail Bakhtin has termed "grotesque realism."[63]

Openings and orifices take the lead in the representation of the body: "an image of impure corporeal bulk with its orifices (mouth, flared nostrils, anus) yawning wider and its lower regions (belly, legs, feet, buttocks, and genitals) given priority over its upper regions (head, 'spirit,' reason)."[64] Although this definition does not do total justice to the form of *waka* that never gave priority to the low, always following strict rules of composition, the reference to the body's lower regions in the two following exchanges between Monokusatarō and the lady of his dreams engendered not only laughter among the Citizens, but also pride for the narrator's ingenuity in dealing with the raw material of popular culture.

In the first exchange the double meaning of the word *fushi*—meaning both "bamboo joint" and "to lie down"—uncovers the presence of Monokusatarō's genitals in the image of a bamboo stick that, according to the man, is well worthy of the woman's beauty. Monokusatarō's poem follows the verse by the woman:

> Karatake o
> Tsue ni tsukitaru
> Mono nareba
> Fushi soigataki
> Hito o miru kana
>
> Since I see
> That the joints are attached
> To your bamboo stick,
> It seems difficult to lie down
> And be joined to you.
>
> Yorozu yo no
> Take no yogoto ni
> Soufushi no
> Nado karatake ni
> Fushinakarubeki
>
> All bamboos,
> Everywhere in the world,
> Have joints:
> Why should my bamboo stick
> Be deprived of its joints?[65]

The female reproductive organs appear as the metaphorical reading of the word *kaki* ("persimmons") in its second meaning of "oyster." The image is concocted by Monokusatarō in a poem that attempts to explain why the woman offers him several chestnuts, pears, and persimmons, together with some salt and a short sword in a single container—a breach of etiquette on the woman's part, since each gift was expected to be presented in a separate tray. Feeling that he has been "treated like a horse or an ox," the man expresses his resentment with such a witty use of poetry that eventually the woman consents to spend the night with him, believing she has found "a lotus flower in the mud, pure gold in a straw wrapper." The grotesque representation of the sexual performance takes place within the classical structure of court poetry, catering to the taste of commoners in their struggle to appropriate the high culture of the aristocracy without losing the identity of their collective origin:

> Isn't it because you want to become one with me *(ware ni hitotsu ni nariawan)* that you put all the fruits in one container *(hitotsu ni shikuretaru)*? Did you give me the chestnuts *(kuri)* to repeatedly let me know *(kurikoto)* that you want me to be here with you? By presenting the pears *(nashi)* are you trying to tell me that no man *(otoko nashi)* is there with you? But how to explain the persimmons *(kaki)* and the salt *(shio)*? Perhaps I can explain them with the following poem:

> | Tsu no kuni no | Since this is the oyster *(kaki)* |
> | Naniwa no ura no | Of Naniwa Bay |
> | Kaki nareba | Of Tsu province, |
> | Umiwataranedo | We don't need to cross the sea |
> | Shio wa tsukikeri | To get salt *(shio)*.[66] |

The Citizens' new attitude toward tradition opens a rent in the fabric of the Japanese medieval episteme. In tracing the differential elements of "The Story of the Lazy Fellow," which highlights the role played by an urban audience in the transformation of what has been generally labeled "medieval," scholars have focused their attention on the very structure of the narrative that on the surface unfolds as the description of the human life of a deity—a genre known as "the Original Ground narrative" *(honjimono)*, which was quite popular during the Kamakura and Muromachi periods. The story of Monokusatarō is no exception, since it follows the traditional pattern: The lazy boy reveals himself as a grandson of Emperor Ninmyō (r. 833–850) who was brought up by peasants of Shinano province after the death of his exiled father. Reinstated as the lord of Kai and Shinano, Monokusatarō dies at 120 years of age, eventually becoming the deity Hotaka no Daimyōjin, while his wife—the girl from the capital—is enshrined as Asai no Gongen.[67]

The Japanese scholar Sakurai Yoshirō has gathered evidence to show the narrator's consistent intention all through the story to present Mono-kusatarō as a deity in order to reduce the reader's surprise at the moment of the man's epiphany. A record of the Hotaka Shrine, the *Sangū Hota-kasha Gozōeitei Nikki* (1501), mentions the custom, widespread in Shinano, of delimiting sacred areas with the erection of four poles—the same structure that appears in the description of Monokusatarō's humble dwelling. Moreover, the food given to him at the beginning of the tale corresponds to a particular kind of rice cake *(mochi)* that a bride and groom offered to the deity on the third night of their marriage cere-mony. This detail supports Monokusatarō's final identity with Hotaka no Daimyōjin since this god was credited with the protection of the newly wed.[68]

The steward of the province *(jitō)* also recognizes in Monokusatarō a sacred presence when, unable to convince him of the need to be either a farmer or a merchant, he eventually orders the villagers to feed him free of charge. Sakurai explains the unrealistic generosity of the government official as a ritual offering that, although it was usually carried out in temples and shrines, in this particular instance was addressed to a human manifestation of a deity—Monokusatarō, alias the god of Hotaka.[69] The steward performs an act of pacification intended to transform a potential threat to the community into a protective shield. This process erases the deity's dangerously irrational and vindictive aspect—the "rough compo-nent" *(ara)* of the god—leaving unchallenged its opposite: "the peaceful, benevolent aspect, reflecting the human order imposed upon chaos,"[70] the deity's "harmonious component" *(niki)*. The successful result of this religious/political ritual is reflected in the transformation undergone by Monokusatarō who, once in contact with an urban reality, loses his lazy side *(monokusa)* and is left with his earnestness and seriousness *(mame)* only.[71]

We cannot doubt the impact on the story of a "medieval" narrative structure. Traces of the Buddhist rationalization of mythical/Shinto thinking are deep and pervasive. Following the path developed by the authors of anecdotal literature *(setsuwa)*, the anonymous author ex-plains "the excess of meaning"[72] that contradicts the general expectation of the workings of the divine, finding an explanation to the strangeness and absurdity of the deity's behavior. The fable is stripped of its strange-ness, and the extraordinary—or mythical—is recycled into the reason-ableness of the religious. But the major departure from medieval modes of narration consists in the fact that, as the literary historian Shinoda Jun'ichi has noted, the new urban bourgeoisie questions and attacks the validity of the structure of the "Original Ground narrative" as a religious fiction to be laughed at rather than believed. Shinoda argues that the debunking of the medieval tradition in "The Story of the Lazy Fellow" occurred during the early Edo period—either the Keichō (1596–1614) or the Genna (1615–1623) eras—during which *Monokusatarō* was allegedly composed.[73]

We perceive the narrator's ironic attitude toward the *honjimono* tradition in the peculiar use that he makes of religious material in a few poetic exchanges between Monokusatarō and the lady from the capital. When she finally accepts the man's courtship, inviting him for a night of pleasure, the lady creates a variation on a poem from the *Kokinshū* on the legend of the god of Mt. Miwa who, after taking the shape of a snake, was exhorted by a woman to join her in her house and become her husband. Although the phallic image does not appear in the *otogizōshi,* the association of the poem with the famous legend provided the missing link to contemporary readers.[74] Before accepting Monokusatarō as her husband, the lady offers him ten sheets of paper *(kami)* that because of associations based on sound—*kami* means both "paper" and "god"—and on a religious tradition—the white paper symbolizes the presence of the divine—leads Monokusatarō to concoct a poetic joke at the expense of the sacred. Monokusatarō's poem says:

Chihayafuru	To be given the paper *(kami)*—
Kami o tsukai ni	Messenger to the almighty
Tabitaru wa	God *(kami):*
Ware o yashiro to	Are you thinking of me
Omou ka ya kimi	As a shrine?[75]

Voicing the skepticism of townsmen, the narrator challenges the plight of "Original Ground narratives" that promise a blissful future life to those who endure the hardships of the present. The final comment in particular subverts the silently accepted reality of traditional cultural patterns. The narrator states that to manifest his Original Ground publicly is a privilege for a deity like Monokusatarō because of the successful outcome that makes human suffering an expression of the divine. Commoners *(bonbu),* however, do not enjoy the same blessings. The unveiling of their Original Ground is only a source of anger *(hara o tate)* and shame, since they know that they will never become deities, and that their pains and suffering know no end.[76]

Another version of the story—"The Account of the Lazy Fellow" *(Monokusatarō Monogatari)*—further emphasizes the fictionality of religious narratives by reinforcing the narrator's irony with a rhetorical exclamation: "Oh, how strange *(okashisa yo)* that while deities enjoy manifesting their Original Ground, commoners get so angry when they do the same!"⁷⁷ Evidently the Citizens were having a hard time believing that they could take pride in the repetitive performance of unrewarding work, and that acceptance of the status quo could take them to the promised land.

The Citizens' Politics of Containment

The tradition of political satire developed by the "Kyoto Boys" *(kyō warabe)*, who would post anonymous lampoons in the capital, surfaces in another genre—the so-called *kyōgen* or "farces"—whose subversive message Tokugawa authorities silenced in the early seventeenth century with an act of compression and then erasure. The institutionalization of subversion occurred with the ritualization of theatrical performances that saw the short and pungent farces of the Muromachi period dwarfed and encapsulated between the staging of its "ennobled" counterpart, the *nō* plays. When the satire resisted domestication, the play was expunged from the repertoire. Only a brief document surviving from the Muromachi period, the *Tenshō Kyōgen Bon* (1578), remains today to confirm the process of desatiricalization that *kyōgen* underwent during the Tokugawa period. It contains the synopses of plays that were the target of governmental censorship.⁷⁸ An example may suffice to clarify the point.

"Petition to the Lord" *(Konoedono no Mōshijō)* is a tribute to the suffering of the medieval peasant who cannot afford to pay the annual tribute to his lord. The petition asks for a tax reduction following a season of meager crops. The anonymous author theatricalizes a peasants' protest in a multitude of "stylized gestures and conventionalized script," putting on stage an actual "ritual of rebellion" that starts with the presentation of a written request.⁷⁹ The farce discloses the daily reality of power abuse in which peasants denounce to the proprietor *(ryōshu)* the greediness of steward-deputies *(jitō-dai)* who were draining their resources.

Peasants disguised their political discontent behind the mask of religious ritual. They addressed their oppressors as "benevolent deities" to whose mercy they entrusted their case. Pledges directed to gods such as Hachiman, the Kumano gods, and other local deities were symbolic representations of the petition. The ritual consisted in burning the written pledges and mixing the ashes with water that crowds of peasants then drank as a collective act of solidarity *(ichimi shinsui)*. The petition itself was then presented to the lord several times, until it was finally accepted. If the request was not granted, the peasants might choose to abandon the land as a sign of protest *(chōsan)*.⁸⁰

"Petition to the Lord" stages this history of rural hardships, explaining the reduced number of peasants in Lord Konoe's fief as a result of the man's repeated refusal to meet their demands. The synopsis reads as follows:

> An attendant comes on stage bringing a petition, approaches Lord Konoe, and meets with him. The lord sits down and looks. The petition is given to the lord. How difficult for the petition to be accepted—how many times the attendant has to go back and forth! The coming and going of messengers is endless like the weaving of thread. It is sad to see the number of people living in the village constantly decreasing and big families growing smaller. The crowing of cocks is silenced, so that nobody knows the arrival of dawn any longer. The seeds of spring plants fly all over, bursting into buds. The moon is covered by clouds, and flowers are struck by the wind. In the same way, the lord is bothered by the petition, which was disguised as a pledge to the deities. The angry lord tears it up, chasing away with his sword the messenger Saemon no Jō. The end.[81]

Tokugawa shoguns promoted a more fictional representation of peasant life by sponsoring congratulatory pieces that advanced a pastoral view of a silenced reality. The *kyōgen* repertoire came to present the farmer as a grateful subject who considers the annual journey to the capital for the payment of the land tax a joyous event affording the happy boor with an opportunity of exposure to an otherwise unknowable urban reality. The world of uprisings *(ikki)* that since the fifteenth century had plagued the country because of the government's unsustainable taxation policy was effaced from the stage where performers disguised as land workers sang the benevolence of a just ruler.

This is the topic of "The Three Laborers" *(Sanninbu)*, a play in which three peasants from the provinces of Owari, Awaji, and Mino are on their way to the capital to pay the customary tribute. The taxpayers join the lord in the aristocratic act of poetic composition, taking part in the celebration of his economic success with the performance of music and dances. Reminded of "the happy event you are experiencing in the capital," the peasants compete in a display of wit singing the blessings bestowed by the sovereign over his subjects. The representative of Mino towers over his colleagues with a pun most appropriate to the major topic of the day: "tunes" and "taxes," which in Japanese share the same sound, *chō:*

> AWAJI PEASANT: Isn't it a matter of rejoicing to come and pay taxes every year?
> OWARI PEASANT: Indeed it is, to come every year to the capital!
> MINO PEASANT: What a happy occasion! A sign of a well-governed era! Your tunes (= taxes) come from different provinces. Forever, forever! I finally left after singing (= paying)![82]

The subversive nature of the Japanese farce became a potent vehicle in the hands of Citizens who resisted the blind acceptance of traditional values based mainly on the doubtful premises of unquestioned precedent, custom, and acquiescence. The explication of actions according to the Buddhist idea of "self-inflicted destiny" (karma) excluded most of the actors of commerce and production from the gaining of spiritual reward, enlightenment. The marginalization of the dealers in animal products, for example, into the limbo of the nonhumans *(hinin)*—the gray area beyond the borders of the social structure—could hardly continue to go unchallenged in an economic world of capital accumulation. The subject's mastery of the dominant class's epistemological apparatus rewrites the history of social stratification, disputing the traditional explanations of privileges and abuses. The tools of the Buddhist philosopher to which hierarchical structures were deeply indebted are presented on stage in the hands of the victims of subjection who now take pleasure in disclosing the unsteady foundations of Buddhist logic.

An attack on Buddhist ideology appears in the farce *Sakon no Samurō* in which the hunter Samurō confronts his exclusion from the community on account of the "impurity" *(kitanai mono)* of his "sinful" activity: the killing of living creatures. The man succeeds in uncovering the contradictory justification of the monk's holiness, forcing the holy man to confess under the threat of the hunter's bow his acquaintance with rice wine, fish, and the pleasures of the flesh. The paradoxical situation derives from the fact that hierarchical society considers the act of consuming "defiled" products—meat in this case—less sinful than the process of producing them. The hunter bases his defense on the same sacred scriptures used by the Zen monk to keep the "sinner" away from the temples' holy ground. A quotation from the third Chinese patriarch of the Zen school, Jian-zhi Chan-shi (d. 606?), shows a commoner beating the man of the Buddhist Law at his own rhetorical game:

> HUNTER: Daruma Daishi says in his writings, "Kill, kill! Should you kill even the smallest measure of time, you will fall into hell as fast as an arrow. . . ." If fault does not exist in one thought, then it cannot be found in the myriads of dharmas. Without fault there is no dharma, without dharma there is no Buddha.
>
> MONK: If this is so, by killing a deer you will inevitably become a deer.
>
> HUNTER: If by killing a deer I become a deer, I will shoot you and become a monk![83]

If we believe—and there is no reason to doubt him—the father of Emperor Go-Hanazono (r. 1429–1464), Go-Sukō In, the challenge to traditional values did not go unpunished. The Tokugawa government was not the first to react strongly to the appearance of free expression. Fifteenth-century aristocrats and high prelates took punitive measures against the actors of farces who found more suitable audiences among the capital's merchants. On the eleventh day of the Third Month 1424, the nobleman portrayed in his diary, the *Kanmon Gyoki,* the customary punishment of a chief actor who excused himself on the ground that "he did not know."

> The farce of the *sarugaku* poked fun at the hardships of the aristocracy. Since this was pure insolence, I ordered my attendant to summon the chief of the troupe and scold him. "This is an imperial residence. How dare you make fun of the aristocrats in their own houses? Your ignorance of etiquette is unforgivable, totally shocking. I am warning you for your own sake. You may learn from knowing that a monk of Mt. Hiei once drew his sword on a *sarugaku* actor for having mocked a monkey.[84] Another actor performing at Ninnaji was punished for making fun of a certain monk's meanness. You should have had more respect for the place where you were performing—to neglect etiquette is unforgivable! I must dismiss you at once from your post." After crying aloud the chief actor apologized repeatedly, saying that he was unaware of etiquette—a very unpleasant scene to witness![85]

In its defiance of accepted traditions, *kyōgen* had a profound impact in questioning the appropriateness of behavioral models based on gender. Not only are peasants standing up to their lords and outcasts challenging the authority of the government's ideologues. Women too escape the margins of power, displacing their lazy husbands from the management of the household, while proposing on stage new definitions of female roles. The representation of women as administrators of small private enterprises attempts to erase the medieval image of female exclusion from the economics of the house. The creation of an alternative center to the male model of production engenders the powerful laughter of an audience that is taken aback by the ambiguity of the situation. While startling the spectator owing to the novelty of a situation that involves the unexpected presence of a working woman, the play also invites him to ponder the feasibility of alternatives and the deception of social structures blindly accepted. The woman running after her husband, a sickle in her hand, in the attempt to hurt a dreamer who is unable to withstand the economic changes of the time, is a recurrent theme in *kyōgen.*[86] Equally popular is the image of the wife who must fight her parasitic husband in the operation of the family business to which the husband is the major threat.[87]

The few examples of *kyōgen* mentioned above indicate the great potential enjoyed by the genre to project a voice that for centuries was either silenced or relegated to the periphery of power. The fulfillment of this potential remained in the hands of a vibrant urban society that attempted to erode traditional privileges by speeding a transformation in the country's economic structure. The appropriation of the genre by the capital's Citizens and by a few independent urban centers provided them with a form of political opposition that they voiced publicly.[88] Yet the assignment of the counterdiscursive voice to the clown on stage and to the world of fantastic production makes of political satire such a carnivalesque act that as a licensed affair it becomes almost ineffectual. To quote Terry Eagleton on this point: "As Shakespeare's Olivia remarks, there is no slander in an allowed fool."[89]

Mikhail Bakhtin's definition of carnival as the revolution of the marginalized fails to do justice to the osmotic movement between dominant and dominated ideologies that takes place in the carnival's clash of opposites. Rather than seeing *kyōgen* simply as the oral expression of the Citizens' political discontent, we should focus more on the process that makes the Citizens use the material of marginalization in the creation of a new ideology—bourgeois ideology—that cannot survive without the continuous presence of the marginalized "other." The carnivalesque act of subversion is then perceived less as an attempt to erase the past and its rules than as a mediation "between a classical/classificatory body and its negations, its Others, what it excludes to create its identity as such."[90]

In the case of the Citizens this mediation can be seen in the formation process of their subjectivity, in which they distinguish themselves from what they originally were—the "popular"—by encoding it in their subjectivity and retaining it as "other." The appropriation of court *(kuge)* manners and military *(buke)* values gives an official identity to the new bourgeoisie that must guarantee the survival of the "difference" in order to claim distinction, while the subversive nature of the "popular" is retained at the level of the political unconscious.[91] The Citizens themselves reappropriate the "other" at the level of fantasy, the imaginary, from which they derive their aesthetic pleasures under the sign of the "other." The incorporation of the alternative voice into mainstream ideology provides a resolution to social contradictions in the aesthetic realm.[92] However subversive the "other" may be, its encompassing into the structure of the newly shaped dominant ideology silences subversion again, making of the "bottom" the simple mimicry of the polite and civilized. The voice of the hegemonic class retains the "other" as the peripheral area of laughter and unavowable utopia, strengthening the "sameness" of hegemonic power.

Thus one can explain the ease enjoyed by Tokugawa authorities in silencing a genre that was already built with a self-silencing device. When in "Suicide by Sickle" *(Kamabara)* the gender conflict becomes a conflict of status, the peasant's verbal threat to behave like a warrior—announcing that he will open his belly with the sickle "as a true peasant would do!"—leaves unscathed the order of social hierarchies. The man's acting according to an "alien" behavioral code, one which is hardly available to members of different social classes, moves the audience to laughter. However, by confining the hidden desire of the "other" in the realm of aesthetic production, the comicality of wishful thinking does little to heal the wounded social body.

In an effort to restore his stained pride the peasant appeals to the values of those who make pride their profession: the warriors. Unable to keep up with his comedy, he abandons his theatrical schemes, realizing that the acceptance of his original status and the performance of manual labor—gathering firewood on the mountain—is substantially less painful than the sickle's blade:

> MAN: If this sickle does not cut, would it hurt? It may be better to sharpen it, so as to die without pain. . . . Woman, I am going to die. Is there anybody who can come and see me die? Anyway, I have made up my mind. Although somebody may come, it will not deter me from my decision. Well, if somebody tries to stop me, there is no reason why I should not stop. . . . Nobody is around today. After all, to die in this manner is to die like a dog. What would my death be worth? Let's recover our composure, and go to work on the mountain.[93]

The play itself searches for harmonious solutions to conflicts, erasing the subversive elements that put the action in motion. When the concept of seniority, for example, which holds a central place in the play of hierarchies, becomes the target of the audience's laughter, the farce does not end with the irreversible disgrace of the old man losing to the energy of impertinent youngsters *(wakashu)*. Although the man is ridiculed as a stubborn old soldier fighting over the preposterous right to spend the night with a page *(chigo)* at an inn of questionable repute—a narrative challenging the validity of traditional rules that would give precedence to the old man—a solution to the seniority debate is found in the convivial reunion of young and old alike, singing war songs together about famous soldiers of the past who met a glorious death in their old age.[94] The act of questioning and contesting recalls a mechanism that erases the question mark in the moment of its formulation.

The setting of the *kyōgen*'s action is another element leading to the success of this politics of containment by silencing the subversive features of reality and displacing them into the aesthetic realm. The extraordinary nature of the farces' background highlights the temporality of a fiction that lasts the duration of a festival, a pilgrimage, or a journey—a brief moment of passage leading to a less volatile reality where the "other" is finally obliterated. Even when social positions are exchanged in the staging of the most exemplary conflict between servants and lords, the fiction only endures for a day, after which the rules of reality are reinstated and the servant runs with all his might in order to escape the painful consequences of the short-lived game.[95]

The Citizens' direct relationship to the domestication of reversal and the creation of a bourgeois ideology feeding on traditional structures of power is best represented in "Criminal by Lots" *(Kuji Zainin)*, a play that stands as a monument to the communalism and independence achieved by the capital's entrepreneurial forces. The farce develops along the lines of decision making in the preparation of a float for the Gion Festival, the major annual celebration of the Citizens' economic success. Sponsored by the capital's wealthiest merchants, this event was an assertion of urban independence from aristocratic, religious, and military power, as well as a parading of the Citizens' economic empowerment.[96] The decision regarding the type of decoration for the float's long pole was, therefore, central to the symbolic self-representation that the urban voice projected to viewers converging from all over the country.

A diversity of opinion ignites the members of the organizing committee. Someone proposes that a strong wild boar be built on the pole ridden by a servant. Another suggests having a *sumō* arena built on the top of a mountain with a fight staged within it. A third organizer launches the idea of a mountain waterfall with a carp ascending it. The servant—Tarō Kaja—of one of the Citizens offers a solution that the majority accepts. The float will look like a scene of retribution: a steep mountain where a criminal suffers the infliction of bodily injuries by a demon who inhabits an idyllic green slope.

Status seems not to matter in a power structure that honors results over precedent and hierarchies. Not only does the brilliance of the servant's idea decide the float; it also determines the choice of impersonators by putting the case in the hands of Fortune and holding a lottery. The Citizens look amused upon the servant/demon beating his master/criminal, apparently unaware that a relaxation of traditional rules may cause their own downfall in a system they have helped to overturn *(geko-kujō)*. In fact, the end of the festival brings about the restoration of the pristine order: the renewed victory of the top over the bottom *(jōkokuge)* in the final silencing of subversion.[97]

The majestic float of the Gion Festival from which the Citizens raised their program of self-determination displaces in the realm of ludization and aesthetic contemplation the subversion of the "other" that surfaced as a constant threat to all forms of power—imperial, shogunal, religious, and urban. The domestication and erasure of their original agenda—a fight against intellectual obfuscation and the silent acceptance of traditional cultural patterns—in the creation of a new identity led the Citizens to uphold a politics of containment that secured them a distinctive place in the Japanese arena of power during the late Middle Ages.

Epilogue

For structures of power that lack a developed state apparatus with mutually reinforcing control among the country's political, religious, and social formations, the power of literary representation and dissemination of ideas through the medium of textual practices—poetic exchanges, announcement of poetic codes, indoctrination by entertainment, fashioning and refashioning of legendary material, staging of images of religious and secular power, appropriation of the means of literary production, and redefinition of the literary canon—carries a special weight in the formation of political distinction. We have examined how each of the fragmented body parts of Japanese medieval authority contributed literary acts and materials to the process of ideological closure in the attempt to create an ideological apparatus that would legitimize their claims to power. With the creation of a large-scale state machine with its "legal practices, i.e., the police, the courts, the prisons, the army, which intervenes directly as a supplementary repressive force,"[1] literary practices become the object of even wider attention on the part of centralized governments.

These considerations indicate the need for further clarification of the cultural politics of the Tokugawa government that we mentioned in relation to the final institutionalization of theatrical practices *(nō* and *kyōgen)* resulting in acts of silencing and erasure. Further research is needed on the neutralizing forces of Tokugawa cultural institutions and on the topic of censorship that since the seventeenth century became a central issue in the process of literary production.[2] Changes in the organization of the means of production—new printing techniques, professionalization of authors, publishers' guilds, government bureaus granting permission for publication—created further tensions between the boundlessness of the text and its appropriation for ideological closure.[3] No matter what degree of engagement an author may be interested in expressing, the appropriation of the work by the institution of aesthetic production inevitably threatens to silence the author's "unrecoverable" intentions. Since "art as an institution neutralizes the political content of the individual work,"[4] this mechanism of "natural" control eventually replaced the need in bourgeois societies for an articulated body of censors.

Among the multiple and divided responses of authors and theoreticians to Tokugawa institutions, agents of ideological closure fashioned literary works publicly defending the epistemological foundations of the shogunate.[5] On the other hand, resistance to the basic tenets of the dominant ideology occurred at both the theoretical and practical levels. Literary theorists and authors displaced their political reaction into the realm of aesthetics, which since the second half of the seventeenth century had begun to constitute itself as an independent field with the development of nativist thought *(kokugaku)*. Like its Western counterpart, the Japanese development of aesthetics was "among other things a response to the problem of political absolutism."[6] An intellectual bourgeoisie dissatisfied with the bureaucracies of the Tokugawa shogunate and alienated from the process of cultural production organized a "professional literary caste" that could confront the cultural politics of the state apparatus.

The Japanese middle-class creators of an alternative code to the *bakufu*'s pragmatic and ethical views of artistic expression combined the attitudes of both their German and French counterparts against the political establishment. Like the German bourgeoisie they "counterposed their new dreams and oppositional ideas" to the "apparatus of the absolute state" as expressed in the military structure of the Tokugawa government. At the same time, because of the reassuring presence of the court and its traditions—the lost paradise that nativists constructed as the unspotted origin of culture—the Japanese bourgeoisie followed the French restorationist politics of *politesse* and *civilité* in the promotion of "ideal" courtly values to be opposed to the "false civilization" of ineffectual military rulers.[7] In their formulation of counterideological discourses, nativists resorted to "the logic and lexicon of sexual domination"[8] either to restore an allegedly primordial "virility" to an effeminate military government or to replace it with a genuine version of courtly "female" sensibility.

Kamo no Mabuchi's (1697–1769) concern with the virility and vitality of "mythical" man led him to search in the most ancient collection of Japanese poetry, the *Man'yōshū*, for the "sincerity *(makoto)*, directness, vitality, manliness *(ooshiku shite)*, and elegance" of the heart of the ancient Japanese before his fall from grace.[9] His restorationist program aimed at reproducing the political structure of the Yamato state—"a manly state *(masurao)*"[10]—under the enlightened guidance of the same bourgeoisie that the erasing power of shogunal authority kept in a state of impotence.

A courtly aesthetics of emotionalism *(mono no aware)* was the response of Motoori Norinaga (1730–1801) to the rationality of the Neo-Confucian model of artistic production—"a serious critique of the established arrangement of authority, inasmuch as it empowered a new subject who was in a position to know."[11] Despite a disagreement on gender, Norinaga's "female" mark of distinction that enabled the bourgeoisie to appropriate the cognitive frame of the court—emotional sensibility—expounded the same message addressed by Mabuchi to "a politically impotent urban bourgeoisie (who could easily identify stylistically with an equally impotent aristocracy), that real power, the power to know things in their essence, belonged to them."[12] Whether or not we accept Norinaga's public praise of the Tokugawa shogunate as proof that his allegiance rested not "with the emperor in Kyoto as nineteenth-century restorationists argued but rather [with] the Tokugawa shogun in Edo,"[13] a middle-class bourgeoisie's erosion of the shogun's monopolistic rights over the field of cultural production cannot easily be neglected.

The nature of literary and historical disciplines has separated these theoretical responses of philosophers and philologists—the area of intellectual historians—from the direct practice of literary production by writers, poets, and playwrights, which remains the exclusive field of "people in literature." We need to overcome this gap in order to clarify the epistemological, social, economic, and political impact of literary artifacts on the process of their production. The issue of conflict between "human feelings" *(ninjō)* and "restraint," "duty," and "obligation" *(giri)* to which Chikamatsu Monzaemon (1653–1725) exposed his characters, showing that "human feelings always triumph over other considerations,"[14] was the same as the one debated by philosophers who were searching for a solution to the repressive stand of political power.[15]

The act of ludization is another characteristic of the literature of the Tokugawa period that underscores resistance to the aesthetic requirements of the shogunate. The explosion in the eighteenth century of comic verses *(kyōka),* "mad prose" *(kyōbun),* and "playful compositions" *(gesaku)* displaced the political discontent of intellectuals into the realm of aesthetics, confining a repressed desire for political action to the periphery of literary production. When an author failed to conceal reality under a thick layer of fantasy, he was imprisoned and fined—showing that the literary act, far from being a frivolous activity, "implied conscious rejection of tradition, orthodoxy, and what [it] perceived as the stifling and perhaps dangerous small-mindedness of the official vision of Japanese society."[16]

This explains the great popularity among Tokugawa readers enjoyed by fantastic stories from China, as well as the decision of a major writer such as Ueda Akinari (1734–1809) to cast his view of reality in the unharmful language of fantasy.[17] The ideal of the "man of letters" *(bunjin)* whose connections with the realm of the supernatural alienates him from the process of political production confines textual discontent to the margins of power, reinforcing the tradition of "reclusive awareness" that makes of intellectuals a resisting voice against the silencing power of political authority. But the institutionalization of counterideological discourses and the government's enticement of intellectuals to perform as part of the institution—as advisors to the ruling class, as the legal heads of private and public schools, or as the legitimate interpreters of the texts of tradition—remained potent tools in the eternal process of cultural/political legitimation.

ABBREVIATIONS

The following abbreviations are used in the notes and bibliography.

BUL   *Biblioteca Universale Laterza*. Bari: Laterza.
CS   *Chūkō Shinsho*. Tokyo: Chūō Kōronsha.
ES   *Edo Sensho*. Tokyo: Yoshikawa Kōbunkan.
GSS   *Grandi Scrittori Stranieri*. Turin: Utet.
HS   *Heibonsha Sensho*. Tokyo: Heibonsha.
IB   *Iwanami Bunko*. Tokyo: Iwanami Shoten.
IS   *Iwanami Shinsho*. Tokyo: Iwanami Shoten.
KB   *Koten Bunko*. Tokyo: Gendai Shichōsha.
KGB   *Kōdansha Gakujutsu Bunko*. Tokyo: Kōdansha.
KGS   *Kōdansha Gendai Shinsho*. Tokyo: Kōdansha.
KNKB   *Kanshō Nihon Koten Bungaku*. Tokyo: Kadokawa Shoten.
KS   *Kasama Sensho*. Tokyo: Kasama Shoin.
MBS   *Minzoku Bungei Sōsho*. Tokyo: Iwazaki Bijutsu Sha.
MS   *Miai Sensho*. Tokyo: Miai Shoten.
NKBT   *Nihon Koten Bungaku Taikei*. Tokyo: Iwanami Shoten.
NKBZ   *Nihon Koten Bungaku Zenshū*. Tokyo: Shōgakukan.
NKZ   *Nihon Koten Zensho*. Tokyo: Asahi Shinbunsha.
NST   *Nihon Shisō Taikei*. Tokyo: Iwanami Shoten.
PBE   *Piccola Biblioteca Einaudi*. Turin: Einaudi.
SNKS   *Shinchō Nihon Koten Shūsei*. Tokyo: Shinchōsha.
TB   *Tōyō Bunko*. Tokyo: Heibonsha.
THL   *Theory and History of Literature*. Minneapolis: University of Minnesota Press.
WBK   *Waka Bungaku Kōza*. Tokyo: Ōfūsha.

NOTES

Whenever I cite a translation, I list the English title first, followed by the work's original Japanese title. Citations of Japanese-language sources at the beginning of a note indicate that I am the translator.

Introduction

1. Michele Marra, *The Aesthetics of Discontent: Politics and Reclusion in Medieval Japanese Literature* (Honolulu: University of Hawaii Press, 1991).

2. See on this point Umberto Eco, *Opera Aperta* (Milan: Bompiani, 1962).

3. This is a point developed by Alberto Asor Rosa, "Letteratura, Testo e Societá," in Alberto Asor Rosa, ed., *Letteratura Italiana,* vol. 1: *Il Letterato e le Istituzioni* (Turin: Einaudi, 1982), p. 29.

4. Alberto Asor Rosa, ed., *Letteratura Italiana,* vol. 1: *Il Letterato e le Istituzioni;* vol. 2: *Produzione e Consumo;* vol. 3: *Le Forme del Testo;* vol. 4: *L'Interpretazione;* vol. 5: *Musica, Teatro, Arti Figurative;* vol. 6: *Questioni;* vol. 7 and 8: *Storia e Geografia della Letteratura Italiana;* vol. 9: *Indici* (Turin: Einaudi, 1982–1991).

5. Pierre Bourdieu, *Distinction: A Social Critique of the Judgement of Taste,* trans. Richard Nice (Cambridge: Harvard University Press, 1984; 1st French ed., 1979), p. 7. See also pp. 1–6, 80–85, and 114–125.

6. Bourdieu, *Distinction,* pp. 249–250.

7. Ibid., p. 228.

8. Ibid., p. 456.

9. Terry Eagleton, *The Ideology of the Aesthetic* (Oxford: Basil Blackwell, 1990), p. 28.

Chapter One

1. Abutsu describes her journey to Kamakura for the purpose of defending the claim of her son in a diary, *The Journal of the Sixteenth-Night Moon (Izayoi Nikki).* For an English translation see Helen Craig McCullough, ed., *Classical Japanese Prose: An Anthology* (Stanford: Stanford University Press, 1990), pp. 340–376.

2. For the English titles of the imperial collections I am indebted to Robert H. Brower and Earl Miner, *Japanese Court Poetry* (Stanford: Stanford University Press, 1961), pp. 482–486.

3. The account by Jien (1155–1225) appears in the historical work *Gukanshō*. See Delmer M. Brown and Ichirō Ishida, *The Future and The Past: A Translation and Study of the Gukanshō, an Interpretative History of Japan Written in 1219* (Berkeley and Los Angeles: University of California Press, 1979), p. 297; Okami Masao and Akamatsu Toshihide, eds., *Gukanshō*, NKBT 86 (Tokyo: Iwanami Shoten, 1967), p. 91.

4. Okami and Akamatsu, *Gukanshō*, p. 93; Brown and Ishida, *The Future and the Past*, p. 300.

5. Ibid., pp. 264–265; pp. 142–143.

6. Iwasa Masashi et al., eds., *Jinnō Shōtōki, Masu Kagami*, NKBT 87 (Tokyo: Iwanami Shoten, 1965), pp. 153–154; H. Paul Varley, trans., *A Chronicle of Gods and Sovereigns: Jinnō Shōtōki of Kitabatake Chikafusa* (New York: Columbia University Press, 1980), pp. 217–218. For a discussion of Kitabatake Chikafusa's historical program see my article "The Conquest of *Mappō*: Jien and Kitabatake Chikafusa," *Japanese Journal of Religious Studies* 12:4 (December 1985): 330–336.

7. Ogi Takashi, ed., *Shin'yō Wakashū: Honbun to Kenkyū* (Tokyo: Kasama Shoin, 1984), pp. 61–62.

8. *Shin'yōshū* 10:1417–1418; Ogi, *Shin'yō Wakashū*, p. 254.

9. Okami and Akamatsu, *Jinnō Shōtōki*, p. 61; Varley, *A Chronicle of Gods and Sovereigns*, p. 77.

10. *Shokugoshūishū* 1350. See *Shinpen Kokka Taikan* 1: *Kashū* (Tokyo: Kadokawa Shoten, 1983), p. 553.

11. *Nanchō Gohyakuban Utaawase* 581. See *Shinpen Kokka Taikan* 5: *Kashū* (Tokyo: Kadokawa Shoten, 1987), p. 743. The metaphor of the "stars" refers to the gathering of courtiers whose poetic activity demonstrates the degree of cultural power enjoyed by their ruler, the emperor/mirror.

12. *Fūga Wakashū* 19:2138–2139; Tsugita Kasumi and Iwasa Miyoko, eds., *Fūga Wakashū* (Tokyo: Miai Shoten, 1974), p. 402.

13. Mizukawa Yoshio, *Takemukigaki Zenshaku* (Tokyo: Kasama Shobō, 1972), p. 9.

14. Ibid., p. 9.

15. Ibid., p. 16.

16. Nishimiya Kazutami, ed., *Kojiki*, SNKS 27 (Tokyo: Shinchōsha, 1979), pp. 50–52; Donald L. Philippi, trans., *Kojiki* (Tokyo: University of Tokyo Press, 1968), pp. 81–86.

17. Mizukawa, *Takemukigaki Zenshaku*, p. 32. Here again the word "stars" is metaphorical for courtier/poets.

18. Varley, *A Chronicle of Gods and Sovereigns*, p. 87; Iwasa, *Jinnō Shōtōki, Masu Kagami*, p. 68.

19. *Shin'yōshū* 16:999; Ogi, *Shin'yō Wakashū*, p. 198.

20. *Shin'yōshū* 6:498; Ogi, *Shin'yō Wakashū*, p. 130. The idea behind this poem is that like the dancer's sleeves—which are turned (that is, rolled over the arm) during the dances—the speaker of the poem would like to re*turn* to the past. The Heavenly Maiden was thought to be the first to have danced the Gosechi dances which were originally performed to celebrate the autumn harvest.

21. Wada Hidematsu, *Shintei Kenmu Nenjū Gyōji Chūkai: Nitchū Gyōji Chūkai,* ed. Tokoro Isamu, *KGB* 895 (Tokyo: Kōdansha, 1989), p. 329.

22. *Shin'yōshū* 9:587; Ogi, *Shin'yō Wakashū,* p. 144.

23. For a discussion of ritual, solidarity, and consensus see David I. Kertzer, *Ritual, Politics, and Power* (New Haven and London: Yale University Press, 1988), pp. 66–69.

24. J. G. A. Pocock, *Politics, Language and Time: Essays on Political Thought and History* (New York: Atheneum, 1971), p. 45.

25. Iwasa Miyoko, *Ametsuchi no Kokoro: Fushimi In Go Uta Hyōshaku* (Tokyo: Kasama Shoin, 1979), p. 139.

26. For an English translation of several excerpts of this legal suit see Robert N. Huey, *Kyōgoku Tamekane: Poetry and Politics in Late Kamakura Japan* (Stanford: Stanford University Press, 1989), pp. 164–167.

27. Quoted in Kubota Jun, "Waka: Seijiteki Kisetsu ni Okeru Waka," *Nanbokuchō: Dōranki no Bungaku,* Special Issue of *Kokubungaku: Kaishaku to Kanshō* (March 1969): 27.

28. Konishi Jin'ichi, *Michi: Chūsei no Rinen,* KGS 420 (Tokyo: Kōdansha, 1975), pp. 76–77; Earl Miner, *An Introduction to Japanese Court Poetry* (Stanford: Stanford University Press, 1968), pp. 125–126.

29. Robert Huey correctly underplays the alleged "modernity" of the Kyōgoku school; Huey, *Kyōgoku Tamekane,* p. 76.

30. Robert N. Huey and Susan Matisoff, trans., "Lord Tamekane's Notes on Poetry: *Tamekanekyō Wakashō,*" in *Monumenta Nipponica* 40:2 (Summer 1985): 138 and 142; Hisamatsu Sen'ichi and Nishio Minoru, eds., *Karonshū, Nōgakuronshū,* NKBT 65 (Tokyo: Iwanami Shoten, 1961), pp. 158 and 161.

31. Junjirō Takakusu, *The Essentials of Buddhist Philosophy,* ed. Wing-Tsit Chan and Charles A. Moore (Honolulu: Office Appliance Co., 1956; 1st ed., 1947) p. 80.

32. In the English translation of the *Tamekanekyō Wakashō,* the word *sōō* is translated as "suitability"; Huey and Matisoff, "Lord Tamekane's Notes on Poetry," p. 134.

33. Iwasa Miyoko, "Kyōgoku Tamekane no Kafū Keisei to Yuishiki Setsu," in Ikeda Toshio, ed., *Sōritsu Nijūshūnen Kinen: Tsurumi Daigaku Bungakubu Ronshū* (Yokohama: Sanbi Insatsu Kabushikigaisha, 1983), pp. 47–67. Iwasa's theory is discussed in Fujihira Haruo, *Karon no Kenkyū* (Tokyo: Perikan Sha, 1988), p. 153.

34. Huey and Matisoff, "Lord Tamekane's Notes on Poetry," p. 142; Hisamatsu and Nishio, *Karonshū, Nōgakuronshū,* pp. 160–161.

35. For a detailed chart of the One Hundred Dharmas see Junjirō Takakusu, *The Essentials of Buddhist Philosophy,* p. 94a.

36. Hisamatsu and Nishio, *Karonshū, Nōgakuronshū,* p. 161.

37. Junjirō Takakusu, *The Essentials of Buddhist Philosophy,* p. 90.

38. See Huey and Matisoff, "Lord Tamekane's Notes on Poetry," p. 133, n. 15.

39. Adapted from Huey and Matisoff, "Lord Tamekane's Notes on Poetry," p. 138; Hisamatsu and Nishio, *Karonshū, Nōgakuronshū,* p. 158.

40. No final agreement has been reached on the question of authorship. See Inoue Muneo, *Chūsei Kadanshi no Kenkyū: Nanbokuchōki* (Tokyo: Meiji Shoin, 1987), p. 39.

41. Okumura Tsuneya, *Kokin Wakashū, SNKS* 19 (Tokyo: Shinchōsha, 1978), p. 379.

42. Sasaki Nobutsuna et al., eds., *Kōchū Nihon Bungaku Ruijū: Zuihitsu Bungaku Shū* (Tokyo: Hakubunkan, 1930), p. 302.

43. Ibid., p. 303.

44. Ibid., p. 312.

45. For Shunzei's use of Tendai philosophy see William R. LaFleur, *The Karma of Words: Buddhism and the Literary Arts in Medieval Japan* (Berkeley: University of California Press, 1983), pp. 90–93.

46. For this information I am indebted to Iwasa Miyoko, *Eifukumon'in: Sono Sei to Uta, KS* 54 (Tokyo: Kasama Shoin, 1976), pp. 40–41.

47. Tsugita Kasumi, ed., *Gyokuyō Wakashū, Iwanami Bunko* (Tokyo: Iwanami Shoten, 1989; 1st ed., 1944), p. 369. For a discussion of this exchange see Nishino Taeko, *Shirasu no Tsuki: Takemukigaki Sakusha Meishi, Eifukumon'in no Uta to Shōgai* (Tokyo: Kokubunsha, 1984), p. 147.

48. Tsugita, *Gyokuyō Wakashū,* p. 376.

49. Nishino, *Shirasu no Tsuki,* p. 198.

50. *Fūga Wakashū* 17:1934–1935; Tsugita Kasumi and Iwasa Miyoko, eds., *Fūga Wakashū* (Tokyo: Miai Shoten, 1974), p. 363.

51. Yamashita Hiroaki, ed., *Taiheiki 2, SNKS* 38 (Tokyo: Shinchōsha, 1980), pp. 171–183.

52. *Fūga Wakashū* 8:736; Tsugita and Iwasa, *Fūga Wakashū,* p. 170. An analogous example appears in *dan* 79 of the *Ise Monogatari* in which the young boy Sadakazu is addressed as a "mighty bamboo" in whose shade the members of his family wish to "find shelter summer and winter." By using floral metaphors in a congratulatory poem aimed at the restoration of power and authority, Eifuku-mon-in follows earlier examples such as the one by the Heian poet Ariwara no Narihira. See Marra, *The Aesthetics of Discontent,* pp. 42–43.

53. Mizukawa, *Takemukigaki Zenshaku,* p. 170.

54. Ibid., p. 184.

55. *Fūga Wakashū* 15:1468–1469; Tsugita and Iwasa, *Fūga Wakashū,* p. 289.

56. *Shinshūi Wakashū* 115–116; Matsushita Daisaburō and Watanabe Fumio, eds., *Kokka Taikan: Kashū* (Tokyo: Kadokawa Shoten, 1951), p. 585.

57. Quoted in Andrew Goble, "Truth, Contradiction and Harmony in Medieval Japan: Emperor Hanazono (1297–1348) and Buddhism," *Journal of the International Association of Buddhist Studies* 12:1 (1989): 48.

58. The following are the two poems in question, the first in its original form and the second in the embellished version by Tameyo:

Amaotome	Flapping are the sleeves
Sode hirugaesu	Of the goddess in the sky:
Yo na yo na no	Every night

Tsuki o kumoi ni
Omoiyaru kana

She must think from afar
Of the moon shining on the palace
above the clouds.

Amaotome
Sode furu yoha no
Kaze samumi
Tsuki o kumoi ni
Omoiyaru kana

Cold is the wind flapping
In the middle of the night
The sleeves of the goddess in the sky:
She must think from afar
Of the moon shining on the palace
above the clouds.

The episode is quoted in Iwasa, *Eifukumon'in: Sono Sei to Uta,* pp. 37–38.

59. This is discussed in Iwasa Miyoko, "Hanazono-in no Eifukumon'in Hihan," *Kokugo to Kokubungaku* (December 1966): 28–37.

60. Helen Craig McCullough, trans., *Kokin Wakashū: The First Imperial Anthology of Japanese Poetry, with Tosa Nikki and Shinsen Waka* (Stanford: Stanford University Press, 1985), p. 257; Okumura Tsuneya, ed., *Kokin Wakashū, SNKS* 19 (Tokyo: Shinchōsha, 1978), pp. 385–386.

61. Murata Masashi, ed., *Shiryō Sanshū: Hanazono Tennō Shinki* 3 (Tokyo: Heibunsha, 1986), p. 265. Hanazono's acquaintance with the preface is proved by an entry from the same diary (seventeenth day, Tenth Month, 1313), according to which Tamekane lectured the emperor on this classic, handing over to Hanazono the secret tradition of the *Kokinshū,* while reading from "a copy made by the brush of Lord Shunzei." See Murata Masashi, ed., *Shiryō Sanshū: Hanazono Tennō Shinki* 1 (Tokyo: Heibunsha, 1982), p. 107.

62. McCullough, *Kokin Wakashū,* p. 258; Okumura, *Kokin Wakashū,* p. 386.

63. Nishino Taeko, *Kōgon-in: Fūga Wakashū Shinsen to Dōran no Yo no Masshiro no Shōgai* (Tokyo: Kokubunsha, 1988), pp. 157–250.

64. Tsugita and Iwasa, *Fūga Wakashū,* pp. 53–54.

65. Ibid., p. 47.

66. McCullough, *Kokin Wakashū,* p. 4; Okumura, *Kokin Wakashū,* p. 14.

67. Tsugita and Iwasa, *Fūga Wakashū,* p. 48.

68. Ibid., p. 50.

69. Ibid., p. 52.

70. *Fūga Wakashū* 8:870. Tsugita and Iwasa, *Fūga Wakashū,* p. 189.

71. *Shingoshūi Wakashū* 1419; *Shinpen Kokka Taikan* 1: *Kashū,* p. 718.

72. Tsugita and Iwasa, *Fūga Wakashū,* p. 52.

73. *Shinsenzai Wakashū* 1987; *Shinpen Kokka Taikan* 1: *Kashū,* p. 641.

74. The idea of *kotodama*—the magical power of words to inform reality—is discussed in David Pollack, *The Fracture of Meaning: Japan's Synthesis of China from the Eighth Through the Eighteenth Centuries* (Princeton: Princeton University Press, 1986), p. 49. See also the chapter "The Kotodama of Names" in H. E. Plutschow, *Chaos and Cosmos: Ritual in Early and Medieval Japanese Literature* (Leiden: E. J. Brill, 1990), pp. 75–87.

75. *Fūga Wakashū* 19:2124; Tsugita and Iwasa, *Fūga Wakashū,* p. 400.

76. *Fūga Wakashū* 19:2187; Tsugita and Iwasa, *Fūga Wakashū,* p. 411.

77. *Fūga Wakashū* 17:1797; Tsugita and Iwasa, *Fūga Wakashū*, p. 340.

78. *Shinsenzai Wakashū* 1745; Matsushita and Watanabe, eds., *Kokka Taikan: Kashū*, p. 569.

79. The Japanese text appears in Nishino, *Kōgon-In*, p. 12.

80. For the cultural legacy of the Kyōgoku school and the appropriation of "the innovative style of *Gyokuyōshū*, 1314, and *Fūgashū*, 1346" by "the Upper and Lower Reizei houses and the disciples of Imagawa Ryōshun, 1325–1420," see Steven D. Carter, "*Waka* in the Age of *Renga*," *Monumenta Nipponica* 36:4 (Winter 1981): 425–426.

81. Robert Edwards, "Exile, Self, and Society," in María-Inés Lagos-Pope, ed., *Exile in Literature* (Lewisburg: Bucknell University Press, 1988), p. 21.

82. Although the reading for this prince's name is often given as Munenaga, I conform to the reading by the historian Mori Shigeaki. See his *Mikotachi no Nanbokuchō: Go-Daigo Tennō no Bunshin*, CS 886 (Tokyo: Chūō Kōronsha, 1988), p. 9.

83. Quoted in Inoue Muneo, "Muneyoshi Shinnō," in Waka Bungakkai, ed., *Chūsei, Kinsei no Kajin*, WBK 7 (Tokyo: Ōfūsha, 1970), p. 241.

84. Yamashita Hiroaki, ed., *Taiheiki 1*, SNKS 15 (Tokyo: Shinchōsha, 1977), p. 25; Helen Craig McCullough, trans., *The Taiheiki: A Chronicle of Medieval Japan* (New York: Columbia University Press, 1959), p. 10.

85. *Shin'yō Wakashū* 1279–1280; Ogi Takashi, *Shin'yō Wakashū: Honbun to Kenkyū* (Tokyo: Kasama Shoin, 1984), p. 233.

86. Quoted in Mori Shigeaki, *Mikotachi no Nanbokuchō: Go-Daigo Tennō no Bunshin*, p. 31.

87. *Shin'yō Wakashū* 7:511; Ogi, *Shin'yō Wakashū*, p. 132.

88. *Rikashū* 190; Matsuda Takeo, ed., *Rikashū*, IB (Tokyo: Iwanami Shoten, 1941), p. 46. For Muneyoshi's biographical data I am indebted to Mori Shigeaki, *Mikotachi no Nanbokuchō*; to Kuramoto Hatsuo, *Muneyoshi Ruten: Shin'yō Wakashū Senja no Shōgai* (Tokyo: Dōgyūsha, 1989); and to Kasahara Kiichirō, *Yoshino Chō to Muneyoshi Shinnō no Seikatsu* (Tokyo: Tōyōkan, 1963).

89. Quoted in Kuramoto, *Muneyoshi Ruten*, p. 105.

90. Edwards, "Exile, Self, and Society," pp. 15–16.

91. Kuramoto, *Muneyoshi Ruten*, p. 78.

92. *Rikashū* 69; Matsuda, *Rikashū*, p. 25.

93. *Rikashū* 720; Matsuda, *Rikashū*, p. 124.

94. *Rikashū* 450; Matsuda, *Rikashū*, p. 85.

95. *Rikashū* 745; Matsuda, *Rikashū*, p. 132.

96. *Rikashū* 717; Matsuda, *Rikashū*, p. 124.

97. *Shin'yō Wakashū* 18:1226; Ogi, *Shin'yō Wakashū*, p. 227.

98. *Rikashū* 897; Matsuda, *Rikashū*, p. 154.

99. *Shin'yō Wakashū* 18:1227; Ogi, *Shin'yō Wakashū*, p. 227.

100. *Shin'yō Wakashū* 17:971; Ogi, *Shin'yō Wakashū*, p. 194.

101. Watanabe Minoru, ed., *Ise Monogatari*, SNKS 2 (Tokyo: Shinchōsha, 1976), p. 23; Helen Craig McCullough, *Tales of Ise: Lyrical Episodes from Tenth-Century Japan* (Stanford: Stanford University Press, 1968), p. 76.

102. *Rikashū* 838; Matsuda, *Rikashū,* p. 145. The poem also appears in *Shin-'yō Wakashū* 19:1319; Ogi, *Shin'yō Wakashū,* p. 239.

103. *Rikashū* 841; Matsuda, *Rikashū,* p. 146.

104. *Rikashū* 676; Matsuda, *Rikashū,* p. 116.

105. *Rikashū* 773; Matsuda, *Rikashū,* p. 138. This exchange also appears in *Shin'yō Wakashū* 7:517–518; Ogi, *Shin'yō Wakashū,* p. 133.

106. *Rikashū* 899; Matsuda, *Rikashū,* p. 154.

107. *Shin'yō Wakashū* 18:1298; Ogi, *Shin'yō Wakashū,* p. 236.

108. *Shin'yō Wakashū* 19:1331–1333; Ogi, *Shin'yō Wakashū,* pp. 241–242.

109. *Shin'yō Wakashū* 6:475; Ogi, *Shin'yō Wakashū,* p. 127.

110. Mori Shigeaki argues that Muneyoshi died in Shinano province around 1385; see Mori, *Mikotachi no Nanbokuchō,* p. 158.

111. *Shin'yō Wakashū* 5:329–330; Ogi, *Shin'yō Wakashū,* p. 223.

Chapter Two

1. J. Thomas Rimer and Yamazaki Masakazu, trans., *On the Art of the Nō Drama: The Major Treatises of Zeami* (Princeton: Princeton University Press, 1984), p. 32; Tanaka Yutaka, ed., *Zeami Geijutsu Ronshū,* SNKS 4 (Tokyo: Shinchōsha, 1976), p. 55.

2. Tamai Kōsuke, *Ben no Naishi Nikki Shinchū* (Tokyo: Taishūkan Shoten, 1966), p. 229.

3. Niunoya Tetsuichi, *Kebiishi: Chūsei no Kegare to Kenryoku,* HS 102 (Tokyo: Heibonsha, 1986), pp. 177–178.

4. Ibid., pp. 200–203.

5. Quoted in Hattori Yukio, "Ushirodo no Kami: Geinō Kami Shinkō ni Kan Suru Ikkōsatsu," in Nihon Bungaku Kenkyū Shiryō Kankō Kai, ed., *Yōkyoku, Kyōgen* (Tokyo: Yūseidō, 1981), p. 21. (This article was originally published in the July 1973 issue of the journal *Bungaku.*)

6. Ibid., p. 23.

7. Yamaji Kōzō, "Okina Sarugaku Saikō: Jō," *Geinō* (February 1985): 17–18.

8. Amano Fumio, "Okina Sarugaku no Seiritsu: Jōgyōdō Shūshōe to no Kanren," *Bungaku* 51:7 (1983): 168–169.

9. Yamaji, "Okina Sarugaku Saikō: Jō," pp. 9–10.

10. Matsuoka Shinpei, "Shōdōgeki no Jidai: Nō no Seiritsu ni Tsuite Ikkōsatsu," *Kokugo to Kokubungaku: Chūsei Bungakushi e no Kairo* (April 1988): 90.

11. Yamaji Kōzō, "Shūshōe no Hen'yō to Chihō Denpa," in Moriya Takeshi, ed., *Geinō to Chinkon: Kanraku to Kyūzai no Dainamizumu* (Tokyo: Shunjūsha, 1988), pp. 61–63.

12. Niunoya, *Kebiishi,* pp. 208–209.

13. Quoted in Yamaji, "Okina Sarugaku Saikō: Jō," p. 12.

14. Yamaji Kōzō, "Okina Sarugaku Saikō: Ge," *Geinō* (March 1985): 16–18.

15. Emiko Ohnuki-Tierney, *The Monkey as Mirror: Symbolic Transformations in Japanese History and Ritual* (Princeton: Princeton University Press, 1987), p. 84.

16. Ibid., p. 85.

17. Niunoya, *Kebiishi,* p. 185, where the expression "children of god" is applied to the performers of *sarugaku.*

18. Quoted in Kyōto Buraku Shi Kenkyūjo, ed., *Chūsei no Minshū to Geinō* (Kyoto: Aunsha, 1986), p. 66.

19. The expression is by Edmund Leach as quoted in Peter Stallybrass and Allon White, *The Politics and Poetics of Transgression* (London: Methuen, 1986), p. 24.

20. Quoted in Yokoi Kiyoshi, *Chūsei Minshū no Seikatsu to Bunka* (Tokyo: Tōkyō Daigaku Shuppankai, 1975), pp. 289–290, n. 2.

21. *Konjaku Monogatari* 29:17; Mabuchi Kazuo et al., eds., *Konjaku Monogatari Shū* 4, *NKBZ* 24 (Tokyo: Shōgakukan, 1976), pp. 377–383.

22. Quoted in Yokoi, *Chūsei Minshū no Seikatsu to Bunka,* p. 271.

23. Quoted in Kōno Katsuyuki, *Shōgaisha no Chūsei* (Kyoto: Bunrikaku, 1987), p. 11.

24. Kyōto Buraku Shi Kenkyūjo, *Chūsei no Minshū to Geinō,* p. 71.

25. The picture appears in Yokoi, *Chūsei Minshū no Seikatsu to Bunka,* pp. 233–234.

26. Ohnuki-Tierney, *The Monkey as Mirror,* pp. 90–91.

27. The text is quoted in Yokoi, *Chūsei Minshū no Seikatsu to Bunka,* pp. 231–232.

28. Ibid., p. 234.

29. Ibid., p. 261, n. 16.

30. This quotation from J. D. Duncan, *Symbols and Social Theory* (New York: Oxford University Press, 1969), pp. 7–8, is discussed in Abner Cohen, *Two-Dimensional Man: An Essay on the Anthropology of Power and Symbolism in Complex Society* (Berkeley and Los Angeles: University of California Press, 1974), p. 37.

31. This story is discussed in Imatani Akira, *Tenbun Hokke no Ran: Busō Suru Machishū* (Tokyo: Heibonsha, 1989), pp. 14–18.

32. Leon Hurvitz, trans., *Scripture of the Lotus Blossom of the Fine Dharma (The Lotus Sūtra)* (New York: Columbia University Press, 1976), pp. 336–337; Sakamoto Yukio and Iwamoto Yutaka, eds., *Hokkekyō: Ge* (Tokyo: Iwanami Shoten, 1967), p. 334.

33. Moriya Takeshi, "Sōron: Bukkyō to Jōdo to Geinō," in Moriya Takeshi, ed., *Geinō to Chinkon,* pp. 15–18; Tokuda Kazuo, "Kyoroku-bon 'Taimadera Engi' Emaki to 'Chūjōhime no Honji,'" in Tokuda Kazuo, *Otogizōshi: Kenkyū* (Tokyo: Miai Shoten, 1988), pp. 385–391.

34. Moriya Takeshi, *Kyō no Geinō: Ōchō kara Ishin made,* CS 555 (Tokyo: Chūō Kōronsha, 1979), pp. 15–16; Tokuda, *Otogizōshi,* pp. 389–390.

35. Tokuda, *Otogizōshi,* p. 390. Even the professionals of the unknown, such as holy men, resorted to this ritual at the end of their life to ensure that no defilement hindered their entrance into the Pure Land. Although our main source is a collection of legendary tales, the *Shasekishū,* there is no reason to dismiss the event as purely fictional. Longing for rebirth in the Pure Land, the holy man of Fukō, Tango province, begged the governor to stage an Amida Welcome Service

on his behalf at the time of his death. The governor agreed, providing the holy man with a chance to reach Amida's paradise: "Costumes for the Buddha and Bodhisattvas and other gear were prepared according to the holy man's directions and sent to him. For many years the priest performed the ceremony of the coming of the holy assemblage, a ritual for dying. As might be expected, the ceremony of welcoming was held during his own final moments, and he came to an auspicious end." See *Shasekishū* 10:9; Robert E. Morrell, *Sand and Pebbles (Shasekishū): The Tales of Mujū Ichien, a Voice for Pluralism in Kamakura Buddhism* (Albany: State University of New York Press, 1985), p. 254; Watanabe Tsunaya, ed., *Shasekishū*, NKBT 85 (Tokyo: Iwanami Shoten, 1966), p. 426.

36. Hōsan-kai of Shitennōji Temple, ed., *Prince Shōtoku and Shitennō-ji Temple: The Seventeen-Article Constitution* (Osaka: Benridō, 1970), pp. 9–10.

37. *Ryōjin Hishō* 2:176; Enoki Katsurō, ed., *Ryōjin Hishō*, SNKS 31 (Tokyo: Shinchōsha, 1979), p. 83.

38. The source is the *Taiki*, the diary of Fujiwara no Yorinaga, as quoted in Moriya, "Sōron: Bukkyō to Jōdo to Geinō," pp. 28–29.

39. Ryukoku University Translation Center, ed., *The Sūtra of Contemplation on the Buddha of Immeasurable Life as Expounded by Śākyamuni Buddha* (Kyoto: Ryukoku University, 1984), p. 27.

40. Koyama Hiroshi et al., eds., *Yōkyoku Shū* 2, NKBZ 34 (Tokyo: Shōgakukan, 1975), pp. 100–101. Another version of this story appears in the sermon ballad *(sekkyō-bushi) Shintokumaru*, first published in 1648, in which the beggar is abandoned at Tennōji's Southern Gate after being cursed to blindness by his stepmother. See Muroki Yatarō, ed., *Sekkyō Shū*, SNKS 8 (Tokyo: Shinchōsha, 1977), pp. 155–207.

41. Niunoya, *Kebiishi*, pp. 138–143.

42. Quoted in Yokoi, *Chūsei Minshū no Seikatsu to Bunka*, p. 255.

43. Niunoya, *Kebiishi*, pp. 183–186.

44. Quoted in Niunoya, *Kebiishi*, pp. 184–185.

45. Quoted in Moriya, *Kyō no Geinō*, p. 76. This passage is discussed in Hyōdō Hiromi, "Monogatari: Shokue to Jōka no Kairo," in Hyōdō Hiromi, Akasaka Norio, and Yamamoto Hiroko, eds., *Monogatari, Sabetsu, Tennōsei*, Firudowāku Shirīzu III (Tokyo: Satsukisha, 1985), p. 178.

46. Kawaguchi Hisao, ed., *Shin Sarugaku Ki*, TB 424 (Tokyo: Heibonsha, 1983), p. 3.

47. Hayashiya Tatsusaburō, *Chūsei Geinōshi no Kenkyū: Kodai kara no Keishō to Sōzō* (Tokyo: Iwanami Shoten, 1960), pp. 320–321.

48. *Man'yōshū* 16:3885; Kojima Noriyuki et al., eds., *Man'yōshū* 4, NKBZ 5 (Tokyo: Shōgakukan, 1975), p. 152.

49. *Man'yōshū* 16:3886; Kojima, *Man'yōshū* 4, pp. 154–155.

50. Quoted in Niunoya, *Kebiishi*, pp. 132–138. See also Moriya, *Kyō no Geinō*, p. 76, who quotes the *Shimo Daigo Nenjū Gyōji* as saying that "priests" of the area annexed *(sanjo hōshi)* to the Karinji—a subtemple of Daigoji—gave eulogizing speeches for the *shūshōe* of the Nagaonomiya Shrine on the sixth day of the First Month.

51. Moriya, *Kyō no Geinō*, p. 77.

52. Hyōdō, "Monogatari," p. 183.

53. Moriya, *Kyō no Geinō,* p. 78.

54. Ibid., p. 80.

55. Quoted in Moriya, *Kyō no Geinō,* p. 81.

56. Ibid., pp. 84–86.

57. The topic of *kanjin hijiri* has been discussed in several articles by Janet R. Goodwin. See her "Alms for Kasagi Temple" in *Journal of Asian Studies* 46:4 (November 1987): 827–841; "Shooing the Dead to Paradise" in *Japanese Journal of Religious Studies* 16:1 (March 1989): 63–80; "Building Bridges and Saving Souls: The Fruits of Evangelism in Medieval Japan" in *Monumenta Nipponica* 44:2 (Summer 1989): 137–149.

58. Matsuoka, "Shōdōgeki no Jidai," pp. 83–84.

59. Quoted in Matsuoka, "Shōdōgeki no Jidai," p. 83.

60. Ibid., p. 85.

61. *Nihon Ryōiki* 3:16. See Kyoko Motomochi Nakamura, trans., *Miraculous Stories from the Japanese Buddhist Tradition: The Nihon Ryōiki of the Monk Kyōkai* (Cambridge: Harvard University Press, 1973), p. 243; Koizumi Osamu, ed., *Nihon Ryōiki, SNKS* 67 (Tokyo: Shinchōsha, 1984), pp. 246–247.

62. For further details see Marra, *The Aesthetics of Discontent,* pp. 51–52.

63. *Konjaku Monogatari* 27:2; Sakakura Atsuyoshi et al., eds., *Konjaku Monogatari Shū: Honchō Sezoku Bu 3, SNKS* 43 (Tokyo: Shinchōsha, 1981), pp. 20–21. A similar version appears in *Uji Shūi Monogatari* 151. See Ōshima Tatehiko, ed., *Uji Shūi Monogatari, SNKS* 71 (Tokyo: Shinchōsha, 1985), pp. 420–421; D. E. Mills, trans., *A Collection of Tales from Uji: A Study and Translation of Uji Shūi Monogatari* (Cambridge: Cambridge University Press, 1970), pp. 368–369.

64. For the translation of the title I am indebted to Robert Borgen, *Sugawara no Michizane and the Early Court* (Cambridge: Council on East Asian Studies, Harvard University, 1986), p. 183.

65. Kojima Noriyuki, ed., *Kaifūsō, Bunka Shūreishū, Honchō Monzui, NKBT* 69 (Tokyo: Iwanami Shoten, 1964), pp. 330–333. According to the *Fusō Ryakki,* the oath was written by Miyoshi Fumie; see Sakakura, *Konjaku Monogatari Shū 3,* pp. 297–298. The reason for the appearance of Tōru's angry spirit was mainly political. When, taking as a pretext the emperor's alleged madness, Fujiwara no Mototsune forced Emperor Yōzei (r. 876–884) to step down from the throne, Tōru—a son of Emperor Saga (r. 809–823)—was prevented by Mototsune from ascending to the throne on the grounds that he had already become a commoner. The new Emperor Kōkō (r. 884–887) was eventually followed by a commoner, Minamoto no Sadami—the Emperor Uda to whom Tōru's spirit appears. Tōru's political frustrations are mentioned in Ishikawa Tōru, ed., *Ōkagami, SNKS* 82 (Tokyo: Shinchōsha, 1989), pp. 62–63; Helen Craig McCullough, trans., *Ōkagami, The Great Mirror: Fujiwara Michinaga (966–1027) and His Times* (Princeton: Princeton University Press, 1980), pp. 93–94.

66. *Jikkinshō* 5:2; Nagatsumi Yasuaki, ed., *Jikkinshō, IB* (Tokyo: Iwanami Shoten, 1942), p. 127. The *Zoku Kojidan* version is quoted in Tokuda Kazuo,

"Kanjin Hijiri to Shaji Engi: Muromachiki o Chūshin to Shite," in Tokuda, *Otogizōshi,* p. 151.

67. The text appears in Tokuda, "Kanjin Hijiri to Shaji Engi," pp. 150–151. The English translation is by Hiroshi Kitagawa and Bruce T. Tsuchida, trans., *The Tale of the Heike: Heike Monogatari* (Tokyo: University of Tokyo Press, 1975), p. 5.

68. Matsuoka, "Shōdōgeki no Jidai," p. 88.

69. The picture appears in Tokuda, "Kanjin Hijiri to Shaji Engi," p. 160.

70. Matsuoka, "Shōdōgeki no Jidai," p. 91.

71. Although the play is now lost and we have only a remaking by his son Zeami *(Tōru),* Kan'ami's work is mentioned in the *Sarugaku Dangi* (An Account of Zeami's Reflections on Art): "Then, when it came to the fierce demon roles, such as in plays such as *Tōru no Otodo,* when [Kan'ami] became a demon and persecuted the Minister, he performed in a serene and magnanimous manner, so that his movement of Delicacy within Strength was moving yet revealed an interior gentleness." See J. Thomas Rimer and Yamazaki Masakazu, trans., *On the Art of the Nō Drama: The Major Treatises of Zeami* (Princeton: Princeton University Press, 1984), pp. 179–180; Tanaka Yutaka, ed., *Zeami Geijutsu Ronshū, SNKS* 4 (Tokyo: Shinchōsha, 1976), p. 182.

In Zeami's *Tōru,* an old monk travels from the eastern provinces to the capital, finally reaching the place where Minamoto no Tōru's villa once stood. An old man informs the monk that this is the place where the minister had his garden built on the model of Shiogama Bay in Michinoku. He says that after his death, Tōru's garden and pond were left in such disrepair that eventually everything disappeared. A man from Kiyomizu Temple appears to the monk, telling him of the appearance of Tōru's ghost in the area. The monk witnesses the strange occurrence. Tōru's ghost vanishes after a brief appearance, leaving the monk alone to observe the minister "entering the capital of the moon." In Zeami's version all references to Tōru's destiny in hell are lost. See Itō Masayoshi, ed., *Yōkyoku Shū: Chū, SNKS* 73 (Tokyo: Shinchōsha, 1986), pp. 397–409.

72. Matsuoka, "Shōdōgeki no Jidai," p. 91.

73. Yamaguchi Masao, "Tennōsei no Shinsō Kōzō," *Chūō Kōron* (November 1976): 90–107.

74. Nakada Norio, Wada Toshimasa, and Kitahara Yasuo, eds., *Kogo Dai Jiten* (Tokyo: Shōgakukan, 1983), p. 611.

75. This widespread joke appears in the "Illustrated Treatise on the Oneness of Demons and Buddhas" *(Mabutsu Ichinyo Ekotoba),* and it is quoted in Iwamoto Yutaka, *Nihon Bukkyōgo Jiten* (Tokyo: Heibonsha, 1988), p. 390.

76. Quoted in Geinōshi Kenkyūkai, ed., *Nihon Geinōshi 2: Kodai, Chūsei* (Tokyo: Hōsei Daigaku Shuppankyoku, 1982), p. 239.

77. For further details see Etsuko Terasaki, " 'Wild Words and Specious Phrases': *Kyōgen Kigo* in the Nō Play *Jinen Koji,*" *Harvard Journal of Asiatic Studies* 49:2 (December 1989): 519–552.

78. Itō, *Yōkyoku Shū: Chū,* p. 131, n. 7.

79. Ibid., p. 131.

80. Ibid., p. 134, n. 6.

81. Ibid., p. 134.

82. Ludization—the idea of a Buddhist cosmology, the Buddhist Six Realms or *rokudō,* conceived "as an arena of play"—is one of the four modes identified by William R. LaFleur as dialectical "escapes from suffering in the six courses," together with infiltration, transcendence, and copenetration. See William R. La-Fleur, *The Karma of Words: Buddhism and the Literary Arts in Medieval Japan* (Berkeley: University of California Press, 1983), pp. 49–59.

83. *Kangin Shū* 131; Kitagawa Tadahiko, ed., *Kangin Shū, Sōan Kouta Shū, SNKS* 53 (Tokyo: Shinchōsha, 1982), p. 76.

84. Itō, *Yōkyoku Shū: Chū,* p. 135.

85. Ibid., pp. 136–137. The passage says:

> WAKI: Well, priest, get out of my boat!
> SHITE: Give me the girl! If I return this garment to you, you won't suffer any loss.
> WAKI: I'd love to return this girl to you, but there is a problem.
> SHITE: What kind of problem?
> WAKI: In my business there is a firm rule *(taihō):* no returns on purchased persons. That's why I can't give you the girl back.
> SHITE: I understand. In my business too we follow a firm rule. If, after meeting with a person who has been sold we leave him without offering our help, we cannot return to our cell. Since I do not want to break either your rule or mine, you can take me to the northern provinces. Otherwise I will not leave your boat.

86. Ibid., p. 138.

87. Jinen Koji narrates a Chinese legend on the origin of boats in China. According to the legend, the idea came to a retainer of King Ko who noticed that the life of a spider was spared by a willow leaf floating on the water. As a result the king conquered the enemy and pacified the country.

88. Ibid., p. 142.

89. Mary Douglas, *Purity and Danger: An Analysis of the Concepts of Pollution and Taboo* (London: Ark Paperbacks, 1984; 1st ed., 1966), p. 67.

90. Quoted in Douglas, *Purity and Danger,* p. 67.

91. For an English translation of *Ukai* see Arthur Waley, *The Nō Plays of Japan* (Tokyo: Tuttle, 1976; 1st ed., 1921), pp. 127–133. A translation of *Utō* appears in Donald Keene, ed., *Anthology of Japanese Literature: From the Earliest Era to the Mid-Nineteenth Century* (New York: Grove Press, 1955), pp. 271–285.

92. *Ryōjin Hishō* 2: 355; Enoki, *Ryōjin Hishō,* pp. 149–150.

93. The attribution of *Ukai* to Enami is made by Zeami's son Motoyoshi in his "Account of Zeami's Reflections on Art" (*Sarugaku Dangi,* 1430). Since the text is said to have had "bad sections which were badly written," Zeami is credited with the rewriting of the text, so that now the play "can be considered as his." See Rimer and Yamazaki, *On The Art of the Nō Drama,* p. 222; Tanaka, *Zeami Geijutsu Ronshū,* p. 227.

94. Itō Masayoshi, ed., *Yōkyoku Shū: Jō, SNKS* 57 (Tokyo: Shinchōsha, 1983), pp. 115–124.

95. Ibid., p. 155.

96. Ibid., p. 151.

97. *Dainihonkoku Hokkekyō Kenki, ge:* 124. See Yoshiko Kurata Dykstra, trans., *Miraculous Tales of the Lotus Sutra from Ancient Japan: The Dainihonkoku Hokekyōkenki of Priest Chingen* (Osaka: Kansai University of Foreign Studies, 1983), pp. 139–140; Inoue Mitsusada and Ōsone Shōsuke, eds., *Ōjōden, Hokke Kenki, NST* 7 (Tokyo: Iwanami Shoten, 1974), p. 209.

98. Dykstra, *Miraculous Tales,* pp. 139–141; Inoue and Ōsone, *Ōjōden, Hokke Kenki,* pp. 208–210. This story is discussed in Hayashi Masahiko, "Etoki to Setsuwa Bungaku: Tateyama Jigoku to Nyonin," in Hayashi Masahiko, *Zōho Nihon no Etoki: Shiryō to Kenkyū* (Tokyo: Miai Shoten, 1984), pp. 182–183. The story also appears in *Konjaku Monogatari* 14:7.

99. *Konjaku Monogatari* 14:8; Mabuchi Kazuo et al., eds., *Konjaku Monogatari Shū:* 1, *NKBZ* 21 (Tokyo: Shōgakukan, 1971), pp. 505–510.

100. The activity of fund-raisers at these temples is mentioned in the diary of Sanjōnishi Sanetaka—*Sanetakakō Ki*—on the twentieth day of the Third Month 1483. The text is quoted in Hayashi, "Etoki to Setsuwa Bungaku," p. 196.

101. Hayashi Masahiko, "Setsuwa Ga 'Tateyama Mandara' no Sekai," in Hayashi, *Zōho Nihon no Etoki,* pp. 210–221.

102. Hyōdō, Akasaka, and Yamamoto, *Monogatari, Sabetsu, Tennōsei,* pp. 58–68.

103. Ibid., pp. 92–106.

104. Itō, *Yōkyoku Shū: Jō,* p. 147.

105. The role played by symbols in the process of socialization is discussed in Cohen, *Two-Dimensional Man,* pp. 41–42.

106. See, for example, Diana Y. Paul, *Women in Buddhism: Images of the Feminine in the Mahāyāna Tradition* (Berkeley, Los Angeles, London: University of California Press, 1985), pp. 77–243.

107. Ibid., p. 31.

108. Hurvitz, *Scripture of the Lotus Blossom of the Fine Dharma,* p. 336; Sakamoto and Iwamoto, *Hokkekyō: Ge,* p. 332.

109. Quoted in Takigawa Masajirō, *Eguchi, Kanzaki: Yūgyō Nyofu, Yūjo, Kugutsume, Zōhohan,* Nihon Rekishi Shinsho (Tokyo: Shibundō, 1965), p. 1.

110. Takigawa Masajirō, *Yūjo no Rekishi,* Nihon Rekishi Shinsho (Tokyo: Shibundō, 1965), p. 57.

111. For a discussion of the Buddhist metaphorical reading of the literary act *(kyōgen kigo)* see Herbert Eugen Plutschow, "Is Poetry a Sin? *Honjisuijaku* and Buddhism Versus Poetry," *Oriens Extremus* 25:2 (1978): 206–218; LaFleur, *The Karma of Words,* pp. 1–25; Marra, *The Aesthetics of Discontent,* pp. 54–59.

112. Enoki, *Ryōjin Hishō,* p. 267.

113. *Jikkinshō* 10:51; Nagatsumi, *Jikkinshō,* p. 293. The poem also appears in *Ryōjin Hishō* 2:235; Enoki, *Ryōjin Hishō,* p. 104.

114. The poem from the *Ryōjin Hishō* says:

Kiku ni okashiki kyō	Sutra chanters whose voices please
yomi wa	the ear:
Tōkaku Takasago no	In Takasago there is Nyōsenbō,
Nyōsenbō	
Eguchi no fuchi ni	In Eguchi, Tayonake no Kimi,
Tayonake no Kimi	
Yodo ni wa Ōgimi Jirōgimi	And how can we forget
	Ōgimi and Jirōgimi from Yodo?

See *Ryōjin Hishō* 2:443; Enoki, *Ryōjin Hishō,* p.183. Since the meaning of *"tōkaku"* is unclear I have omitted it in my translation.

115. *Ryōjin Hishō* 2:422; Enoki, *Ryōjin Hishō,* p. 175.

116. Carmen Blacker, *The Catalpa Bow: A Study of Shamanistic Practices in Japan* (London: Allen & Unwin, 1975), p. 29.

117. *Kojidan* 221; Kobayashi Yasuharu, ed., *Kojidan: Jō,* KB 60 (Tokyo: Gendai Shichōsha, 1981), p. 239. A *tanka* version of this poem by Senkei Hōshi appears in the *Ryōjin Hishō.* This slightly different version reads:

Gokuraku wa	Although I hear
Harukeki hodo to	That the Pure Land
Kikishikado	Is very far away,
Tsutomete itaru	Still it is a place
Tokoro narikeri	That can be reached swiftly.

See *Ryōjin Hishō* 2:564; Enoki, *Ryōjin Hishō,* p. 221.

118. Mircea Eliade, *Shamanism: Archaic Techniques of Ecstasy* (Princeton: Princeton University Press, 1964; 1st French ed., 1951), p. 73; see also pp. 79–81.

119. The picture appears in Abe Yasurō, "Seizoku no Tawamure to Shite no Geinō: Yūjo, Shirabyōshi, Kusemai no Monogatari o Megurite," in Moriya Takeshi, ed., *Geinō to Chinkon,* p. 177.

120. *Ryōjin Hishō* 2:168; Enoki, *Ryōjin Hishō,* p. 80.

121. Abe, "Seizoku no Tawamure to Shite no Geinō," p. 178.

122. *Kojidan* 3:291; Kobayashi, *Kojidan: Jō,* pp. 303–304. *Senjūshō* 6:10; Nishio Kōichi, ed., *Senjūshō,* IB (Tokyo: Iwanami Shoten, 1970), pp. 163–164.

123. William R. LaFleur translates the exchange as follows:

Yo no naka o	It is hard, perhaps,
Itou made koso	To hate and part with the world;
Katakarame	But you are stingy
Kari no yadori o	Even with the night I ask of you,
Oshimu kimi kana	A place in your soon-left inn.

The response by a "woman of pleasure":

Ie o izuru	It's because I heard
Hito to shi kikeba	You're no longer bound to life
Kari no yado ni	As a householder

Kokoro tomu na to   That I'm loath to let you get attached
Omou bakari zo   To this inn of brief, bought, stays.

See William R. LaFleur, *Mirror for the Moon: A Selection of Poems by Saigyo (1118–1190)* (New York: New Directions, 1978), p. 37; *Sankashū* 752–753; Gotō Shigeo, ed., *Sankashū, SNKS* 49 (Tokyo: Shinchōsha, 1982), pp. 206–207. This exchange also appears in Kuwabara Hiroshi, trans., *Saigyō Monogatari, KGB* 497 (Tokyo: Kōdansha, 1981), pp. 198–201, and in the *Shin Kokin Wakashū* 978–979. The *Shin Kokinshū*'s preface *(kotobagaki)* to the first poem says that Saigyō was on his way to Tennōji when he was caught by rain and, therefore, asked for a night's lodging. The woman's reply is said to have been composed by the courtesan Tae (Tae *yūjo*). See Kubota Jun, ed., *Shin Kokin Wakashū: Jō, SNKS* 24 (Tokyo: Shinchōsha, 1978), pp. 334–335.

124. *Senjūshō* 9:8; Nishio, *Senjūshō*, pp. 294–298. Another story from the same collection focuses on the Eguchi courtesan. In the Ninth Month 1178, a monk visits the western provinces with an acolyte. At Eguchi Hashimoto they notice the house of a well-known courtesan whose religious songs speak of rebirth in Amida's paradise. The nun living in the house invites the two monks to spend the night with her until the storm is over. In a session of linked poetry *(renga)* the woman shows her uncommon ability to cap verses. The monks can only conclude that she "must have been the beloved nun of Eguchi"—an explicit reference to Saigyō's spiritual guide. See *Senjūshō* 5:11; Nishio, *Senjūshō*, pp. 150–152.

125. Nihon Gakujutsu Shinkōkai, ed., *The Noh Drama: Ten Plays from the Japanese* (Tokyo: Tuttle, 1973), p. 123; Itō, *Yōkyoku Shū: Jō*, p. 201.

126. Nihon Gakujutsu Shinkōkai, *The Noh Drama*, p. 124; Itō, *Yōkyoku Shū*, p. 201.

127. D. E. Mills, "Murasaki Shikibu—Saint or Sinner?" in *Bulletin of the Japan Society of London* (1979): 4–12; Marra, *The Aesthetics of Discontent*, p. 57; Linda M. Sylte, "Zenchiku's 'A Genji Requiem' and Mishima's Modern Adaptation" (M.A. thesis, Washington University, 1980).

128. *Izumi Shikibu Shū;* Matsushita Daisaburō, ed., *Zoku Kokka Taikan* (Tokyo: Kadokawa Shoten, 1958), p. 637, n. 40,461. For a discussion of this poem see Saeki Junko, *Yūjo no Bunka Shi: Hare no Onnatachi, CS* 853 (Tokyo: Chūō Kōronsha, 1987), p. 63. The Ōsaka Barrier is a narrow pass through a range of mountains separating Kyoto from the area of Lake Biwa. Because of its literal meaning, "Meeting Slope," the pass became a *locus classicus* in the Japanese literary tradition. See Susan Matisoff, *The Legend of Semimaru, Blind Musician of Japan* (New York: Columbia University Press, 1978), pp. 6–14.

129. Ōshima Tatehiko, ed., *Otogizōshi Shū, NKBZ* 36 (Tokyo: Shōgakukan, 1974), pp. 385–393.

130. During a sutra-copying ceremony, the holy man hesitates to accept Miyaki's offerings because of the woman's sinful profession. When Miyaki enlightens Shōkū to the truth of the universal participation in Buddha nature, the holy man accepts her donation. Awakened to the evil of discrimination, Shōkū responds with a poem:

Tsu no kuni no	What kind of thing
Naniwa no koto ka	Is not within the Law,
Nori naranu	Even in Naniwa in Tsu?
Asobitawabure	I hear that the Law applies
Made to koso kike	Even to gambling and sex.

See *Go Shūi Shū* 20:1199; adapted from Robert E. Morrell, "The Buddhist Poetry in the *Goshūishū*," *Monumenta Nipponica* 28:1 (Spring 1973): 100; Fujimoto Kazue, ed., *Go Shūi Waka Shū* 4, *KGB* 587 (Tokyo: Kōdansha, 1983), pp. 409–411.

131. The exchange takes place in the form of poetry. To Kūya's poem,

Gokuraku wa	The upright person
Naoki hito koso	Will certainly reach
Mairu nare	Paradise:
Magareru koto o	Stop forever
Nagaku todome yo	Your crooked behavior!

Izumi replies:

Hijiri dani	If at least you, holy man,
Kokoro ni irete	Would guide me
Michibikaba	With all your strength,
Magaru magaru mo	I might well be able to reach it,
Mairitsuki namu	Even if by a crooked road.

See Kobayashi, *Kojidan: Jō*, p. 302.

132. The fictional relationship between Izumi Shikibu and Dōmyō may have been prompted by the fact that the poetess had an affair with Dōmyō's father, Fujiwara no Michitsuna—brother of Michinaga—as we know from her private collection, the *Izumi Shikibu Shū*. See Ōshima Tatehiko, "Izumi Shikibu no Setsuwa," in his *Otogizōshi to Minkan Bungei, MBS* 12 (Tokyo: Iwazaki Bijutsu Sha, 1967), p. 128. The names of Izumi and Dōmyō appear together in a poem from the *Ryōjin Hishō* that lists the names of famous poets:

Waka ni sugurete medetaki wa	The most excellent and wonderful poets:
Hitomaru Akihito Ono no Komachi	Hitomaro, Akahito, Ono no Komachi,
Mitsune Tsurayuki Mibu no Tadamine	Mitsune, Tsurayuki, Mibu no Tadamine,
Henjō Dōmyō Izumi Shikibu.	Henjō, Dōmyō, and Izumi Shikibu.

See *Ryōjin Hishō* 1:3; Enoki, *Ryōjin Hishō*, p. 18. Although Dōmyō was considered one of the Thirty-Six Poetic Geniuses *(sanjūrokkasen)* and the *Ōkagami* praises him as a "great expert on Japanese poetry," his achievements do not warrant the comparison with such venerated giants of the poetic tradition as Hitomaro and Tsurayuki. The listing of Dōmyō's name is probably the result of the mental connection that medieval Japanese made between the holy man and the famous poet Izumi Shikibu. See Joseph K. Yamagiwa, trans., *The Ōkagami: A Japanese Historical Tale* (Tokyo: Tuttle, 1977), p. 153.

As a poet Dōmyō was known for his witty use of language. The section on lust (*kōshoku*) from the collection of legendary tales known as *Kokonchomonjū* relates that, while riding on the same cart with Izumi Shikibu, Dōmyō was careful to sit with his back turned to the woman because, should he be enticed by the woman's smile, he would fall from the cart, thus betraying his disregard for the Buddhist precepts. In the poem accompanying the event, the holy man compares Izumi's smile to the shape of an opening burr laughing at a chestnut about to fall to the ground:

Yoshi ya yoshi	What can I do?
Mukaji ya mukaji	Shall I turn towards you or not?
Igaguri no	By meeting with your smile
Emi mo ainaba	—A chestnut in its opening burr—
Ochi mo koso sure	I will certainly fall down.

See *Kokonchomonjū* 8:11, no. 318; Nishio Kōichi and Kobayashi Yasuharu, eds., *Kokonchomonjū: Jō, SNKS* 59 (Tokyo: Shinchōsha, 1983), pp. 380–381.

In another episode from the same collection, the inhabitants of a mountain village offer some food to Dōmyō, who is undergoing ascetic training. The villagers explain the nature of the food offered: "buckwheat which entirely covers the field." Realizing that the consumption of food may jeopardize the goal of his spiritual exercises, Dōmyō comes up with a poetic pun on the Japanese word *shishi*, which means both "wild boar" and "flesh."

Hitahaete	I feel that
Tori dani suenu	The wild boar will certainly visit
Somamugi ni	This field of buckwheat,
Shishi tsukinubeki	Whose surface is entirely covered,
Kokochi koso sure	And where birds can never stop.

The poem implies that while the wild boar will certainly come *(shishi tsukinubeki)* to eat the buckwheat, the consumption of so much food will cause the holy man to put on weight *(shishi tsukinubeki)* and fail his religious undertakings. See *Kokonchomonjū* 18:28, no. 616; Nishio Kōichi and Kobayashi Yasuharu, eds., *Kokonchomonjū: Ge, SNKS* 76 (Tokyo: Shinchōsha, 1986), p. 306.

133. *Konjaku Monogatari* 12:36; Mabuchi Kazuo et al., eds., *Konjaku Monogatari Shū* 1, NKBZ 21 (Tokyo: Shōgakukan, 1971), pp. 334–335.

134. Quoted in Ōshima, "Izumi Shikibu no Setsuwa," p. 130.

135. *Konjaku Monogatari* 12:36; Mabuchi, *Konjaku Monogatari Shū* 1, pp. 332–333.

136. Ōshima Tatehiko, ed., *Uji Shūi Monogatari, SNKS* 71 (Tokyo: Shinchōsha, 1985), pp. 21–22; D. E. Mills, trans., *A Collection of Tales from Uji: A Study and Translation of Uji Shūi Monogatari* (Cambridge: Cambridge University Press, 1970), pp. 135–136.

137. *Uji Shūi Monogatari* 1:1; Mills, *A Collection of Tales from Uji,* p. 135; Ōshima, *Uji Shūi Monogatari,* p. 21.

138. Although missing in the version of the *Izumi Shikibu Shū,* this detail

appears in the postscript to the poem by the Kibune deity in the version of the *Go Shūi Waka Shū* 20:1165; Fujimoto, *Go Shūi Waka Shū* 4, p. 363.

139. Abandoned by her lover, Izumi visits the Kibune Shrine and, noticing a few fireflies on the sacred stream of the compound, recites the following poem:

Mono omoeba	Deep in my thoughts
Sawa no hotaru mo	It looks as if
Wagami yori	These fireflies in the stream
Akugare izuru	Were my spirit
Tama ka to zo miru	Fleeing my body.

The god answers:

Okuyama ni	Don't be so overcome by thoughts
Tagirite otsuru	As to feel that your spirit is falling
Takitsuse no	Like pearls
Tama chiru bakari	In the rapids of a cascade
Mono na omoi so	Flowing into the deep mountain.

See *Izumi Shikibu Shū* 125–126; Nomura Seiichi, ed., *Izumi Shikibu Nikki, Izumi Shikibu Shū*, SNKS 42 (Tokyo: Shinchōsha, 1981), p. 129; *Go Shūi Waka Shū* 1164–1165; Fujimoto, *Go Shūi Waka Shū* 4, pp. 361–363.

140. See a few examples in F. Kurausu, *Meicho Edai: Sei Fūzoku no Nihon Shi,* Kawade Bunko (Tokyo: Kawade Shobō, 1988), p. 73, 79, 89, 99. For the courtesans' devotion to *dōsojin* see Saeki, *Yūjo no Bunka Shi*, p. 66.

141. Ōshima, *Uji Shūi Monogatari*, p. 22; Mills, *A Collection of Tales from Uji*, p. 136.

142. *Uji Shūi Monogatari* 1:2; Ōshima, *Uji Shūi Monogatari*, p. 23; Mills, *A Collection of Tales from Uji*, p. 137.

143. Hurvitz, *Scripture of the Lotus Blossom of the Fine Dharma*, p. 133; Sakamoto Yukio and Iwamoto Yutaka, eds., *Hokkekyō: Chū*, IB (Tokyo: Iwanami Shoten, 1964), p. 20.

144. Adapted from Edwin A. Cranston, trans., *The Izumi Shikibu Diary: A Romance of the Heian Court* (Cambridge: Harvard University Press, 1969), p. 6; Ōshima, *Otogizōshi Shū*, pp. 385–393.

145. Ōshima, "Izumi Shikibu no Setsuwa," pp. 139–141.

146. James H. Foard, "Seiganji: The Buddhist Orientation of a Noh Play," *Monumenta Nipponica* 35:4 (Winter 1980): 438.

147. Foard, "Seiganji," p. 452; Sanari Kentarō, ed., *Yōkyoku Taikan* 3 (Tokyo: Meiji Shoin, 1964), p. 1562.

148. *Hosshinshū* 6:10; Miki Sumito, ed., *Hōjōki, Hosshinshū*, SNKS 5 (Tokyo: Shinchōsha, 1976), pp. 280–281.

149. The statement is by Shunzei no Musume (1171–1251) as reported in her *Nameless Book (Mumyōzōshi)*. See Michele Marra, trans., "*Mumyōzōshi*: Part 3," *Monumenta Nipponica* 39:4 (Winter 1984): 427; Kuwabara Hiroshi, ed., *Mumyōzōshi*, SNKS 7 (Tokyo: Shinchōsha, 1976), p. 114. The emphasis is mine.

150. Hosokawa Ryōichi, *Onna no Chūsei: Ono no Komachi, Tomoe, Sono*

Hoka (Tokyo: Nihon Editā Sukūru, 1989), p. 263. For the first poem I have used the slightly different version that appears in Hyōdō, "Monogatari: Shokue to Jōka no Kairo," p. 204.

151. McCullough, *Kokin Wakashū*, p. 7; Okumura, *Kokin Waka Shū*, p. 23.

152. W. G. Aston, trans., *Nihongi: Chronicles of Japan from the Earliest Times to A.D. 697* (Tokyo: Tuttle, 1980; 1st ed., 1896), p. 318; Sakamoto Tarō et al., eds., *Nihon Shoki: Jō, NKBT* 67 (Tokyo: Iwanami Shoten, 1965), p. 440.

153. *Kojidan* 2:127. See Kobayashi, *Kojidan: Jō,* pp. 140–141; Yanase Kazuo, *Mumyōshō Zenkō* (Tokyo: Katō Chūdōkan, 1980), pp. 448–456; Hilda Kato, "The *Mumyōshō* of Kamo no Chōmei and Its Significance in Japanese Literature," *Monumenta Nipponica* 23:3–4 (1968): 422–424.

154. Arthur Waley, *The Nō Plays of Japan* (Tokyo: Tuttle, 1976; 1st ed., 1921), p. 115; Itō, *Yōkyoku Shū: Chū, SNKS* 73 (Tokyo: Shinchōsha, 1986), p. 254.

155. Itō, *Yōkyoku Shū: Chū,* p. 256.

156. Ibid., p. 256.

157. Waley, *The Nō Plays of Japan,* p. 120; Itō, *Yōkyoku Shū: Chū,* p. 258.

158. Waley, *The Nō Plays of Japan,* p. 124; Itō, *Yōkyoku Shū: Chū,* p. 260.

159. This translation is by McCullough, *Kokin Wakashū* 9:409, p. 98.

160. Ōshima, *Otogizōshi Shū,* pp. 111–112.

161. Kitagawa Tadahiko, *Zeami, CS* 292 (Tokyo: Chūō Kōronsha, 1972), p. 14.

162. Stephen Orgel, *The Illusion of Power: Political Theater in the English Renaissance* (Berkeley: University of California Press, 1975), p. 1.

163. Quoted in Kitagawa, *Zeami,* p. 31.

164. The *Emperor's Visit to the Kitayama Villa (Kitayamadono Gyōkō Ki)* mentions the event, although the names of the actors are not reported. Kitagawa Tadahiko infers Zeami's presence from the free access that the playwright enjoyed to Yoshimitsu's house; Kitagawa, *Zeami,* p. 36.

165. Tanaka, *Zeami Geijutsu Ronshū,* pp. 248–249; Rimer and Yamazaki, *On the Art of the Nō Drama,* pp. 241–242.

166. Kitagawa, *Zeami,* pp. 41–42.

167. Ibid., p. 164.

168. Rimer and Yamazaki, *On the Art of the Nō Drama,* p. 42; Tanaka, *Zeami Geijutsu Ronshū,* p. 67. The addition in brackets is mine. I have discussed Zeami's "Flower" and the impact of Buddhist thought on the theory and practice of *nō* in my article, "Zeami and Nō: A Path Towards Enlightenment," *Journal of Asian Culture* 12 (1988): 37–67.

169. The relationship of Zeami to members of the Southern court is traced in the *Kanze Fukuda Genealogy (Kanze Fukuda Keizu),* according to which Zeami's mother was a sister of the Southern general Kusunoki Masashige. Although the reliability of this source is marred by the fact that it was produced during the late Edo period, a few historical circumstances sustain the thesis that Zeami's exile may have been prompted by his ties with the Southern court. We have records placing Zeami's son Motomasa at the Amagawa Shrine in the Yoshino area—the headquarters of the Southern court—where he wrote a prayer to the god of music

Benzaiten, a petition to restore himself and his father to the glory of the past. Motomasa died in Ise province, which had long been occupied by Southern troops. Since we cannot trace with any certainty a blood relationship between Zeami and members of the Southern court, we may speculate that the loss of Ashikaga patronage may have induced Zeami and his descendants to look for new patrons in an alternative center of power: what was left of the Yoshino court after reunification. See Kitagawa, *Zeami,* pp. 168–171. On the subject of Zeami's exile see Susan Matisoff, "*Kintōsho:* Zeami's Song of Exile," *Monumenta Nipponica* 32:4 (Winter 1977): 441–458, and Susan Matisoff, "Images of Exile and Pilgrimage: Zeami's *Kintōsho,*" *Monumenta Nipponica* 34:4 (Winter 1979): 449–465.

170. Louis Adrian Montrose, " 'Eliza, Queene of Shepheardes,' and the Pastoral of Power," *English Literary Renaissance* 10:2 (Spring 1980): 155.

171. Ibid., p. 164. On the pastoral as an assertion of royal power see Orgel, *The Illusion of Power,* pp. 49–50.

172. Montrose, " 'Eliza, Queene of Shepheardes,' " p. 178.

173. Orgel, *The Illusion of Power,* p. 52.

174. Ibid., p. 88.

175. Jonathan Goldberg, *James I and the Politics of Literature: Jonson, Shakespeare, Donne, and Their Contemporaries* (Stanford: Stanford University Press, 1989; 1st ed., 1983), p. 33.

176. For a detailed analysis in English of the *gozan* system see Martin Collcutt, *Five Mountains: The Rinzai Zen Monastic Institution in Medieval Japan* (Cambridge: Council on East Asian Studies, Harvard University, 1981).

177. Imatani Akira, *Muromachi no Ōken: Ashikaga Yoshimitsu no Ōken Sandatsu Keikaku,* CS 978 (Tokyo: Chūō Kōronsha, 1990), pp. 119–120.

178. Ibid., p. 122.

179. Ibid., pp. 122–123.

180. Nippon Gakujutsu Shinkōkai, *The Noh Drama: Ten Plays from the Japanese* (Tokyo: Tuttle, 1973; 1st ed., 1955), pp. 10–11 and 16–17; Itō Masayoshi, *Yōkyoku Shū: Chū,* SNKS 73 (Tokyo: Shinchōsha, 1986), pp. 286–287 and 291–292.

181. Nippon Gakujutsu Shinkōkai, *The Noh Drama,* pp. 50 and 52; Itō, *Yōkyoku Shū: Chū,* pp. 115–116.

182. Nippon Gakujutsu Shinkōkai, *The Noh Drama,* p. 54; Itō, *Yōkyoku Shū: Chū,* p. 117.

183. Quoted in Hyōdō, "Monogatari: Shokue to Jōka no Kairo," p. 193.

184. Ibid., pp. 192–195.

Chapter Three

1. For the filiation of several *otogizōshi* from *setsuwa* see Tokuda, *Otogizōshi: Kenkyū,* pp. 26–46; for the history of sermon-ballads see Sekiyama Kazuo, *Sekkyō no Rekishi: Bukkyō to Wagei,* IS 64 (Tokyo: Iwanami Shoten, 1978).

2. To this day the relationship between what is traditionally called Shintoism, religious Taoism, and other popular beliefs has not been satisfactorily clarified. Nevertheless, it is imperative to avoid using the term "Shinto" to identify an alleg-

edly indigenous religion to which members of Buddhist institutions addressed their message of evangelization. See Kuroda Toshio, "Shintō in the History of Japanese Religion," trans. James C. Dobbins and Suzanne Gay, *Journal of Japanese Studies* 7:1 (Winter 1981): 1–21.

3. H. Paul Varley, trans., *A Chronicle of Gods and Sovereigns: Jinnō Shōtōki of Kitabatake Chikafusa* (New York: Columbia University Press, 1980), p. 269; Iwasa Masashi et al., eds., *Jinnō Shōtōki, Masu Kagami,* NKBT 87 (Tokyo: Iwanami Shoten, 1965), p. 193.

4. The expression *kyō warabe* already appears during the Heian period, when Fujiwara no Akihira mentioned the jokes of "the boys" in his *Shin Sarugaku Ki* (1064). See Kawaguchi, *Shin Sarugaku Ki,* pp. 3–4.

5. *Gunsho Ruijū* 25 (1933), pp. 503–504. The text also appears in Satō Shin'ichi, *Nanbokuchō no Dōran,* Nihon no Rekishi 9 (Tokyo: Chūō Kōron Sha, 1974), pp. 96–98. For a discussion of the lampoon see Nagazumi Yasuaki, Uwayokote Masataka, and Sakurai Yoshirō, eds., *Taiheiki no Sekai: Henkaku no Jidai o Yomu* (Tokyo: Nihon Hōsō Shuppan Kyōkai, 1987), pp. 251–254.

6. The medieval chronicle *Taiheiki* contains twenty-three lampoons addressed to the Northern and Southern courts and to the governments of both the Kamakura and Muromachi periods. One notes that the presumed author of the *Taiheiki,* Kojima Hōshi, has been recently shown to have been residing in the area of Nijō Kawara, where the lampoon translated here was disclosed. The custom of using the banks of the Kamo River as a favorite site for graffiti can be easily related to Kojima's acquaintance with the art of satire. See Gotō Meisei, "Bunshin," *Gunzō* 11 (1988): 128–142; Sakurai Yoshirō, "Machishū Bunka no Senkuteki Keitai: *Taiheiki* to Kyō Warabe to," in Sakurai Yoshirō, *Chūsei Nihonjin no Shii to Hyōgen* (Tokyo: Miraisha, 1970), pp. 166–179.

7. Quoted in Yokoi Kiyoshi, *Gekokujō no Bunka* (Tokyo: Tōkyō Daigaku Shuppan Kai, 1980), p. 55.

8. For the role played by the two wheels of the cart of government see Kuroda Toshio, *Ōbō to Buppō: Chūseishi no Kōzu,* Hōzō Sensho 23 (Kyoto: Hōzōkan, 1983), pp. 8–22.

9. Oyamada Tomokiyo (1782–1847) established this date in the first half of the nineteenth century. Kishi Shōzō argues that the *Shintōshū* was compiled approximately between 1354 and 1358. See Kishi Shōzō, trans., *Shintōshū,* TB 94 (Tokyo: Heibonsha, 1967), pp. 298–300; see also Barbara Ruch, "Medieval Jongleurs and the Making of a National Literature," in John W. Hall and Toyoda Takeshi, eds., *Japan in the Muromachi Age* (Berkeley: University of California Press, 1977), pp. 150–151.

10. See Origuchi's *Nihon Bungaku Keimō* as quoted in Kishi Shōzō, "*Shintōshū:* Sōsetsu Honbun Kanshō," in Nishio Kōichi and Kishi Shōzō, eds., *Chūsei Setsuwa Shū: Kokonchomonjū, Hosshinshū, Shintōshū,* KNKB 23 (Tokyo: Kadokawa Shoten, 1977), p. 278.

11. For Kikuchi Ryōichi's position see Kishi, *Shintōshū,* p. 297; Iwasaki Takeo, *Sanshō-dayū Kō: Chūsei no Sekkyōgatari,* HS 23 (Tokyo: Heibonsha, 1973), p. 229.

12. Robert Borgen and Marian Ury, "Readable Japanese Mythology: Selec-

tions from *Nihon Shoki* and *Kojiki*," *Journal of the Association of Teachers of Japanese* 24:1 (April 1990): 71. Although a little less readable, the standard translation remains Donald L. Philippi, trans., *Kojiki* (Tokyo: University of Tokyo Press, 1968), p. 85; Nishimiya Kazutami, ed., *Kojiki*, SNKS 27 (Tokyo: Shinchōsha, 1979), pp. 51–52.

13. Varley, *A Chronicle of Gods and Sovereigns*, p. 77; Iwasa, *Jinnō Shōtōki, Masu Kagami*, p. 61.

14. Varley, *A Chronicle of Gods and Sovereigns*, p. 87; Iwasa, *Jinnō Shōtōki, Masu Kagami*, pp. 68–69.

15. Kondō Yoshihiro, ed., *Shintōshū: Tōyō Bunko Bon* (Tokyo: Kadokawa Shoten, 1959), pp. 240–241; Kishi, *Shintōshū*, pp. 157–158.

16. Kondō, *Shintōshū*, p. 241; Kishi, *Shintōshū*, p. 158.

17. Kondō, *Shintōshū*, p. 55; Kishi, *Shintōshū*, p. 15.

18. Kondō, *Shintōshū*, pp. 54–55; Kishi, *Shintōshū*, pp. 15–16.

19. Aston, *Chronicles of Japan*, pp. 115–116; Sakamoto, *Nihon Shoki*, p. 196.

20. Kondō, *Shintōshū*, p. 57; Kishi, *Shintōshū*, p. 18.

21. In addition to these twelve deities, the story mentions Bishamonten and Aizen'ō as the Original Grounds of Kannokura who is worshiped at the Shingū Shrine, Miroku Bosatsu as the Original Ground of Raiden Hachidai Kongō Dōji, and Shichibutsu Yakushi as the Original Ground of Asuka Daigyōji. See Kondō, *Shintōshū*, pp. 45–46; Kishi, *Shintōshū*, pp. 3–4.

22. The story appears in Ōe no Masafusa's *Honchō Shinsen Den*. See Inoue Mitsusada and Ōsone Shōsuke, eds., *Ōjōden, Hokke Kenki*, NST 7 (Tokyo: Iwanami Shoten, 1974), pp. 258–259; Silvio Calzolari, *Il Dio Incatenato, Honchō Shinsen Den di Ōe no Masafusa: Storie di Santi e Immortali Taoisti nel Giappone dell' Epoca Heian (794–1185)* (Florence: Sansoni, 1984), pp. 57–61. I have discussed the Buddhist appropriation of Japanese popular beliefs in my review of Calzolari's book in *Monumenta Nipponica* 41:4 (Winter 1986): 495–497.

23. *Gunsho Ruijū* 26, pp. 235–256.

24. Aston, *Nihongi*, p. 21; Sakamoto, *Nihon Shoki: Jō*, p. 90.

25. Aston, *Nihongi*, p. 114; Sakamoto, *Nihon Shoki: Jō*, p. 194.

26. Nishimiya, *Kojiki*, p. 39; Philippi, *Kojiki*, p. 65.

27. Tanigawa Ken'ichi, *Tokoyo Ron: Nihonjin no Tamashi no Yukue*, HS 81 (Tokyo: Heibonsha, 1983), pp. 19–40.

28. Quoted in Katō Takahisa, "Kumano Sanzan Shinkō no Kenkyū," in Katō Takahisa, *Jinja no Shiteki Kenkyū* (Tokyo: Ōfūsha, 1976), pp. 31–32.

29. In the *otogizōshi* version of this story, *The Original Ground of Suwa (Suwa no Honji)*, the holy man Kūya Shōnin replaces Kandai Shōjō. See Matsumoto Ryūshin, ed., *Otogizōshi Shū*, SNKS 34 (Tokyo: Shinchōsha, 1980), p. 286.

30. Kondō, *Shintōshū*, p. 335; Kishi, *Shintōshū*, p. 285. The same line, *gojin ujō, suihō fushō, koshuku ninjū, dōshō butsuka*, appears in the *otogizōshi* version; Matsumoto, *Otogizōshi Shū*, p. 287.

31. For a discussion of the expression *wakō dōjin* see Morrell, *Sand and Pebbles*, p. 338.

32. Ichiko Teiji, ed., *Otogizōshi, NKBT* 38 (Tokyo: Iwanami Shoten, 1958), pp. 411–433. The much more detailed *Shintōshū* version appears in Kondō, *Shintōshū,* pp. 46–55, and in Kishi, *Shintōshū,* pp. 4–15.

33. Kondō, *Shintōshū,* pp. 47 and 51; Kishi, *Shintōshū,* pp. 5 and 11.

34. Matsumoto, *Otogizōshi Shū,* p. 262.

35. Ibid., pp. 251–287. For the source of this story in the *Shintōshū* see Kondō, *Shintōshū,* pp. 295–335; Kishi, *Shintōshū,* pp. 238–286.

36. Iwasaki Takeo, *Sanshō-dayū Kō: Chūsei no Sekkyōgatari, HS* 23 (Tokyo: Heibonsha, 1973), pp. 26–28; Muroki Yatarō, ed., *Sekkyōshū, SNKS* 8 (Tokyo: Shinchōsha, 1977), pp. 404–406; Araki Shigeru and Yamamoto Kichizō, eds., *Sekkyō-bushi: Sanshō-dayū, Oguri Hangan, TB* 243 (Tokyo: Heibonsha, 1973), pp. 307–310. For an introduction to the genre and its major works in English see Nobuko Ishii, "Sekkyō-bushi," *Monumenta Nipponica* 44:3 (Autumn 1989): 283–307.

37. Quoted in Iwasaki, *Sanshō-dayū Kō,* p. 27.

38. Muroki, *Sekkyōshū,* pp. 81–152. For a modern version of this story see Mori Ōgai's novella *Sanshō Dayū* (Sanshō the Steward; 1915) in David Dilworth and J. Thomas Rimer, eds., *The Incident at Sakai and Other Stories* (Honolulu: University of Hawaii Press, 1977), pp. 123–148.

39. Hayashiya Tatsusaburō, *Kodai Kokka no Kaitai* (Tokyo: Tōkyō Daigaku Shuppan Kai, 1955), pp. 323–325.

40. Anno Masaki, *Genin Ron: Chūsei no Ijin to Kyōkai* (Tokyo: Nihon Editā Sukūru Shuppanbu, 1987), pp. 118–119.

41. There is no definitive agreement among scholars as to whether Kanayaki Jizō is the Original Ground of Tsushiōmaru, Anju no Hime, or their father Masauji. See Anno, *Genin Ron,* pp. 110–115.

42. Muroki, *Sekkyōshū,* pp. 211–298. The same pattern applies to the hero of *Aigo no Waka,* who is eventually worshiped as Sannō Gongen—the god of earth, water, and agriculture—after having been killed by that same agricultural society that he is now protecting. See Muroki, *Sekkyōshū,* pp. 301–344.

Chapter Four

1. V. Dixon Morris, "Sakai: From *Shōen* to Port City," in John W. Hall and Toyoda Takeshi, eds., *Japan in the Muromachi Age* (Berkeley: University of California Press, 1977), pp. 145–158; V. Dixon Morris, "The City of Sakai and Urban Autonomy," in George Elison and Bardwell L. Smith, eds., *Warlords, Artists, and Commoners: Japan in the Sixteenth Century* (Honolulu: University of Hawaii Press, 1981), pp. 23–54.

2. Hayashiya Tatsusaburō, *Machishū: Kyōto ni okeru "Shimin" Keisei Shi, CS* 59 (Tokyo: Chūō Kōron Sha, 1964), pp. 103–104.

3. Hayashiya, *Machishū,* p. 139. The songs accompanying the dances of the Citizens were collected in 1518 in the *Kangin Shū.* See Kitagawa Tadahiko, ed., *Kangin Shū, Sōan Kouta Shū, SNKS* 53 (Tokyo: Shinchōsha, 1982).

4. Hayashiya, *Machishū,* pp. 173–177.

5. Sasaki Gin'ya, *Muromachi Bakufu,* Nihon no Rekishi 13 (Tokyo: Shōgakukan, 1975), pp. 336–343. See also Imatani Akira, *Tenbun Hokke no Ran: Busō Suru Machishū* (Tokyo: Heibonsha, 1989).

6. Quoted in Hayashiya, *Machishū,* p. 118; see also pp. 115–117.

7. On this subject see H. Paul Varley, *The Ōnin War: History of Its Origins and Background with a Selective Translation of The Chronicle of Ōnin* (New York: Columbia University Press, 1967).

8. Quoted in Hayashiya, *Machishū,* pp. 106–107. See also Imatani Akira, *Tokitsugu Gyōki: Kuge Shakai to Machishū Bunka no Setten* (Tokyo: Kabushiki Kaisha Soshiete, 1980), pp. 189–190.

9. Hayashiya, *Machishū,* pp. 200–201. For the role played by the *Ise Monogatari* in the Japanese court see Marra, *The Aesthetics of Discontent,* pp. 35–53.

10. Like most definitions of genres, the expression *otogizōshi* suffers from the inflation of differentiated material—about four hundred stories compiled in the span of three centuries. The historical reason for the inclusion of this massive gathering of Muromachi narratives in the category of *otogizōshi* goes back to 1801, when Ozaki Masayoshi, in his survey of literature *Gunsho Ikkan,* classified as *otogizōshi* twenty-three stories that Shibukawa Seiemon had originally collected under the title of *Otogi Bunko* ("Library of Narratives") around 1661–1672. These stories are: *Bunshō Sōshi, Hachikazuki, Komachi Sōshi, Onzōshi Shimawatari, Karaito Sōshi, Kowata Kitsune, Nanakusa Sōshi, Sarugenji Sōshi, Monokusatarō, Sazareishi, Hamaguri no Sōshi, Koatsumori, Nijūshikō, Bondenkoku, Nose Saru Sōshi, Neko no Sōshi, Hamaide Sōshi, Izumi Shikibu, Issun Bōshi, Saiki, Urashima Tarō, Yokobue Sōshi,* and *Shuten Dōji.*

Since then hundreds of stories have been added to the genre. The diversified nature of this rich and heterogeneous material presents literary historians with the challenge of classification. The Japanese medievalist Ichiko Teiji has provided the classical model of subdivisions, deriving it from the plots and characters of each story. His "Aristocracy Pieces" (*kuge mono*) deal with the hardships of noblemen whose trials are a prerequisite for the fulfillment of their love. This category also includes stories about persecuted stepdaughters and biographies of poets. Examples are: *Shinobine Monogatari, Akizuki Monogatari, Iwaya no Sōshi, Hachikazuki, Hanayo no Hime, Komachi Sōshi,* and *Izumi Shikibu.*

"Monks or Religious Pieces" (*sōryo* or *shukyō mono*) include portraits of trainees and monks breaking the precepts, stories of religious awakening, biographies of priests, origins of temples (*honji mono*) and shrines (*engi*), and Buddhist sermons. A few examples are: *Aki no Yo no Nagamonogatari, Ashibiki, Oyou no Ama, Sasayakidake, Sannin Hōshi, Koya Monogatari, Saiki, Kumano no Honji, Bondenkoku,* and *Suwa no Honji.*

"Warrior Pieces" (*buke mono*) introduce the subject of fights against demons, material from the Genpei war, and stories of loyalty and vengeance. A few examples: *Tamura no Sōshi, Shūten Dōji, Rashōmon, Onzōshi Shimawatari, Jōruri Monogatari, Hogan Miyako Banashi, Yokobue Sōshi, Koatsumori, Karaito Sōshi, Hamade Sōshi, Akashi no Saburō, Morokado Monogatari,* and *Muramatsu no Monogatari.*

"Commoner Pieces" (*shōmin mono*) include humorous stories of people's ingenuity, examples of worldly success, and congratulatory pieces such as *Fukutomi Sōshi, Urihime Monogatari, Bunshō Sōshi, Sarugenji Sōshi, Monokusatarō, Issunbōshi, Matsutake Monogatari, Nanagusa Sōshi, Sazareishi,* and *Kootoko no Sōshi.*

"Stories of Foreign Lands" *(ikoku mono)* deal with the customs of real and imaginary foreign countries, as in the case of *Yokihi Monogatari, Nijūshikō, Rushi Chōja, Homyō Dōji, Hōrai Monogatari,* and *Furo Fushi.*

Finally, "Nonhuman Pieces" *(irui mono)* portray animals or supernatural beings who behave like human beings and intermarry with them. Examples are: *Urashima Tarō, Hamaguri no Sōshi, Kowata Kitsune, Nezumi no Sōshi, Okoze, Shōjin Gyorui Monogatari, Arokassen Monogatari, Engaku, Suzume no Hosshin,* and *Neko no Sōshi.*

See Ichiko Teiji, *Chūsei Shōsetsu no Kenkyū* (Tokyo: Tōkyō Daigaku Shuppan Kai, 1955). The same classification is followed by Ōshima Tatehiko, ed., *Otogizōshi Shū, NKBZ* 36 (Tokyo: Shōgakukan, 1974), pp. 9–14.

11. Kidō Saizō, ed., *Tsurezuregusa, SNKS* 10 (Tokyo: Shinchōsha, 1977), pp. 138–139; Donald Keene, trans., *Essays in Idleness: The Tsurezuregusa of Kenkō* (New York: Columbia University Press, 1967), pp. 104–105. For Kenkō's assessment of Muromachi Japan, see Marra, *The Aesthetics of Discontent,* pp. 127–152.

12. Keene, *Essays in Idleness,* p. 179; Kidō, *Tsurezuregusa,* p. 228.

13. Keene, *Essays in Idleness,* p. 178; Kidō, *Tsurezuregusa,* p. 227. The emphasis is mine.

14. The influence on *Bunshō Sōshi* exerted by medieval writings on the ethical codes of merchants is analyzed in Sakurai Yoshirō, "*Bunshō Sōshi* no Seiritsu ni Tsuite: Chūsei Shōnin no Shii Kōzō to Sono Bunkateki Hyōgen Keitai no Bunseki," in his *Chūsei Nihonjin no Shii to Hyōgen* (Tokyo: Miraisha, 1970), pp. 300–327.

15. James T. Araki, "Bunshō Sōshi: The Tale of Bunshō, the Saltmaker," *Monumenta Nipponica* 38:3 (Autumn 1983): 223; Ōshima Tatehiko, ed., *Otogizōshi Shū, NKBZ* 36 (Tokyo: Shōgakukan 1974), p. 42.

16. Araki, "*Bunshō Sōshi,*" p. 225; Ōshima, *Otogizōshi Shū,* p. 44.

17. The narrator's decision to include the character "lotus" in both names of Bunshō's daughters indicates a further relationship between the producers/consumers of this story—the Citizens *(machishū)*—and the Hokke sect that made the title of the *Lotus Sutra (Hokkekyō)* an icon of salvation. I thank Bruce Coats for pointing this out to me.

18. The significant role played by Bunshō's daughters is analyzed in Satake Akihiro, " 'Bunshō Sōshi' Saidoku," in Nihon Bungaku Kenkyū Shiryō Kankōkai, ed., *Otogizōshi* (Tokyo: Yūseidō, 1974), pp. 126–132.

19. Araki, "Bunshō Sōshi," p. 235; Ōshima, *Otogizōshi Shū,* p. 64.

20. Araki, "Bunshō Sōshi," p. 238; Ōshima, *Otogizōshi Shū,* p. 69.

21. Araki, "Bunshō Sōshi," p. 239; Ōshima, *Otogizōshi Shū,* p. 70.

22. Ōshima, *Otogizōshi Shū,* pp. 387–388.

23. Ibid., p. 389.

24. The date 1474 originally advanced by Araki Yoshio has been accepted by Ōshima Tatehiko. See his " 'Sarugenji Sōshi' no Seiritsu," in Ōshima Tatehiko, *Otogizōshi to Minkan Bungei, MBS* 12 (Tokyo: Iwazaki Bijutsu Sha, 1967), p. 123.

25. The campaign is known as the *Hiyoshi Sarugaku Kanjin Nō;* quoted in Itō Masayoshi, *Yōkyoku Shū: Jō,* p. 394.

26. This is a variation of the following poem from the *Kokin Rokujō:*

Au koto o	If you keep on
Akogi no shima ni	Meeting and pulling [the nets]
Hiku tabi no	At Akogi Island
Tabikasanaraba	Eventually
Hito mo shirinan	People will find out.

See Matsushita, *Zoku Kokka Taikan,* p. 522:32381.

27. This is a quotation from a poem by Kyūzai Hōshi which is included in the *Tsukuba Shū,* a collection of linked verses:

Kusa no na mo	Even the names of plants
Tokoro ni yorite	Change
Kawaru nari	According to places:
Naniwa no ashi wa	The rushes of Naniwa become
Ise no hamaogi	The beach reeds of Ise.

See *Tsukuba Shū* 1333; Fukui Kyūzō, ed., *Tsukuba Shū: Ge, NKZ* (Tokyo: Asahi Shinbunsha, 1951), p. 109.

28. This is a variation of a poem by Emperor Go-Saga (r. 1242–1246) collected in the *Shoku Gosenshū* that praises the refinement of a fisherman. Fearing that the smoke rising from the furnace may hide the moon from view during the production of salt, the man puts out the fire beneath the furnace. The poem says:

Shiogama no	The smoke rising in the bay
Ura no kemuri wa	Of Shiogama—the Salt Furnace
Taenikeri	Has ceased:
Tsuki min to te no	Is it perhaps the work of a fisher
Ama no shiwaza ka	Wishing to see the moon?

See Matsushita Daisaburō and Watanabe Fumio, eds., *Kokka Taikan: Kashū,* p. 245:339.

29. Itō, *Yōkyoku Shū: Jō,* pp. 28–29.

30. Haruo Shirane discusses this point in his *Bridge of Dreams: A Poetics of "The Tale of Genji"* (Stanford: Stanford University Press, 1987), pp. 29–30.

31. For a discussion of the code of *miyabi* see Marra, *The Aesthetics of Discontent,* pp. 35–53.

32. *Ise Monogatari* 27. See Helen Craig McCullough, trans., *Tales of Ise: Lyrical Episodes from Tenth-Century Japan* (Stanford: Stanford University Press, 1968), p. 92; Watanabe Minoru, ed., *Ise Monogatari, SNKS* 2 (Tokyo: Shinchōsha, 1978), p. 45. The *to* of the fourth line is omitted in the *otogizōshi* version. See Ōshima, *Otogizōshi Shū,* p. 205.

33. McCullough, *Tales of Ise,* p. 92; Watanabe, *Ise Monogatari,* p. 45.

34. Ōshima, *Otogizōshi Shū,* p. 208.

35. Ibid., p. 222.

36. The "Story of Genji the Monkey" has the following version:

Shiogi toru	You will soon be found out
Agokigaura ni	If you keep on

Hiku ami mo	Throwing the nets
Tabi kasanareba	In Akogi Bay
Araware zo suru	Where salt is made.

See Ōshima, *Otogizōshi Shū,* p. 224. This poem is discussed by Kubota Jun, "Otogizōshi no Waka," in Ichiko Teiji and Noma Kōshin, eds., *Otogizōshi, Kanazōshi, KNKB* 26 (Tokyo: Kadokawa Shoten, 1976), pp. 310–313.

37. The story introduces another parody of the structure courtesan/bodhisattva by further appropriating material from the *Genpei Seisuiki.* The scene in question portrays the love of Moritō, who is better known by the religious name of Mongaku, for the married woman Tennyo Gozen. The woman's mother, Ama Gozen, must decide whether to let the man inside the house, and thus have her daughter's honor stained, or to allow Moritō to die of love in front of the house, thus causing the entire family to become the victim of the man's angry spirit. Ama Gozen justifies her daughter's adultery on the ground that the girl is acting out of compassion for the man—a "religious savior" leading Moritō onto the path of enlightenment. The narrator's irony bursts into the following passage:

"How pitiful! If I let the man meet with my daughter I will cause her to commit the sin of adultery. But if the man dies, we will suffer his anger for a long time. What shall I do?" she thought. "The Buddha prohibits the taking of life, and once you are dead, you cannot come back from that world. *To help people is the duty of the bodhisattva!*"

See Ōshima, *Otogizōshi Shū,* p. 210. The emphasis is mine.

38. The poem says:

Wagi moko ga	How sad it is
Nemidaregami o	To look at the sleep-disheveled hair
Sarusawa no	Of my beloved
Ike no tamamo to	Transformed into the weeds
Miru zo kanashiki	Of Sarusawa Pond.

See *Yamato Monogatari* 150; Sakakura Atsuyoshi et al., eds., *Taketori Monogatari, Ise Monogatari, Yamato Monogatari, NKBT* 9 (Tokyo: Iwanami Shoten, 1959), pp. 322–323; Ōshima, *Otogizōshi Shū,* p. 227.

39. Sarugenji's contribution to *The Tale of Genji* reads as follows:

Sarusawa no	Are those willows
Ike no yanagi ya	Of Sarusawa Pond
Wagi moko ga	A memento
Nemidaregami no	Of the sleep-disheveled hair
Katami naruran	Of my beloved?

See Ōshima, *Otogizōshi Shū,* p. 227. Although the *Yamato Monogatari,* as well as medieval anecdotal collections such as the *Fukuro Zōshi* and the *Jikkinshō,* record the story of the girl abandoned by the emperor, no mention of Genji's visit to Sarusawa Pond is ever made in the *Genji Monogatari.* See *Fukuro Zōshi* 31; Ōzawa Tomio et al., eds., *Fukuro Zōshi Chūshaku: Jō* (Tokyo: Hanawa Shobō, 1974), p. 135.

40. Izumi's poem appears in the *Hachiman Gudōkun,* in which it is recited by the bodhisattva Hachiman:

Hinomoto ni	In Japan
Iwaware tamou	I doubt there is anyone
Iwashimizu	Who has never visited
Mairanu hito wa	Iwashimizu Shrine,
Araji to zo omou	The sacred place of worship.

See Ōshima, *Otogizōshi Shū,* p. 228.

41. Ibid., p. 229.

42. See Jacques Le Goff, "The Several Middle Ages of Jules Michelet," in Jacques Le Goff, *Time, Work, and Culture in the Middle Ages,* trans. Arthur Goldhammer (Chicago: University of Chicago Press, 1980), pp. 3–28.

43. See Garin's essay on the crisis of medieval thought in Eugenio Garin, *Medioevo e Rinascimento, BUL* 124 (Rome and Bari: Laterza, 1984; 1st ed., 1954), pp. 13–45.

44. On the transformation of political institutions see Lauro Martines, *Power and Imagination: City-States in Renaissance Italy* (Baltimore: Johns Hopkins University Press, 1979), pp. 7–110.

45. See Jacques Le Goff, "Labor, Techniques, and Craftsmen in the Value Systems of the Early Middle Ages (Fifth to Tenth Centuries)," in his *Time, Work, and Culture in the Middle Ages,* pp. 71–86.

46. See Norbert Elias, *The Court Society* (New York: Pantheon Books, 1983; 1st German ed., 1969), pp. 153–157, 238–239.

47. Michel Foucault, *The Order of Things: An Archeology of the Human Sciences* (New York: Vintage Books, 1973; 1st French ed., 1966), pp. 50–77.

48. Michel Foucault, *The Archeology of Knowledge* and *The Discourse on Language* (New York: Pantheon Books, 1972; 1st French ed., 1971), pp. 166–177.

49. Jesse M. Gellrich, *The Idea of the Book in the Middle Ages: Language Theory, Mythology, and Fiction* (Ithaca and London: Cornell University Press, 1985), pp. 252–253.

50. Kenneth P. Kirkwood, *Renaissance in Japan: A Cultural Survey of the Seventeenth Century* (Tokyo: Tuttle, 1970).

51. Jin'ichi Konishi, *A History of Japanese Literature* 1: *The Archaic and Ancient Ages,* trans. Aileen Gatten and Nicholas Teele (Princeton: Princeton University Press, 1984), p. 57.

52. LaFleur, *The Karma of Words,* p. 9.

53. LaFleur's *The Karma of Words,* whose subtitle is *Buddhism and the Literary Arts in Medieval Japan,* covers texts of the ninth century such as the *Nihon Ryōiki,* as well as Bashō's *Oku no Hosomichi,* compiled in 1689. Following LaFleur's periodization, I discussed in my *Aesthetics of Discontent*—subtitled *Politics and Reclusion in Medieval Japanese Literature*—texts of the ninth century such as the *Taketori Monogatari* and the *Ise Monogatari* as well as concentrating on more traditionally "medieval" works of the Kamakura and Muromachi periods.

54. Ōshima, *Otogizōshi Shū*, p. 232. For a complete translation of the story see Virginia Skord, trans., *Tales of Tears and Laughter: Short Fiction of Medieval Japan* (Honolulu: University of Hawaii Press, 1991), pp. 185–204.

55. Ōshima, *Otogizōshi Shū*, pp. 231–232.

56. "The capital looked much better than Shinano province. The Eastern and Western Hills (Higashiyama and Nishiyama), the imperial palace *(gosho-dairi)*, temples and shrines presented an awesome view—something that cannot find expression in words. No trace could be found of Monokusatarō's weary look *(monokusagenaru keshiki)*." See Ōshima, *Otogizōshi Shū*, p. 238.

57. Ibid., pp. 238–239.

58. Ibid., pp. 240–241.

59. Ibid., p. 251.

60. To the lady's words,

Kyō yori wa	From today
Waga nagusami ni	What shall I use
Nani ka sen	To entertain myself?

Monokusatarō answers:

Kotowari nareba	Nothing can I say, since quite
Mono mo iwarezu	Reasonable is your sorrow.

See Ōshima, *Otogizōshi Shū*, p. 251.

61. "I have met you in Ōhara, Shizuhara, Seriu village, Kōdō, Kawasaki, Nakayama, Chōraku Temple, Kiyomizu, Rokuhara, Rokkakudō, Saga, Hōrin Temple, Uzumasa, Daigo, Kurusu, Kohatayama, Yodo, Yahata, Sumiyoshi, Kurama Temple, Tenjin Shrine in Gojō, Kibune Shrine, Hiyoshi Shrine, Gion, Kitano, Kamo, Kasuga, and many other places; what does this mean, what does this mean?" See Ōshima, *Otogizōshi Shū*, p. 242.

62. The discovery of the lady's address prompts Monokusatarō to display his knowledge of the basics for an understanding of the literary tradition. At the lady's suggestion of the location of her house "at the bottom of the pine" *(matsu no moto* 松のもと*)*, he sees in the pun Akashi Bay, in today's Hyōgo prefecture. The explanation comes from the fact that the character *matsu* 松 (pine) is the first part of the compound *taimatsu* 松明 (pine torch), the second character of which is *akari* 明 (light). To be at the bottom of the pine meant to be in the city of the "light-stone" 明石, which is Akashi city.

In another puzzle the lady mentions "the village where the sun goes down" *(higururu sato* 日暮るる里*)*. Thinking that the place must be dark *(kurai* 暗*)*, Monokusatarō feels that the woman's villa is located in the area known as Kurama on the east side of the capital.

When the lady refers to "Torch Lane" (Tomoshibi no Kōji 燈火の小路), he associates the torch with the idea of oil, thus answering that the woman must live in "Oil Lane" (Abura no Kōji 油の小路), which was located east of Horikawa Street.

When she refers to the "Village of Shame" (Hazukashi no Sato 恥づかしの里), the man is reminded of the expression "abiding one's shame" *(haji o shinobu*

恥を忍ぶ), concluding that the solution to the puzzle must be the village of Shinobu no Sato しのぶの里, which scholars identify with present-day Fukuoka city.

The name "Tunic Village" (Uwagi no Sato 表着の里) makes him think of a precious textile, brocade (*nishiki* 錦), and of the following response: "Then your place must be in Nishiki no Kōji 錦の小路—'Brocade Lane,' " north of Shijō Street.

When the woman mentions the "Country of Seduction" (Nagusamu Kuni 慰む国), the man remembers the verse *koishite ō mi* 恋して逢ふ身 ("the person whom loving I met") and, through sound associations, recalls Ōmi province 近江国 in present-day Shiga prefecture.

Monokusatarō interprets "The Cloudless Village" (Kumorinaki Sato) as Kagami no Shuku ("Mirror Town") of Shiga prefecture because of the mirror's unclouded surface.

He then associates the "Autumn Country" (Aki suru Kuni 秋する国) with the harvest of rice plants (*inaba* 稲葉), suggesting that the lady's place must be Inaba Inaba 因幡, in the eastern part of what is today Tottori prefecture.

Finally, asked to decipher the expression "Twenty Years Country" (Hatachi no Kuni 二十の国), Monokusatarō suggests Wakasa province (Wakasa no Kuni 若狭国)—literally, "The Country of Youth"—in the western part of Fukui prefecture, owing to the association between "twenty years" and "youth." See Ōshima, *Otogizōshi Shū*, p. 243.

63. M. Bakhtin, *Rabelais and His World,* trans. Helene Iswolsky (Cambridge: MIT Press, 1968), p. 20.

64. Stallybrass and White, *The Politics and Poetics of Transgression,* pp. 8–9.

65. Ōshima, *Otogizōshi Shū*, p. 244.

66. Ibid., pp. 248–249.

67. Ibid., pp. 254–256.

68. Sakurai Yoshirō, *Kamigami no Henbō: Shaji Engi no Sekai Kara* (Tokyo: Tōkyō Daigaku Shuppan Kai, 1976), p. 214.

69. Ibid., p. 215.

70. H. E. Plutschow, *Chaos and Cosmos: Ritual in Early and Medieval Japanese Literature* (Leiden: E. J. Brill, 1990), p. 28.

71. Monokusatarō's dual aspect is analyzed in Satake Akihiro, "Muchi to Gudon: Monokusatarō no Yukue," in Satake Akihiro, *Gekokujō no Bungaku* (Tokyo: Chikuma Shobō, 1967), pp. 65–89.

72. The expression is by Marcel Detienne, *The Creation of Mythology,* trans. Margaret Cook (Chicago and London: University of Chicago Press, 1986; 1st French ed., 1981), p. 10.

73. Shinoda Jun'ichi, "Musō *Monokusatarō* Ron," in Taniyama Shigeru Kyōju Taishoku Kinen Jigyō Jikkō Iinkai, ed., *Taniyama Shigeru Kyōju Taishoku Kinen: Kokugo Kokubungaku Ronshū* (Tokyo: Hanawa Shobō, 1972), p. 227.

74. The *Kokinshū* (992) poem says:

> Wa ga io wa   I live in a cell
> Miwa no yamamoto   At the foot of Mt. Miwa:
> Koishiku wa   Should you miss me,

Toburaikimase	Please come and pay a visit—
Sugi tateru kado	The gate where the cedar stands.

Adapted from McCullough, *Kokin Wakashū,* pp. 214–215; Okumura, *Kokin Wakashū,* pp. 332–333. The lady's variation is:

Omou nara	If you think of me
Toite mo kimase	Please come and pay a visit:
Waga yado wa	My cell
Karatachibana no	Is the gate where the gromwell
Murasaki no kado	And the Chinese orange stand.

See Ōshima, *Otogizōshi Shū,* p. 244. Asami Kazuhiko discusses this poem in " 'Monokusatarō' no Uta yori," in Nihon Bungaku Kenkyū Shiryō Kankōkai, ed., *Otogizōshi* (Tokyo: Yūseidō, 1985), pp. 133–141.

75. Ōshima, *Otogizōshi Shū,* pp. 249–250.

76. Ibid., p. 255.

77. The text is quoted in Shinoda, "Musō *Monokusatarō* Ron," p. 223.

78. The synopses appear in Furukawa Hisashi, ed., *Kyōgen Shū: Ge, NKZ* 73 (Tokyo: Asahi Shinbun Sha, 1956), pp. 231–332. The transformation experienced by the genre during the Tokugawa period is discussed in William R. LaFleur, "Society Upside-Down: *Kyōgen* as Satire and as Ritual," in his *Karma of Words,* pp. 133–148.

79. The quotations are from Thomas Keirstead, "The Theatre of Protest: Petitions, Oaths, and Rebellion in the *Shōen," Journal of Japanese Studies* 16:2 (Summer 1990): 370 and 388.

80. Yokoi Kiyoshi, "Minshū Bunka no Kaika," in Geinōshi Kenkyūkai, ed., *Nihon Geinōshi 3: Chūsei* (Tokyo: Hōsei Daigaku Shuppankyoku, 1983), pp. 208–209.

81. Furukawa, *Kyōgen Shū,* pp. 285–286.

82. Nonomura Kaizō and Andō Tsunejirō, eds., *Kyōgen Shūsei* (Tokyo: Nōgaku Shorin, 1974; 1st ed., 1931), p. 198.

83. Koyama Hiroshi, ed., *Kyōgen Shū: Ge, NKBT* 43 (Tokyo: Iwanami Shoten, 1961), p. 267.

84. Monkeys were believed to be messengers of the mountain deity that was venerated as a protector of Mt. Hiei. See Ohnuki-Tierney, *The Monkey as Mirror,* p. 43.

85. The text is quoted in Koyama Hiroshi, ed., *Kyōgen Shū: Jō, NKBT* 42 (Tokyo: Iwanami Shoten, 1960), p. 13. For a brief discussion of the text see Sugiura Minpei, *Sengoku Ransei no Bungaku, IS* 557 (Tokyo: Iwanami Shoten, 1965), p. 141.

86. This is the central scene of "Suicide by Sickle" *(Kamabara),* in which male pride is channeled in the lament of a lazy farmer who, addressing his neighbor, has a hard time digesting this sudden exchange of sexual roles: "Although he may be bundled in straw, a man is still a man!" See Nonomura and Andō, *Kyōgen Shūsei,* p. 104.

87. In "Tarō from the Riverbank" *(Kawara Tarō)* the wife is in charge of the sale of rice wine at the market by the Kamo River. The only role that the husband

plays in managing the household is his excessive consumption of *sake,* which the woman tries unsuccessfully to halt. The man even goes so far as to publicize his wine as sour so that he can feast on the unsold liquor. The woman finally allows him a drink but not before pouring it on his face. See Nonomura and Andō, *Kyōgen Shūsei,* p. 103.

88. This was the conclusion of the epilogue in my *Aesthetics of Discontent.* There, introducing the topic of the Citizens, I was led by some sort of Bakhtinian unconscious to state that they "could raise more loudly their voices of political discontent, which the recluses were forced to confine to the margins of power" (p. 154.) The present study allows me to define more precisely the degree of assimilation of the "tradition of subversion" into the dominant ideology that the Citizens themselves were creating.

89. Terry Eagleton, *Walter Benjamin: Towards a Revolutionary Criticism* (London: Verso, 1981), p. 148.

90. Stallybrass and White, *The Politics and Poetics of Transgression,* p. 26.

91. Here I am following a scheme provided by Stallybrass and White, *The Politics and Poetics of Transgression,* p. 193.

92. See on this point Fredric Jameson, *The Political Unconscious: Narrative as a Socially Symbolic Act* (Ithaca: Cornell University Press, 1981), p. 79.

93. Nonomura and Andō, *Kyōgen Shūsei,* pp. 105–106.

94. This is the topic of the play "The Old Soldier" *(Rōmusha).* See Sasano Ken, ed., *Nō, Kyōgen: Chū, IB* (Tokyo: Iwanami Shoten, 1943), pp. 500–508.

95. This is the case of "The Two Lords" *(Futari Daimyō),* in which a servant (Tarō Kaja) who has been entrusted with a sword threatens the two men. The warriors find themselves naked in the street, imitating fighting cocks and angry dogs and singing popular tunes. The servant's dream lasts only a day. See Kitagawa Tadahiko and Yasuda Akira, eds., *Kyōgen Shū, NKBZ 35* (Tokyo: Shōgakukan, 1972), pp. 147–169.

96. The Gion Festival is discussed in Hayashiya, *Machishū,* pp. 124–136.

97. Nonomura and Andō, *Kyōgen Shūsei,* pp. 134–137.

Epilogue

1. Louis Althusser, "Ideology and Ideological State Apparatuses (Notes Towards an Investigation)," in his *Essays on Ideology* (London: Verso, 1984; 1st French ed., 1970), p. 11.

2. The problem is discussed in Konta Yōzō, *Edo no Kinsho, ES 6* (Tokyo: Yoshikawa Kōbunkan, 1981).

3. For these new developments see Blake Morgan Young, *Ueda Akinari* (Vancouver: University of British Columbia, 1982), p. 19.

4. Peter Burger, *Theory of the Avant-Garde, THL 4* (Minneapolis: University of Minnesota Press, 1984), p. 90.

5. For a defense of Neo-Confucianism see the *Kiyomizu Monogatari* as discussed in Herman Ooms, *Tokugawa Ideology: Early Constructs, 1570–1680* (Princeton: Princeton University Press, 1985), pp. 151–160.

6. Eagleton, *The Ideology of the Aesthetic,* p. 14.

7. Norbert Elias, *The Civilizing Process* 1: *The History of Manners,* trans.

Edmund Jephcott (New York: Pantheon Books, 1978; 1st Swiss ed., 1939), pp. 18 and 39–40.

8. Bourdieu, *Distinction,* p. 382.

9. Peter Nosco, *Remembering Paradise: Nativism and Nostalgia in Eighteenth-Century Japan* (Cambridge and London: Council on East Asian Studies, Harvard University, 1990), p. 123.

10. Ibid., p. 144.

11. H. D. Harootunian, *Things Seen and Unseen: Discourse and Ideology in Tokugawa Nativism* (Chicago and London: University of Chicago Press, 1988), p. 98.

12. Ibid., pp. 112–113.

13. Nosco, *Remembering Paradise,* p. 220.

14. Donald Keene, "Characteristic Responses to Confucianism in Tokugawa Literature," in Peter Nosco, ed., *Confucianism and Tokugawa Culture* (Princeton: Princeton University Press, 1984), p. 123.

15. For an attempt to relate the philosophy of Itō Jinsai to Chikamatsu's poetics see David Pollack, *The Fracture of Meaning: Japan's Synthesis of China from the Eighth Through the Eighteenth Centuries* (Princeton: Princeton University Press, 1986), pp. 204–209.

16. Robert W. Leutner, *Shikitei Sanba and the Comic Tradition in Edo Fiction* (Cambridge and London: Council on East Asian Studies, Harvard University, 1985), p. 42. Despite the political consciousness of this statement as well as an enlightening passage on the arrest of Shikitei Sanba because of his satirical pieces dealing "with current events or recognizable contemporary individuals or groups" (p. 31), Leutner's conclusions undermine his own findings, advancing again the thesis of the "innocent nature" of the literary act: "Nor have we any hint here of the frustration and discontent that common sense and instinct tell us the rigid and authoritarian style of *bakufu* rule must have engendered. But neither Sanba nor his readers thought of fiction as a medium for social protest; far from it. Even now fiction remains, except for a distinct minority of its readers and practitioners, a reassuring entertainment, a medium that confirms, if sometimes in round-about ways, the conventional pieties, which do not include a vision of life as bleak and unsusceptible to improvement. And so on the human level, too, *Ukiyoburo* is a sentimental work." See Leutner, *Shikitei Sanba and the Comic Tradition in Edo Fiction,* p. 109. For a discussion of "sentimental readings" of the Japanese classics see Marra, *The Aesthetics of Discontent,* pp. 1–7.

17. For a discussion of the relationship between Akinari and the nativist movement, as well as Akinari's dispute with Norinaga over matters of phonetics and myths, see Young, *Ueda Akinari,* pp. 79–87, although the political relevance of this intellectual exchange between the writer and the philosopher is not examined. The argument recently advanced regarding Akinari's "effort to subordinate ethical concerns to the demands of art" does not do justice to the political implications of Akinari's writing. See Dennis Washburn, "Ghostwriters and Literary Haunts: Subordinating Ethics to Art in *Ugetsu Monogatari*," *Monumenta Nipponica* 45:1 (Spring 1990): 43.

GLOSSARY

Abutsu　阿仏

Aigo no Waka　愛護の若

Aizen'ō　愛染王

Akogi　阿漕

Amida Nyorai　阿弥陀如来

Ankō　安康

Antoku　安徳

Ariwara no Narihira　在原業平

aruki miko　歩き巫女

Ashikaga Tadayoshi　足利真義

Ashikaga Takauji　足利尊氏

Ashikaga Yoshiakira　足利義詮

Ashikaga Yoshimasa　足利義政

Ashikaga Yoshimitsu　足利義満

Ashikaga Yoshimochi　足利義持

Ashikaga Yoshinori　足利義教

Ashikaga Yoshitsugu　足利義嗣

Asukai Masaari　飛鳥井雅有

Awataguchi Sarugaku Ki
　粟田口猿楽記

bakufu　幕府

Baramon Sōjō　婆羅門僧正

Ben no Naishi Nikki　弁内侍日記

Bishamonten　毘沙門天

biwa hōshi　琵琶法師

Bunkyō Hifuron　文鏡秘府論

Bunshō Sōshi　文正草子

buppō　仏法

Chigo no Miya　児の宮

Chikamatsu Monzaemon
　近松門左衛門

Chingen　鎮源

Chiyokane　千代包

Chōkan Kanmon　長寛甚文

Chōkei　長慶

Chōken　澄憲

chokusenshū　勅撰集

Chōri Yurai Ki　長吏由来記

Chūin Michimasa　中院通勝

Chūin Sadahira　中院定平

Chūjōhime　中将姫

chūsei　中世

Chūsendai no Ran　中先代の乱

Chūyūki　中右記

Daigo　醍醐

Daigo Nenjū Gyōji　醍醐年中行事

Daigoji Zōjiki　醍醐寺雑事記

Daikakuji　大覚寺

Dainichi Nyorai　大日如来

Dainihonkoku Hokkekyō Kenki
　大日本国法華経験記

Dairi Hyakuban Utaawase　内裏
　百番歌合

Dajōin Jisha Zōjiki　大乗院
　寺社雑事記

dengaku　田楽

Dōmyō Ajari　道命阿闍梨

Ebina no Naami　海老名南阿弥

Eguchi　江口

Eifukumon-in　永福門院

Eifukumon-in Hyakuban Onjika-
　awase　永福門院百番御自歌合

213

Eizon 叡尊

En no Gyōja 役行者

Enami no Saemongorō 榎並の左
衛門五郎

Enkyō Ryōkyō Sochinjō 延慶
両卿訴陳状

Enkyū Kimon 延久記文

Enseimon-in Shindainagon 延政門
院新大納言

eta 穢多

etoki hōshi 絵解法師

Fudaraku 補陀落

fuen 浮艶

Fūga Wakashū 風雅和歌集

Fugen Bosatsu 普賢菩薩

Fugen Bosatsu Kanpotsu Hon
普賢菩薩観発品

Fujitsugu Nyūdō 藤次入道

Fujiwara no Akihira 藤原明衡

Fujiwara no Michinaga 藤原道長

Fujiwara no Shunzei 藤原俊成

Fujiwara no Tadamichi 藤原忠通

Fujiwara no Tameie 藤原為家

Fujiwara no Tamemori 藤原為守

Fujiwara no Teika 藤原定家

Fujiwara no Yasumasa 藤原保昌

fujumon 諷誦文

Fukumaru 福丸

Fūshikaden 風姿花伝

Fushimi 伏見

Fushimi In Goshū 伏見院御集

gekokujō 下剋上

Genji Ippon Kyō 源氏一品経

Genji Monogatari 源氏物語

Genkimon-in 玄輝門院

Genpei Seisuiki 源平盛衰記

Genshin 源信

Go-Daigo 後醍醐

Go-Fukakusa 後深草

Go-Fushimi 後伏見

Go-Hanazono 後花園

Go-Kameyama 後亀山

Go-Kōgon 後光厳

Go-Komatsu 後小松

Go-Murakami 後村上

Go-Nijō 後二条

Go-Reizei 後冷泉

Go-Saga 後嵯峨

Go-Shirakawa 後白河

Go-Sukō 後崇光

Go-Toba 後鳥羽

Go-Uda 後宇多

Go-Yōzei 後陽成

Gogumaiki 後愚昧記

Goryōsha Bukkiryō 御霊社服忌令

Gosho Ōji 五所王子

Goshūishū 後拾遺集

Gosuiden no Nyōgo 五衰殿の女御

Gōyōki 迎陽記

Gyokuyō Wakashū 玉葉和歌集

Hakusan Ōkagami 白山大鏡

Hamuro Nagamune 葉室長宗

Hanazono 花園

Hanazono Tennō Shinki
花園天皇宸記

Heike Monogatari 平家物語

Heike Nōkyō 平家納経

Higashi Nijō-in 東二条院

Higyō Yasha 飛行夜叉

Hijiri no Miya 聖の宮

hinin 非人

Hino Meishi 日野名子

Hino Sukeaki 日野資明

Hino Toshimitsu 日野俊光

Hiryū Gongen 飛滝権現

Hōbutsushū 宝物集

Hōjō 北条

Hokke Hakkō 法華八講

Hokkekyō 法華経

Hon'ami Kōetsu 本阿弥光悦

Hon'ami Motomitsu 本阿弥本光

Honchō Monzui 本朝文粋

Honchō Mudaishi 本朝無題詩

honji 本地

Hosokawa Takakuni　細川高国
Hosokawa Yoriyuki　細川頼之
Hosokawa Yūsai　細川幽斎
Hosshinshū　発心集
Hossō　法相
Hyōhanki　兵範記
Ichijō Kanera　一条兼良
Ihara Saikaku　井原西鶴
Ii Michimasa　井伊道政
Imagawa Ryōshun　今川了俊
imi　忌
Inryōken Nichiroku　蔭凉軒日録
Inuwaka　犬若
Ippen Shōnin　一遍上人
Ise Monogatari　伊勢物語
Iyahito Shinnō　弥仁親王
Izayoi Nikki　十六夜日記
Izumi Shikibu　和泉式部
Izumi Shikibu Nikki　和泉式部日記
Izumi Shikibu Shū　和泉式部集
jashō　邪正
Jian-zhi Chan-shi　金智禅師
Jien　慈円
Jikkinshō　十訓抄
Jimyōin　持明院
Jinen Koji　自然居士
Jinmu　神武
Jinnō Shōtōki　神皇正統記
jisei　自性
jisei no kimi　治世の君
jitō　地頭
Jizō Bosatsu　地蔵菩薩
Jōgyōdō Raiyuki　常行堂来由記
jōkokuge　上剋下
Jōshōji Nenjū Sōsetsuchō
　成勝寺年中相折帳
Jūgosho　十五所
Jūichimen Kannon　十一面観音
junchokusenshū　准勅撰集
Kagami no Miya no Koto　鏡の宮の事
Kagenki　嘉元記

Kamabara　鎌腹
Kameyama　亀山
Kamo no Chōmei　鴨長明
Kamo no Mabuchi　賀茂真淵
Kan'ami Kiyotsugu　観阿弥清次
Kanchūki　勘仲記
Kaneyoshi Shinnō　懐良親王
Kangin Shū　閑吟集
kanjin hijiri　勧進聖
Kanmon Gyoki　看聞御記
Kanmuryōjukyō　観無量寿経
Kannon Bosatsu　観音菩薩
kanrei　管領
Kanshi Naishinnō　惟子内親王
Kantō moshitsugi　関東申次
Kanze Fukuda Keizu　観世福田系図
Kasuga Akikuni　春日顕国
Kasuga Onmōde no Ki　春日御詣記
kawaramono　河原者
Kazan-in Iechika　花山院家親
Kazan-in Iemasa　花山院家雅
Kazan-in Nagachika　花山院長親
kebiishi　検非違使
kechien　結縁
Kegonkyō　華厳経
Keikō　経幸
Keishi Naishinnō　瓊子内親王
Kenkō　兼好
Kenmu Nenjū Gyōji　建武年中行事
Kennaiki　建内記
Kenshinmon-in　顕親門院
Kesadayū　袈裟大夫
Ki no Arimasa　紀在昌
Ki no Tsurayuki　紀貫之
Kikumasa　菊正
Kikutake　菊武
Kitabatake Akiyoshi　北畠顕能
Kitabatake Chikafusa　北畠親房
Kitanosha Hikitsuke　北野社引付
Kitayamadono Gyōkō
　Ki　北山殿行幸記
Kō no Morofuyu　高師冬

Kōgimon-in　広義門院
Kōgon　光厳
Koinu　小犬
Kojidan　古事談
Kojiki　古事記
Kojima Hōshi　小嶋法師
Kokin Rokujō　古今六帖
Kokinshū　古今集
Kokonchomonjū　古今著聞集
Komachi Sōshi　小町草子
Komori no Miya　子守の宮
Kōmyō　光明
Konjaku Monogatari　今昔物語
Konoedono no Mōshijō
　木の△殿の申ぢやう
Kōrei　孝霊
Kōun Kuden　耕雲口伝
kugutsu　傀儡
Kuji Zainin　闇罪人
Kujō Takahiro　九条隆博
Kujō Yoshitsune　九条良経
Kūkai　空海
Kumano bikuni　熊野比丘尼
Kumano Gongen Go Suijaku Engi
　熊野権現御垂迹緑起
Kumano Gongen no Koto　熊野
　権現の事
Kumano no Go Honji no Sōshi
　熊野の御本地のさうし
Kuninaga Shinnō　邦良親王
Kusunoki Masashige　楠木正成
Kusunoki Masayoshi　楠木正儀
Kusunoki Masayuki　楠木正行
Kūya Shōnin　空也上人
kyō warabe　京童
kyōgen　狂言
Kyōgoku-in　京極院
Kyōgoku Tameaki　京極為明
Kyōgoku Tamefuji　京極為藤
Kyōgoku Tamekane　京極為兼
Kyōgoku Tameko　京極為子
Kyōgoku Tamenori　京極為教

Kyōkai　景戒
machinin　町人
machishū　町衆
Madarajin　摩多羅神
Mansai Jugō Nikki　満済准后日記
Man'yōshū　万葉集
Meishukushū　明宿集
Mii Zokutōki　三井続燈記
Minamoto no Akikane　源顕兼
Minamoto no Tōru　源融
Miroku Bosatsu　弥勒菩薩
Monju Bosatsu　文殊菩薩
Monokusatarō　物くさ太郎
Monokusatarō Monogatari
　懶太郎物語
Moriyoshi Shinnō　護良親王
Moromori Ki　師守記
Motomasa　元雅
Motoori Norinaga　本居宣長
Motoyoshi　元能
mukaekō　迎講
Mumyōshō　無名抄
Mumyōzōshi　無名草子
Muneyoshi Shinnō　宗良親王
Murasaki Shikibu　紫式部
Musō Kokushi　夢窓国師
Myōgoki　名語記
naishi　内侍
Naka no Gozen　中の御前
Nanbokuchō　南北朝
Nanchō Gohyakuban Utaawase
　南朝五百番歌合
Naohito Shinnō　直仁親王
Nichiren Shōnin　日蓮上人
Nichizō　日像
Nihon Kōki　日本後記
Nihon Ryōiki　日本霊異記
Nihon Shoki　日本書紀
Nijō Kawara Rakusho　二条河
　原落書
Nijō Noriyoshi no Musume
　二条教良女

Nijō Tamefuji　二条為藤
Nijō Tamemichi　二条為道
Nijō Tamesada　二条為定
Nijō Tametō　二条為遠
Nijō Tameuji　二条為氏
Nijō Tameyo　二条為世
Nijō Yoshimoto　二条良基
Nintoku　仁徳
Nise Monogatari　仁勢物語
Nishi no Gozen　西の御前
Nisshin　日親
nissōkan　日想観
Nitchū Gyōji　日中行事
Nitta Yoshimune　新田義宗
Nitta Yoshisada　新田義定
nō　能
Nomori no Kagami　野守鏡
Nyaku Itchi Ōji　若一王子
Nyoirin Kannon　如意輪観音
ōbō　王法
Ōdai Nenjū Gyōji　往代年中行事
Ōe no Masafusa　大江匡房
Ogasawara Sadamune　小笠原貞宗
Oguri　小栗
On'ami　音阿弥
oni-nō　鬼能
Ōnin　王仁
onmyōji　陰陽師
Ono no Komachi　小野小町
Oshikōji Kintada　押小路公忠
otogizōshi　御伽草子
Raii　頼意
Rakuchū Rakugaizu　洛中洛外図
rakusho　落書
Reizei Tamesuke　冷泉為相
Renzen　蓮禅
Rikashū　李花集
Rokkaku Sadayori　六角定頼
rokudō　六道
Rokujō Arifusa　六条有房
Ryōjin Hishō　梁塵秘抄
Ryōjin Hishō Kudenshū　梁塵秘抄口伝集

Ryūgen Sōjō Nikki　隆源僧正日記
Ryūju Bosatsu　竜樹菩薩
Ryūten　竜天
Saichō　最澄
Saigyō　西行
Saigyō Monogatari　西行物語
Saionji Kinhira　西園寺公衡
Saionji Kinmune　西園寺公宗
Saionji Kinshige　西園寺公重
Saionji Kinsuke　西園寺公相
Saionji Kintsune　西園寺公経
Saionji Sanehira　西園寺実衡
Saionji Sanekane　西園寺実兼
Saionji Saneo　西園寺実雄
Saionji Sanetoshi　西園寺実俊
Saionji Saneuji　西園寺実氏
Saionji Yoshiko　西園寺禧子
saka hinin　坂非人
Sakamoto Ryōma　坂本竜馬
Sanemori　実盛
Sanetakakō Ki　実隆公記
Sangū Hotakasha Gozōeitei Nikki　三宮穂高社御造営定日記
sanjo　散所
sanjo hinin　散所非人
sanjo hōshi　散所法師
Sanjōnishi Sanetaka　三条西実隆
Sankashū　山家集
Sanninbu　三人夫
Sanshō-dayū　山椒太夫
Sansho Gongen　三所権現
sanzai hinin　散在非人
sarugaku　猿楽
Sarugaku Dangi　申楽談儀
Sarugenji Sōshi　猿源氏草子
Seiganji　誓願寺
Seikaku　聖覚
Sekiso Ōrai　尺素往来
sekkyō-bushi　説経節
sekkyō-hijiri　説教聖
Semimaru　蟬丸
Senju Kannon　千手観音

Senjūshō　撰集抄
senmin　賤民
senzu manzai　千秋万歳
Seppō Myōgen Ron　説法明眼論
setsuwa　説話
Shaka Nyorai　釈迦如来
Shasekishū　沙石集
Shih Ching　詩経
Shijō Takasuke　四条隆資
Shin Sarugaku Ki　新猿楽記
Shingosenshū　新後撰集
Shinkokinshū　新古今集
Shinsenzai Wakashū　新千載和歌集
Shinshūishū　新拾遺集
Shintōshū　神道集
Shin'yō Wakashū　新葉和歌集
Shinzokukokinshū　新続古今集
Shō Kannon　請観音
shōen　荘園
Shōjō Gongen　証誠権現
Shoku Goshūi Wakashū　続後
　拾遺和歌集
Shōkū Shōnin　性空上人
shokunin　職人
Shōkunmon-in　昭訓門院
Shokusenzaishū　続千載集
shōmonji　声聞師
shugenja　修験者
shugo　守護
shuku hinin　宿非人
shūshōe　修正会
sōdai　惣代
Son'un　尊雲
sōō　相応
Sotoba Komachi　卒都婆小町
suijaku　垂迹
Suisaki　水左記
suke　典侍
Sukō　崇光
Suminokura Soan　角倉素庵
Sutoku　崇徳

Suwa Daimyōjin Ekotoba
　諏訪大明神絵詞
Suwa Engi no Koto　諏訪縁起の事
Suwa no Honji　諏訪の本地
Tachibana no Michisada　橘道貞
Taiheiki　太平記
Taima Mandara So　当麻曼陀羅疏
Taira no Kiyomori　平清盛
Taira no Tsunechika　平経親
Takasago　高砂
Takayoshi Shinnō　尊良親王
Takemukigaki　竹むきが記
Tamekanekyō Wakashō　為兼卿
　和歌抄
Tateyama Mandara　立山曼茶羅
Tendai　天台
Tengu Zōshi　天狗草子
Tenshō Kyōgen Bon　天正狂言本
tesarugaku　手猿楽
Tōin Kinkage　洞院公蔭
Tōin Kinkata　洞院公賢
Tōin Saneyo　洞院実世
Tokitsugu Gyōki　言継卿記
tokuseiryō　徳政令
Tokutaka　徳高
Tōru no Otodo　融の大臣
tsuina　追儺
Tsuneyoshi Shinnō　恒良親王
Tsurezuregusa　徒然草
Uda　宇多
Ueda Akinari　上田秋成
Uesugi Noriaki　上杉憲顕
Uji Shūi Monogatari　宇治拾遺物語
Ukai　鵜飼
ushirodo no sarugaku　後戸の猿楽
Utō　善知鳥
wakō dōjin　和光同塵
Wuxing Dayi　五行大義
Xiao Ji　蕭吉
Xuan-zang　玄奘
yabuiri　藪入

Yakushi Nyorai　薬師如来
Yamashina Ke Raiki　山科家礼記
Yamashina Tokitsugu　山科言継
Yamato Monogatari　大和物語
Yasuhito Shinnō　康仁親王
yatagarasu　八咫烏
yojō　余情
Yoroboshi　弱法師
Yoshida Sadafusa　吉田定房
Yoshidake Hinamiki　吉田家日次記
Yosho Myōjin　四所明神
Yūgyō Shōnin　遊行上人

Yuishiki　唯識
yūjo　遊女
Yūyo Seisō　酉誉聖聡
Zeami Motokiyo　世阿弥元清
Zekkai Chūshin　絶海中津
Zenchiku　禅竹
Zenji no Miya　禅師の宮
Zenzai　善財
Zōami　増阿弥
Zoku Kojidan　続古事談
zushi　呪師

BIBLIOGRAPHY

Works in Japanese

Abe, Yasurō. "Seizoku no Tawamure to Shite no Geinō: Yūjō, Shirabyōshi, Kuse-mai no Monogatari o Megurite." In Moriya Takeshi, *Geinō to Chinkon: Kanraku to Kyūzai no Dainamizumu*. Tokyo: Shunjūsha, 1988.

Amano, Fumio. "Okina Sarugaku no Seiritsu: Jōgyōdō Shūshōe to no Kanren." *Bungaku* 51:7 (1983): 166–177.

Anno, Masaki. *Genin Ron: Chūsei no Ijin to Kyōkai*. Tokyo: Nihon Editā Sukūru Shuppanbu, 1987.

Araki, Shigeru, and Yamamoto Kichizō, eds. *Sekkyō-Bushi: Sanshō-Dayū, Oguri Hangan*. TB 243. Tokyo: Heibonsha, 1973.

Asami, Kazuhiko. " 'Monokusatarō' no Uta yori." In Nihon Bungaku Kenkyū Shiryō Kankōkai, ed., *Otogizōshi*. Tokyo: Yūseidō, 1985 (1st ed., 1974).

Enoki, Katsurō, ed. *Ryōjin Hishō*. SNKS 31. Tokyo: Shinchōsha, 1979.

Fujihira, Haruo. *Karon no Kenkyū*. Tokyo: Perikan Sha, 1988.

Fujimoto, Kazue, trans. *Goshūiwakashū* 4. KGB 587. Tokyo: Kōdansha, 1983.

Fukui, Kyūzō, ed. *Tsukuba Shū: Ge*. NKZ 74. Tokyo: Asahi Shinbunsha, 1951.

Furukawa, Hisashi, ed. *Kyōgen Shū: Ge*. NKZ 73. Tokyo: Asahi Shinbunsha, 1956.

Geinōshi Kenkyūkai, ed. *Nihon Geinōshi 2: Kodai, Chūsei*. Tokyo: Hōsei Daigaku Shuppan Kyoku, 1982.

Gotō, Meisei. "Bunshin." *Gunzō* 11 (1988): 128–142.

Gotō, Shigeo, ed. *Sankashū*. SNKS 49. Tokyo: Shinchōsha, 1982.

Haga, Kōshirō. "Shōgun no Kyōto: Gaisetsu." In Haga Kōshirō et al., eds., *Jinbutsu Nihon no Rekishi* 8: *Shōgun no Kyōto*. Tokyo: Shōgakukan, 1975.

Hattori, Yukio. "Ushirodo no Kami: Geinōkami Shinkō ni Kan Suru Ikkōsatsu." In Nihon Bungaku Kenkyū Shiryō Kankōkai, ed., *Yōkyoku, Kyōgen*. Tokyo: Yūseidō, 1981.

Hayashi, Masahiko. *Zōho Nihon no Etoki: Shiryō to Kenkyū*. Tokyo: Miai Shoten, 1984.

Hayashiya, Tatsusaburō. *Chūsei Bunka no Kichō*. Tokyo: Tōkyō Daigaku Shuppan Kai, 1953.

———. *Chūsei Geinōshi no Kenkyū: Kodai kara no Keishō to Sōzō*. Tokyo: Iwanami Shoten, 1960.

221

———. *Kodai Kokka no Kaitai*. Tokyo: Tōkyō Daigaku Shuppan Kai, 1955.

———. *Machishū: Kyōto ni Okeru "Shimin" Keisei Shi*. CS 59. Tokyo: Chūō Kōronsha, 1964.

Hisamatsu, Sen'ichi, and Nishio Minoru, eds. *Karonshū, Nōgakuronshū*. NKBT 65. Tokyo: Iwanami Shoten, 1961.

Hosokawa, Ryōichi. *Onna no Chūsei: Ono no Komachi, Tomoe, Sono Hoka*. Tokyo: Nihon Editā Skūru, 1989.

Hyōdō, Hiromi. "Monogatari: Shokue to Jōka no Kairo." In Hyōdō Hiromi, Akasaka Norio, and Yamamoto Hiroko, eds., *Monogatari, Sabetsu, Tennōsei*. Firudowāku Shirīzu III. Tokyo: Satsukisha, 1985.

Ichiko, Teiji. *Chūsei Shōsetsu no Kenkyū*. Tokyo: Tōkyō Daigaku Shuppan Kai, 1955.

———, ed. *Otogizōshi*. NKBT 38. Tokyo: Iwanami Shoten, 1958.

Ichiko, Teiji, and Noma Kōshin, eds. *Otogizōshi, Kanazōshi*. KNKB 26. Tokyo: Kadokawa Shoten, 1976.

Ienaga, Saburō. *Sarugaku no Shisōteki Kōsatsu*. Tokyo: Hōsei Daigaku Shuppan Kyoku, 1980.

Iguchi, Makiji. "Tamekane Karon to Bukkyō Shisō." *Kokubungaku Kenkyū* 72 (1980): 35–44.

Imatani, Akira. *Muromachi no Ōken: Ashikaga Yoshimitsu no Ōken Sandatsu Keikaku*. CS 978. Tokyo: Chūō Kōronsha, 1990.

———. *Tenbun Hokke no Ran: Busō Suru Machishū*. Tokyo: Heibonsha, 1989.

———. *Tokitsugu Gyōki: Kuge Shakai to Machishū Bunka no Setten*. Tokyo: Kabushiki Kaisha Soshiete, 1980.

Inoue, Mitsusada, and Ōsone Shōsuke, eds. *Ōjōden, Hokke Kenki*. NST 7. Tokyo: Iwanami Shoten, 1974.

Inoue, Muneo. *Chūsei Kadaishi no Kenkyū: Nanbokuchōki*. Tokyo: Meiji Shoin, 1987.

———. "Muneyoshi Shinnō." In Waka Bungakkai, ed., *Chūsei, Kinsei no Kajin*. WBK 7. Tokyo: Ōfūsha, 1970.

Ishikawa, Tōru, ed. *Ōkagami*. SNKS 82. Tokyo: Shinchōsha, 1989.

Itō, Masayoshi, ed. *Yōkyoku Shū: Jō*. SNKS 57. Tokyo: Shinchōsha, 1983.

———. *Yōkyoku Shū: Chū*. SNKS 73. Tokyo: Shinchōsha, 1986.

Itō, Sei. *Shinhokuchō no Hito to Bungaku*. MS 6. Tokyo: Miai Shoten, 1979.

Iwamoto, Yutaka. *Nihon Bukkyōgo Jiten*. Tokyo: Heibonsha, 1988.

Iwasa, Masashi, et al., eds. *Jinnō Shōtōki, Masu Kagami*. NKBT 87. Tokyo: Iwanami Shoten, 1965.

Iwasa, Miyoko. *Ametsuchi no Kokoro: Fushimi In Go Uta Hyōshaku*. Tokyo: Kasama Shoin, 1979.

———. *Eifukumon'in: Sono Sei to Uta*. KS 54. Tokyo: Kasama Shoin, 1976.

———. "Hanazono-in no Eifukumon'in Hihan." *Kokugo to Kokubungaku* (December 1966): 28–37.

———. "Kyōgoku Tamekane no Kafū Keisei to Yuishiki Setsu." In Ikeda Toshio, ed., *Sōritsu Nijūshūnen Kinen: Tsurumi Daigaku Bungakubu Ronshū*. Yokohama: Sanbi Insatsu Kabushikigaisha, 1983.

Iwasaki, Takeo. *Sanshō-Dayū Kō: Chūsei no Sekkyōgatari*. HS 23. Tokyo: Heibonsha, 1973.

Kasahara, Kiichirō. *Yoshino Chō to Muneyoshi Shinnō no Seikatsu.* Tokyo: Tō-yōkan, 1963.

Katō, Takahisa. "Kumano Sanzan Shinkō no Kenkyū." In Katō Takahisa, *Jinja no Shiteki Kenkyū.* Tokyo: Ōfūsha, 1976.

Kawaguchi, Hisao, ed. *Shin Sarugaku Ki. TB* 424. Tokyo: Heibonsha, 1983.

Kawazoe, Shōji. *Imagawa Ryōshun.* Tokyo: Yoshikawa Kōbunkan, 1964.

Kidō, Saizō, ed. *Tsurezuregusa. SNKS* 10. Tokyo: Shinchōsha, 1977.

Kishi, Shōzō, trans. *Shintōshū. TB* 94. Tokyo: Heibonsha, 1983.

———. *"Shintōshū: Sōsetsu, Honbun Kanshō."* In Nishio Kōichi and Kishi Shōzō, eds., *Chūsei Setsuwa Shū: Kokonchomonjū, Hosshinshū, Shintōshū. KNKB* 23. Tokyo: Kadokawa Shoten, 1977.

Kitagawa, Tadahiko, ed. *Kangin Shū, Sōan Kouta Shū. SNKS* 53. Tokyo: Shinchōsha, 1982.

———. *Zeami. CS* 292. Tokyo: Chūō Kōronsha, 1972.

Kitagawa, Tadahiko, and Yasuda Akira, eds. *Kyōgen Shū. NKBZ* 35. Tokyo: Shōgakukan, 1972.

Kobayashi, Tomoaki. *Chūsei Bungaku no Shisō.* Tokyo: Shibundō, 1964.

Kobayashi, Yasuharu, ed. *Kojidan: Jō. KB* 60. Tokyo: Gendai Shichōsha, 1981.

Koizumi, Osamu, ed. *Nihon Ryōiki. SNKS* 67. Tokyo: Shinchōsha, 1984.

Kojima, Noriyuki, ed. *Kaifūsō, Bunka Shūreishū, Honchō Monzui. NKBT* 69. Tokyo: Iwanami Shoten, 1964.

Kojima, Noriyuki, Kinoshita Masatoshi, and Satake Akihiro, eds. *Man'yōshū* 4. *NKBZ* 5. Tokyo: Shōgakukan, 1975.

Kondō, Yoshihiro. *Shintōshū: Tōyō Bunko Bon.* Tokyo: Kadokawa Shoten, 1959.

Konishi, Jin'ichi. *Michi: Chūsei no Rinen. KGS* 420. Tokyo: Kōdansha, 1975.

Kōno, Katsuyuki. *Shōgaisha no Chūsei.* Kyoto: Bunrikaku, 1987.

Konta, Yōzō. *Edo no Kinsho. ES* 6. Tokyo: Yoshikawa Kōbunkan, 1981.

Koyama, Hiroshi, ed. *Kyōgen Shū: Jō. NKBT* 42. Tokyo: Iwanami Shoten, 1960.

Koyama, Hiroshi, et al., eds. *Kyōgen Shū: Ge. NKBT* 43. Tokyo: Iwanami Shoten, 1961.

Kubota, Jun. "Otogizōshi no Waka." In Ichiko Teiji and Noma Kōshin, eds., *Otogizōshi, Kanazōshi. KNKB* 26. Tokyo: Kadokawa Shoten, 1976.

———, ed. *Shin Kokin Wakashū: Jō. SNKS* 24. Tokyo: Shinchōsha, 1978.

———, ed. *Shin Kokin Wakashū: Ge. SNKS* 30. Tokyo: Shinchōsha, 1979.

———. "Waka: Seijiteki Kisetsu ni Okeru Waka." *Nanbokuchō: Dōranki no Bungaku,* Special Issue of *Kokubungaku: Kaishaku to Kanshō* (March 1969): 24–32.

Kuramoto, Hatsuo. *Muneyoshi Ruten: Shin'yōwakashū Senja no Shōgai.* Tokyo: Dōgyūsha, 1989.

Kurausu, F. *Meicho Edai: Sei Fūzoku no Nihon Shi.* Kawade Bunko 781A. Tokyo: Kawade Shobō, 1988.

Kuroda, Hideo. *Sugata no Shigusa no Chūseishi: Ezu to Emaki no Fūkei kara.* Tokyo: Heibonsha, 1986.

Kuroda, Toshio. *Ōbō to Buppō: Chūseishi no Kōzu.* Hōzō Sensho 23. Kyoto: Hōzōkan, 1983.

Kuwabara, Hiroshi, ed. *Mumyōzōshi. SNKS* 7. Tokyo: Shinchōsha, 1976.

———, trans. *Saigyō Monogatari. KGB* 497. Tokyo: Kōdansha, 1981.

Kyōto Buraku Shi Kenkyūjo, ed. *Chūsei no Minshū to Geinō.* Kyoto: Aunsha, 1986.

Mabuchi, Kazuo, Kunisaki Fumimaro, and Konno Tōru, eds. *Konjaku Monogatari Shū* 1–4. *NKBZ* 21–24. Tokyo: Shōgakukan, 1971–1976.

Matsuda, Takeo, ed. *Rikashū. IB* 2712–2713. Tokyo: Iwanami Shoten, 1941.

Matsumoto, Ryūshin, ed. *Otogizōshi Shū. SNKS* 34. Tokyo: Shinchōsha, 1980.

Matsuoka, Shinpei. "Shōdōgeki no Jidai: Nō no Seiritsu ni Tsuite Ikkōsatsu." *Kokugo to Kokubungaku: Chūsei Bungakushi e no Kairo* (April 1988): 81–92.

Matsushita, Daisaburō, ed. *Zoku Kokka Taikan.* Tokyo: Kadokawa Shoten, 1958.

Matsushita, Daisaburō, and Watanabe Fumio, eds. *Kokka Taikan: Kashū.* Tokyo: Kadokawa Shoten, 1951.

Mizukawa Yoshio. *Takemukigaki Zenshaku.* Tokyo: Kasama Shobō, 1972.

Mori, Shigeaki. *Kenmu Seiken: Go-Daigo Tennō no Jidai.* Kyōikusha Rekishi Shinsho: Nihon Shi 60. Tokyo: Kyōikusha, 1980.

———. *Mikotachi no Nanbokuchō: Go-Daigo Tennō no Bunshin. CS* 886. Tokyo: Chūō Kōronsha, 1988.

Moriya, Takeshi. *Kyō no Geinō: Ōchō kara Ishin made. CS* 555. Tokyo: Chūō Kōronsha, 1979.

Murata, Masashi, ed. *Shiryō Sanshū: Hanazono Tennō Shinki* 1. Tokyo: Heibunsha, 1982.

———. *Shiryō Sanshū: Hanazono Tennō Shinki* 3. Tokyo: Heibunsha, 1986.

Muroki, Yatarō, ed. *Sekkyōshū. SNKS* 8. Tokyo: Shinchōsha, 1977.

Nagai, Michiko. "Ashikaga Yoshimitsu." In Haga Kōshirō et al., eds., *Jinbutsu Nihon no Rekishi* 8: *Shōgun no Kyōto.* Tokyo: Shōgakukan, 1975.

Nagazumi, Yasuaki, ed. *Jikkinshō. IB* 30-120-1. Tokyo: Iwanami Shoten, 1983 (1st ed., 1942).

Nagazumi, Yasuaki, Uwayokote Masataka, and Sakurai Yoshirō. *Taiheiki no Sekai: Henkaku no Jidai o Yomu.* Tokyo: Nihon Hōsō Shuppan Kyōkai, 1987.

Nakada, Norio, Wada Toshimasa, and Kitahara Yasuo, eds. *Kogo Daijiten.* Tokyo: Shōgakukan, 1983.

Nakamura Yūjirō. "Toposu to Nō: Hakusan to Tateyama ni Furete." *Kokubungaku: Nō, Tōtaru Media no Seisei* 31:10 (September 1986): 32–35.

Nishimiya, Kazutami, ed. *Kojiki. SNKS* 27. Tokyo: Shinchōsha, 1979.

Nishino, Taeko. *Kōgon-in: Fūga Wakashū Shinsen to Dōran no Yo no Masshiro no Shōgai.* Tokyo: Kokubunsha, 1988.

———. *Shirasu no Tsuki: Takemukigaki Sakusha Meishi, Eifukumon'in no Uta to Shōgai.* Tokyo: Kokubunsha, 1984.

Nishio, Kōichi, ed. *Senjūshō. IB* 30-024-1. Tokyo: Iwanami Shoten, 1970.

Nishio, Kōichi, and Kishi Shōzō, eds. *Chūsei Setsuwa Shū: Kokonchomonjū, Hosshinshū, Shintōshū. KNKB* 23. Tokyo: Kadokawa Shoten, 1977.

Nishio, Kōichi, and Kobayashi Yasuharu, eds. *Kokonchomonjū: Jō. SNKS 59.* Tokyo: Shinchōsha, 1983.

Nishio, Kōichi, and Kobayashi Yasuharu, eds. *Kokonchomonjū: Ge. SNKS 76.* Tokyo: Shinchōsha, 1986.

Niunoya, Tetsuichi. *Kebiishi: Chūsei no Kegare to Kenryoku. HS 102.* Tokyo: Heibonsha, 1986.

Nomura, Seiichi, ed. *Izumi Shikibu Nikki, Izumi Shikibu Shū. SNKS 42.* Tokyo: Shinchōsha, 1981.

Nonomura, Kaizō, and Andō Tsunejirō, eds. *Kyōgen Shūsei.* Tokyo: Nōgaku Shorin, 1974 (1st ed., 1931).

Ogi, Takashi, ed. *Shin'yō Wakashū: Honbun to Kenkyū.* Tokyo: Kasama Shoin, 1984.

Okumura, Tsuneya, ed. *Kokin Wakashū. SNKS 19.* Tokyo: Shinchōsha, 1978.

Ōshima, Tatehiko. "Izumi Shikibu no Setsuwa." In Ōshima Tatehiko, *Otogizōshi to Minkan Bungei. MBS 12.* Tokyo: Iwazaki Bijutsu Sha, 1967.

———, ed. *Otogizōshi Shū. NKBZ 36.* Tokyo: Shōgakukan, 1974.

———. "'Sarugenji Sōshi' no Seiritsu." In Ōshima Tatehiko, *Otogizōshi to Minkan Bungei. MBS 12.* Tokyo: Iwazaki Bijutsu Sha, 1967.

———, ed. *Uji Shūi Monogatari. SNKS 71.* Tokyo: Shinchōsha, 1985.

Ōzawa, Tomio, et al., eds. *Fukuro Zōshi Chūshaku: Jō.* Tokyo: Hanawa Shobō, 1974.

Saeki, Junko. *Yūjo no Bunka Shi: Hare no Onnatachi. CS 853.* Tokyo: Chūō Kōronsha, 1987.

Sakakura, Atsuyoshi, et al., eds. *Taketori Monogatari, Ise Monogatari, Yamato Monogatari. NKBT 9.* Tokyo: Iwanami Shoten, 1959.

Sakakura, Atsuyoshi, Honda Giken, and Kawabata Yoshiaki, eds. *Konjaku Monogatari Shū: Honchō Sezoku Bu 3. SNKS 43.* Tokyo: Shinchōsha, 1981.

Sakamoto, Tarō, et al., eds. *Nihon Shoki: Jō-Ge. NKBT 67–68.* Tokyo: Iwanami Shoten, 1965.

Sakamoto, Yukio, and Iwamoto Yutaka, eds. *Hokkekyō: Jō-Chū-Ge.* Tokyo: Iwanami Shoten, 1962–1967.

Sakurai, Yoshirō. "Bunshō Sōshi no Seiritsu ni Tsuite: Chūsei Shōnin no Shii Kōzō to Sono Bunkateki Hyōgen Keitai no Bunseki." In Sakurai Yoshirō, *Chūsei Nihonjin no Shii to Hyōgen.* Tokyo: Miraisha, 1970.

———. *Kamigami no Henbō: Shaji Engi no Sekai kara.* Tokyo: Tōkyō Daigaku Shuppan Kai, 1976.

———. "Machishū Bunka no Senkuteki Keitai: *Taiheiki* to Kyōwarabe to." In Sakurai Yoshirō, *Chūsei Nihonjin no Shii to Hyōgen.* Tokyo: Miraisha, 1970.

Sanari, Kentarō, ed. *Yōkyoku Taikan 3.* Tokyo: Meiji Shoin, 1964.

Sasaki, Gin'ya. *Muromachi Bakufu.* Nihon no Rekishi 13. Tokyo: Shōgakukan, 1975.

Sasaki, Nobutsuna, et al., eds. *Kōchū Nihon Bungaku Ruijū: Zuihitsu Bungaku Shū.* Tokyo: Hakubunkan, 1930.

Sasano, Ken, ed. *Nō, Kyōgen: Chū.* Tokyo: Iwanami Shoten, 1943.

Satake, Akihiro. " 'Bunshō Sōshi' Saidoku." In Nihon Bungaku Kenkyū Shiryō Kankōkai, ed., *Otogizōshi*. Tokyo: Yūseidō, 1985 (1st ed., 1974).

———. "Muchi to Gudon: Monokusatarō no Yukue." In Satake Akihiro, *Gekokujō no Bungaku*. Tokyo: Chikuma Shobō, 1967.

Satō, Shin'ichi. *Nanbokuchō no Dōran*. Nihon no Rekishi 9. Tokyo: Chūō Kōronsha, 1974.

Sekiyama, Kazuo. *Sekkyō no Rekishi: Bukkyō to Wagei. IS* 64. Tokyo: Iwanami Shoten, 1978.

Shinoda, Jun'ichi. "Musō *Monokusatarō* Ron." In Taniyama Shigeru Kyōju Taishoku Kinen Jigyō Jikkō Iinkai, *Taniyama Shigeru Kyōju Taishoku Kinen: Kokugo Kokubungaku Ronshū*. Tokyo: Hanawa Shobō, 1972.

Shinpen Kokka Taikan Henshūiinkai. *Shinpen Kokka Taikan* 1. Tokyo: Kadokawa Shoten, 1983.

Sugiura, Minpei. *Sengoku Ransei no Bungaku. IS* 557. Tokyo: Iwanami Shoten, 1965.

Takigawa, Masajirō. *Eguchi, Kanzaki: Yūgyō Nyofu, Yūjo, Kugutsume, Zōhohan*. Nihon Rekishi Shinsho. Tokyo: Shibundō, 1965.

———. *Yūjo no Rekishi*. Nihon Rekishi Shinsho. Tokyo: Shibundō, 1965.

Tamai, Kōsuke. *Ben no Naishi Nikki Shinchū*. Tokyo: Taishūkan Shoten, 1966.

Tanaka, Yutaka, ed. *Zeami Geijutsu Ronshū. SNKS* 4. Tokyo: Shinchōsha, 1976.

Tanigawa, Ken'ichi. *Tokoyo Ron: Nihonjin no Tamashi no Yukue. HS* 81. Tokyo: Heibonsha, 1983.

Toita, Michizō. *Kan'ami to Zeami. IS* E77. Tokyo: Iwanami Shoten, 1969.

Tokuda, Kazuo. "Kanjin Hijiri to Shaji Engi: Muromachiki o Chūshin to Shite." In Tokuda Kazuo, *Otogizōshi: Kenkyū*. Tokyo: Miai Shoten, 1988.

———. "Kyōroku-Bon 'Taimadera Engi' Emaki to 'Chūjōhime no Honji.' " In Tokuda Kazuo, *Otogizōshi: Kenkyū*. Tokyo: Miai Shoten, 1988.

Tokue, Motomasa. " 'Mukoiri Jinen Koji' Kō." *Kokugo to Kokubungaku* (July 1968): 27–41.

Tsugita, Kasumi. "Eifukumon'in." In Waka Bungaku, ed., *Chūsei, Kinsei no Kajin. WBK* 7. Tokyo: Ōfūsha, 1970.

———, ed. *Gyokuyō Wakashū. IB* 30-137-1. Tokyo: Iwanami Shoten, 1989 (1st ed., 1944).

Tsugita, Kasumi, and Iwasa Miyoko, eds. *Fūga Wakashū*. Tokyo: Miai Shoten, 1974.

Wada, Hidematsu. *Shintei Kenmu Nenjū Gyōji Chūkai, Nitchū Gyōji Chūkai*. Edited by Tokoro Isamu. *KGB* 895. Tokyo: Kōdansha, 1989.

Watanabe, Minoru, ed. *Ise Monogatari. SNKS* 2. Tokyo: Shinchōsha, 1976.

Watanabe, Tsunaya, ed. *Shasekishū. NKBT* 85. Tokyo: Iwanami Shoten, 1966.

Yamaguchi, Masao. "Tennōsei no Shinsō Kōzō." *Chūō Kōron* (November 1976): 90–107.

———. "Tennōsei no Shōchōteki Kūkan." *Chūō Kōron* (December 1976): 178–196.

Yamaguchi, Masao, and Matsuoka Shinpei. "Taidan: Tōtaru Media to Shite no Nō." *Kokubungaku* 31:10 (September 1986): 6–35.

Yamaji, Kōzō. "Okina Sarugaku Saikō: Jō." *Geinō* (February 1985): 8–19.
———. "Okina Sarugaku Saikō: Ge." *Geinō* (March 1985): 8–18.
———. "Shūshōe no Hen'yō to Chihō Denpa." In Moriya Takeshi, ed., *Geinō to Chinkon: Kangaku to Kyūzai no Dainamizumu.* Tokyo: Shunjūsha, 1988.
Yamashita, Hiroaki, ed. *Taiheiki 1. SNKS 15.* Tokyo: Shinchōsha, 1977.
Yanase, Kazuo, ed. *Mumyōsho Zenkō.* Tokyo: Chūdōkan, 1980.
Yokoi, Kiyoshi. *Chūsei Minshū no Seikatsu Bunka.* Tokyo: Tōkyō Daigaku Shuppan Kai, 1975.
———. *Gekokujō no Bunka.* Tokyo: Tōkyō Daigaku Shuppan Kai, 1980.
———. "Minshū Bunka no Kaika." In Geinōshi Kenkyūkai, ed., *Nihon Geinōshi 3: Chūsei.* Tokyo: Hōsei Daigaku Shuppankyoku, 1983.
———. "Shokue Shisō no Chūseiteki Kōzō: Kami to Tennō to 'Senmin' to." *Kokubungaku: Kaishaku to Kanshō* 11 (1972): 79–88.

Works in Western Languages

Althusser, Louis. *Essays on Ideology.* London: Verso, 1984.
Araki, James T. "*Bunshō Sōshi:* The Tale of Bunshō, the Saltmaker." *Monumenta Nipponica* 38:3 (Autumn 1983): 221–249.
Asor Rosa, Alberto, ed. *Letteratura Italiana.* 9 vols. Turin: Einaudi, 1982–1991.
Aston, W. G. *Nihongi: Chronicles of Japan from the Earliest Times to A.D. 697.* Tokyo: Tuttle, 1980 (1st ed., 1896).
Bakhtin, Mikhail. *Rabelais and His World.* Translated by Helene Iswolsky. Cambridge: MIT Press, 1968.
Blacker, Carmen. *The Catalpa Bow: A Study of Shamanistic Practices in Japan.* London: Allen & Unwin, 1975.
Borgen, Robert. *Sugawara no Michizane and the Early Court.* Cambridge: Council on East Asian Studies, Harvard University, 1986.
Borgen, Robert, and Marian Ury. "Readable Japanese Mythology: Selections from *Nihon Shoki* and *Kojiki.*" *Journal of the Association of Teachers of Japanese* 24:1 (April 1990): 61–97.
Bourdieu, Pierre. *Distinction: A Social Critique of the Judgement of Taste.* Translated by Richard Nice. Cambridge: Harvard University Press, 1984 (French ed., 1979).
Brown, Delmer M., and Ichirō Ishida. *The Future and the Past: A Translation and Study of the Gukanshō, an Interpretative History of Japan Written in 1219.* Berkeley and Los Angeles: University of California Press, 1979.
Burger, Peter. *Theory of the Avant-Garde.* Translated by Michael Shaw. *THL* 4. Minneapolis: University of Minnesota Press, 1984.
Calzolari, Silvio. *Il Dio Incatenato, Honchō Shinsen Den di Ōe no Masafusa: Storie di Santi e Immortali Taoisti nel Giappone dell' Epoca Heian (794–1185).* Florence: Sansoni, 1984.
Carter, Steven D. "*Waka* in the Age of *Renga.*" *Monumenta Nipponica* 36:4 (Winter 1981): 425–444.
Cohen, Abner. *Two-Dimensional Man: An Essay on the Anthropology of Power and Symbolism in Complex Society.* Berkeley, Los Angeles, London: University of California Press, 1974.

Collcutt, Martin. *Five Mountains: The Rinzai Zen Monastic Institution in Medieval Japan.* Cambridge: Council on East Asian Studies, Harvard University, 1981.

Cranston, Edwin A., trans. *The Izumi Shikibu Diary: A Romance of the Heian Court.* Cambridge: Harvard University Press, 1969.

Detienne, Marcel. *The Creation of Mythology.* Translated by Margaret Cook. Chicago and London: University of Chicago Press, 1986 (French ed., 1981).

Dilworth, David, and J. Thomas Rimer, eds. *The Incident at Sakai and Other Stories.* Honolulu: University of Hawaii Press, 1977.

Douglas, Mary. *Purity and Danger: An Analysis of the Concepts of Pollution and Taboo.* London: Ark Paperbacks, 1984 (1st ed., 1966).

Dykstra, Kurata Yoshiko, trans. *Miraculous Tales of the Lotus Sutra from Ancient Japan: The Dainihonkoku Hokekyōkenki of Priest Chingen.* Osaka: Kansai University of Foreign Studies, 1983.

Eagleton, Terry. *The Ideology of the Aesthetic.* Oxford: Basil Blackwell, 1990.

———. *Walter Benjamin: Towards a Revolutionary Criticism.* London: Verso, 1981.

Eco, Umberto. *Opera Aperta.* Milan: Bompiani, 1962.

Edwards, Robert. "Exile, Self, and Society." In María-Inés Lagos-Pope, ed., *Exile in Literature.* Lewisburg: Bucknell University Press, 1988.

Eliade, Mircea. *Shamanism: Archaic Techniques of Ecstasy.* Princeton: Princeton University Press, 1964 (French ed., 1951).

Elias, Norbert. *The Civilizing Process 1: The History of Manners.* Translated by Edmund Jephcott. New York: Pantheon Books, 1978 (Swiss ed., 1939).

———. *The Court Society.* Translated by Edmund Jephcott. New York: Pantheon Books, 1983 (German ed., 1969).

Foard, James H. "*Seiganji:* The Buddhist Orientation of a Noh Play." *Monumenta Nipponica* 35:4 (Winter 1980): 437–456.

Foucault, Michel. *The Archeology of Knowledge and The Discourse on Language.* New York: Pantheon Books, 1972 (French ed., 1971).

———. *The Order of Things: An Archeology of the Human Sciences.* New York: Vintage Books, 1973 (French ed., 1966).

Garin, Eugenio. *Medioevo e Rinascimento. BUL* 124. Rome and Bari: Laterza, 1984 (1st ed., 1954).

Gellrich, Jesse M. *The Idea of the Book in the Middle Ages: Language Theory, Mythology, and Fiction.* Ithaca and London: Cornell University Press, 1985.

Ginzburg, Carlo. *I Benandanti: Stregoneria e Culti Agrari tra Cinquecento e Seicento. PBE* 197. Turin: Einaudi, 1966.

———. *Storia Notturna: Una Decifrazione del Sabba.* Turin: Einaudi, 1989.

Goble, Andrew Edmund. "Go-Daigo and the Kenmu Restoration." Ph.D. dissertation, Stanford University, 1987.

———. "Truth, Contradiction and Harmony in Medieval Japan: Emperor Hanazono (1297–1348) and Buddhism." *Journal of the International Association of Buddhist Studies* 12:1 (1989): 21–63.

Goldberg, Jonathan. *James I and the Politics of Literature: Jonson, Shakespeare, Donne, and Their Contemporaries.* Stanford: Stanford University Press, 1989 (1st ed., 1983).

―――. "The Politics of Renaissance Literature: A Review Essay." *ELH* 49:2 (Summer 1982): 514–542.

Goodwin, Janet R. "Alms for Kasagi Temple." *Journal of Asian Studies* 46:4 (November 1987): 827–841.

―――. "Building Bridges and Saving Souls: The Fruits of Evangelism in Medieval Japan." *Monumenta Nipponica* 44:2 (Summer 1989): 137–149.

―――. "Shooing the Dead to Paradise." *Japanese Journal of Religious Studies* 16:1 (March 1989): 63–80.

Greenblatt, Stephen. "Invisible Bullets: Renaissance Authority and Its Subversion." *Glyph: Johns Hopkins Textual Studies* 8 (1981): 40–61.

―――. "Murdering Peasants: Status, Genre, and the Representation of Rebellion." In Stephen Greenblatt, ed., *Representing the English Renaissance.* Berkeley, Los Angeles, London: University of California Press, 1988.

Harootunian, H. D. *Things Seen and Unseen: Discourse and Ideology in Tokugawa Nativism.* Chicago and London: University of Chicago Press, 1988.

Hōsan-kai of Shitennōji Temple, ed. *Prince Shōtoku and Shitennō-ji Temple: The Seventeen-Article Constitution.* Osaka: Benridō, 1970.

Huey, Robert N. *Kyōgoku Tamekane: Poetry and Politics in Late Kamakura Japan.* Stanford: Stanford University Press, 1989.

―――. "The Medievalization of Poetic Practice." *Harvard Journal of Asiatic Studies* 50:2 (1990): 651–668.

Huey, Robert N., and Susan Matisoff, trans. "Lord Tamekane's Notes on Poetry: *Tamekanekyō Wakashō.*" *Monumenta Nipponica* 40:2 (Summer 1985): 127–146.

Hurvitz, Leon, trans. *Scripture of the Lotus Blossom of the Fine Dharma* (*The Lotus Sūtra*). New York: Columbia University Press, 1976.

Ishii, Nobuko. "*Sekkyō-Bushi.*" *Monumenta Nipponica* 44:3 (Autumn 1989): 283–307.

Jameson, Fredric. *The Political Unconscious: Narrative as a Socially Symbolic Act.* Ithaca: Cornell University Press, 1981.

Kato, Hilda. "The *Mumyōshō* of Kamo no Chōmei and Its Significance in Japanese Literature." *Monumenta Nipponica* 23:3–4 (1968): 321–430.

Keene, Donald, ed. *Anthology of Japanese Literature: From the Earliest Era to the Mid-Nineteenth Century.* New York: Grove Press, 1955.

―――. "Characteristic Responses to Confucianism in Tokugawa Literature." In Peter Nosco, ed., *Confucianism and Tokugawa Culture.* Princeton: Princeton University Press, 1984.

―――, trans. *Essays in Idleness: The Tsurezuregusa of Kenkō.* New York: Columbia University Press, 1967.

Keirstead, Thomas. "The Theater of Protest: Petitions, Oaths, and Rebellion in the *Shōen.*" *Journal of Japanese Studies* 16:2 (Summer 1990): 357–388.

Kertzer, David I. *Ritual, Politics, and Power.* New Haven and London: Yale University Press, 1988.

Kirkwood, Kenneth P. *Renaissance in Japan: A Cultural Survey of the Seventeenth Century.* Tokyo: Tuttle, 1970.

Kitagawa, Hiroshi, and Bruce T. Tsuchida, trans. *The Tale of the Heike: Heike Monogatari.* Tokyo: University of Tokyo Press, 1975.

Kōgen, Mizuno. *Buddhist Sutras: Origin, Development, Transmission.* Tokyo: Kōsei Publishing Co., 1982.

Konishi, Jin'ichi. *A History of Japanese Literature 1: The Archaic and Ancient Ages.* Translated by Aileen Gatten and Nicholas Teele. Princeton: Princeton University Press, 1984.

Kramer, Lloyd S. "Literature, Criticism, and Historical Imagination: The Literary Challenge of Hayden White and Dominick LaCapra." In Lynn Hunt, ed., *The New Cultural History.* Berkeley, Los Angeles, London: University of California Press, 1989.

Kuroda, Toshio. "Shintō in the History of Japanese Religion." Translated by James C. Dobbins and Suzanne Gay. *Journal of Japanese Studies* 7:1 (Winter 1981): 1–21.

LaFleur, William R. *The Karma of Words: Buddhism and the Literary Arts in Medieval Japan.* Berkeley, Los Angeles, London: University of California Press, 1983.

———, trans. *Mirror for the Moon: A Selection of Poems by Saigyō (1118–1190).* New York: New Directions Paperbook, 1978.

Le Goff, Jacques. *Time, Work, and Culture in the Middle Ages.* Translated by Arthur Goldhammer. Chicago: University of Chicago Press, 1980.

Leutner, Robert W. *Shikitei Sanba and the Comic Tradition in Edo Fiction.* Cambridge and London: Council on East Asian Studies, Harvard University, 1985.

Liu, Alan. "The Power of Formalism: The New Historicism." *ELH* 56:4 (Winter 1989): 721–771.

McCullough, Helen Craig, trans. *Kokin Wakashū: The First Imperial Anthology of Japanese Poetry, with Tosa Nikki and Shinsen Waka.* Stanford: Stanford University Press, 1985.

———. *Ōkagami, The Great Mirror: Fujiwara Michinaga (966–1027) and His Times.* Princeton: Princeton University Press, 1980.

———. *The Taiheiki: A Chronicle of Medieval Japan.* New York: Columbia University Press, 1959.

———. *Tales of Ise: Lyrical Episodes from Tenth-Century Japan.* Stanford: Stanford University Press, 1968.

Marra, Michele. *The Aesthetics of Discontent: Politics and Reclusion in Medieval Japanese Literature.* Honolulu: University of Hawaii Press, 1991.

———. "The Buddhist Mythmaking of Defilement: Sacred Courtesans in Medieval Japan." *The Journal of Asian Studies* 52:1 (February 1993): 49–65.

———. "The Conquest of *Mappō:* Jien and Kitabatake Chikafusa." *Japanese Journal of Religious Studies* 12:4 (December 1985): 319–341.

———. "The Development of *Mappō* Thought in Japan." *Japanese Journal of Religious Studies* 15:1 (March 1988): 25–54 and 15:4 (December 1988): 287–305.

————. "Major Japanese Theorists of Poetry: From Ki no Tsurayuki to Kamo no Chōmei." *Ōsaka Gaikokugo Daigaku Gakuhō* 67 (1984): 27–35.

————. "The Michizane Legend as Seen in the Nō Drama, *Raiden*." *Ōsaka Gaikokugo Daigaku Gakuhō* 64 (1984): 437–446.

————, trans. "*Mumyōzōshi*: Introduction and Translation." *Monumenta Nipponica* 39:2 (Summer 1984): 115–145; 39:3 (Autumn 1984): 281–305; 39:4 (Winter 1984): 409–434.

————, trans. *I Racconti di Ise (Ise Monogatari)*. Turin: Einaudi, 1985.

————. "Review: Silvio Calzolari, *Il Dio Incatenato, Honchō Shinsen Den di Ōe no Masafusa: Storie di Santi e Immortali Taoisti nel Giappone dell' Epoca Heian (794–1185)*." *Monumenta Nipponica* 41:4 (Winter 1986): 495–497.

————. "Semi-Recluses (*Tonseisha*) and Impermanence (*Mujō*):Kamo no Chōmei and Urabe Kenkō." *Japanese Journal of Religious Studies* 11:4 (December 1984): 313–350.

————, trans. *Storie di Mercanti: Il Magazzino Eterno del Giappone, I Calcoli del Mondo*. GSS 57. Turin: Utet, 1983.

————. "Zeami and Nō: A Path Towards Enlightenment." *Journal of Asian Culture* 12 (1988): 37–67.

Martines, Lauro. *Power and Imagination: City-States in Renaissance Italy*. Baltimore: Johns Hopkins University Press, 1979.

Matisoff, Susan. "Images of Exile and Pilgrimage: Zeami's *Kintōsho*." *Monumenta Nipponica* 34:4 (Winter 1979): 449–465.

————. "*Kintōsho*: Zeami's Song of Exile." *Monumenta Nipponica* 32:4 (Winter 1977): 441–458.

————. *The Legend of Semimaru, Blind Musician of Japan*. New York: Columbia University Press, 1978.

Mills, D. E., trans. *A Collection of Tales from Uji: A Study and Translation of Uji Shūi Monogatari*. Cambridge: Cambridge University Press, 1970.

————. "Murasaki Shikibu: Saint or Sinner?" *Bulletin of the Japan Society of London* (1979): 4–13.

Miner, Earl. *An Introduction to Japanese Court Poetry*. Stanford: Stanford University Press, 1968.

————. "Waka: Features of Its Constitution and Development." *Harvard Journal of Asiatic Studies* 50:2 (1990): 669–706.

Montrose, Louis Adrian. " 'Eliza, Queene of Shepheardes,' and the Pastoral of Power." *English Literary Renaissance* 10:2 (Spring 1980): 153–182.

Morrell, Robert E. "The Buddhist Poetry in the *Goshūishū*." *Monumenta Nipponica* 28:1 (Spring 1973): 87–100.

————. *Sand and Pebbles (Shasekishū): The Tales of Mujū Ichien, a Voice for Pluralism in Kamakura Buddhism*. Albany: State University of New York Press, 1985.

Morris, V. Dixon. "The City of Sakai and Urban Autonomy." In George Elison and Bardwell L. Smith, eds., *Warlords, Artists, and Commoners: Japan in the Sixteenth Century*. Honolulu: University of Hawaii Press, 1981.

————. "Sakai: From *Shōen* to Port City." In John W. Hall and Toyoda Takeshi, eds., *Japan in the Muromachi Age*. Berkeley, Los Angeles, London: University of California Press, 1977.

Morris, Mark. "*Waka* and Form, *Waka* and History." *Harvard Journal of Asiatic Studies* 46:2 (December 1986): 551–610.

Nakamura, Kyoko Motomochi, trans. *Miraculous Stories from the Japanese Buddhist Tradition: The Nihon Ryōiki of the Monk Kyōkai*. Cambridge: Harvard University Press, 1973.

Nippon Gakujutsu Shinkōkai, ed. *The Noh Drama: Ten Plays from the Japanese*. Tokyo: Tuttle, 1973 (1st ed., 1955).

Nosco, Peter. *Remembering Paradise: Nativism and Nostalgia in Eighteenth-Century Japan*. Cambridge and London: Council on East Asian Studies, Harvard University, 1990.

Ohnuki-Tierney, Emiko. *The Monkey as Mirror: Symbolic Transformations in Japanese History and Ritual*. Princeton: Princeton University Press, 1987.

Ooms, Herman. *Tokugawa Ideology: Early Constructs, 1570–1680*. Princeton: Princeton University Press, 1985.

Orgel, Stephen. *The Illusion of Power: Political Theater in the English Renaissance*. Berkeley, Los Angeles, London: University of California Press, 1975.

Ortolani, Benito. "Zenchiku Aesthetics of the Nō Theatre." *Riverdale Studies* 3 (1976): 1–28.

Paul, Diana Y. *Women in Buddhism: Images of the Feminine in the Mahāyāna Tradition*. Berkeley, Los Angeles, London: University of California Press, 1985.

Philippi, Donald L., trans. *Kojiki*. Tokyo: University of Tokyo Press, 1968.

Plutschow, H. E. *Chaos and Cosmos: Ritual in Early and Medieval Japanese Literature*. Leiden: E. J. Brill, 1990.

———. "Is Poetry a Sin? *Honjisuijaku* and Buddhism Versus Poetry." *Oriens Extremus* 25:2 (1978): 206–218.

Pocock, J. G. A. *Politics, Language and Time: Essays on Political Thought and History*. New York: Atheneum, 1971.

Pollack, David. *The Fracture of Meaning: Japan's Synthesis of China from the Eighth Through the Eighteenth Centuries*. Princeton: Princeton University Press, 1986.

Rimer, J. Thomas, and Yamazaki Masakazu, trans. *On the Art of the Nō Drama: The Major Treatises of Zeami*. Princeton: Princeton University Press, 1984.

Ruch, Barbara. "Medieval Jongleurs and the Making of a National Literature." In John W. Hall and Toyoda Takeshi, eds., *Japan in the Muromachi Age*. Berkeley, Los Angeles, London: University of California Press, 1977.

———. "The Other Side of Culture in Medieval Japan." In Kozo Yamamura, ed., *The Cambridge History of Japan 3: Medieval Japan*. Cambridge: Cambridge University Press, 1990.

Ryukoku University Translation Center, ed. *The Sūtra of Contemplation on the Buddha of Immeasurable Life as Expounded by Śākyamuni Buddha*. Kyoto: Ryukoku University, 1984.

Shirane, Haruo. *The Bridge of Dreams: A Poetics of "The Tale of Genji."* Stanford: Stanford University Press, 1987.

————. "Lyricism and Intertextuality: An Approach to Shunzei's Poetics." *Harvard Journal of Asiatic Studies* 50:1 (1990): 71–85.

Skord, Virginia, trans. *Tales of Tears and Laughter: Short Fiction of Medieval Japan.* Honolulu: University of Hawaii Press, 1991.

Stallybrass, Peter, and Allon White. *The Politics and Poetics of Transgression.* London: Methuen, 1986.

Sylte, Linda M. "Zenchiku's 'A Genji Requiem' and Mishima's Modern Adaptation." M.A. thesis, Washington University, 1980.

Takakusu, Junjirō. *The Essentials of Buddhist Philosophy.* Edited by Wing-Tsit Chan and Charles A. Moore. Honolulu: Office Appliance Co., 1956 (1st ed., 1947).

Terasaki, Etsuko. " 'Wild Words and Specious Phrases': *Kyōgen Kigo* in the *Nō* Play *Jinen Koji.*" *Harvard Journal of Asiatic Studies* 49:2 (December 1989): 519–552.

Therborn, Goran. *The Ideology of Power and the Power of Ideology.* London: Verso, 1980.

Varley, H. Paul, trans. *A Chronicle of Gods and Sovereigns: Jinnō Shōtōki of Kitabatake Chikafusa.* New York: Columbia University Press, 1980.

————. *The Ōnin War: History of Its Origins and Background with a Selective Translation of the Chronicle of Ōnin.* New York: Columbia University Press, 1967.

Waley, Arthur. *The Nō Plays of Japan.* Tokyo: Tuttle, 1976 (1st ed., 1921).

Washburn, Dennis. "Ghostwriters and Literary Haunts: Subordinating Ethics to Art in *Ugetsu Monogatari.*" *Monumenta Nipponica* 45:1 (Spring 1990): 39–74.

Yamagiwa, Joseph K., trans. *The Ōkagami: A Japanese Historical Tale.* Tokyo: Tuttle, 1977.

Young, Blake Morgan. *Ueda Akinari.* Vancouver: University of British Columbia Press, 1982.

INDEX

HAWAI

Production Notes

Composition and paging were done on the
Quadex Composing System and typesetting
on the Compugraphic 8400 by the design
and production staff of University of
Hawaii Press.

The text and display typeface is Sabon.

Offset presswork and binding were done by
The Maple-Vail Book Manufacturing Group.
Text paper is Writers RR Offset, basis 50.